The Collect
in Anglican Liturgy

The Collect
in Anglican Liturgy

Texts and Sources 1549–1989

Alcuin Club Collection Number 72

Compiled and edited by
Martin R. Dudley

The Alcuin Club

A Liturgical Press Book

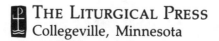
THE LITURGICAL PRESS
Collegeville, Minnesota

Cover design by David Manahan, O.S.B.

Copyright © 1994 The Alcuin Club, Runcorn, Chesire, United Kingdom. Published by The Liturgical Press, Collegeville, Minnesota 56321. Printed in the United States of America.

1	2	3	4	5	6	7	8

Library of Congress Cataloging-in-Publication Data

The collect in Anglican liturgy : texts and sources, 1549–1989 /
  Martin R. Dudley, editor.
      p.   cm. — (Alcuin Club collection ; no. 72)
  Includes bibliographical references and indexes.
  ISBN 0-8146-2308-5
    1. Collects—History and criticism.   2. Anglican
Communion—Liturgy—History.   I. Dudley, Martin.
II. Series: Alcuin Club collections ; no. 72.
BX5141.A1A6   no. 72
[BX5145.A62]
264'.036—dc20   94-3741
                                         CIP

CONTENTS

ACKNOWLEDGEMENTS

The copyright of collects is a most complex matter. Permission has been sought from the known copyright holders of the various prayer books (except for the American *Book of Common Prayer* 1928 and 1978 which are not in copyright). Each collection contains material previously in copyright elsewhere, and the compiler is aware that he may have inadvertently violated a copyright. He hopes to produce a full list of copyrights in relation to collects and would be glad to be supplied with further information.

Original collects from *Alternative Collects 1985*, © 1985 the Anglican Church of Australia Trust Corporation, published by AIO Press are reproduced with permission.

Collects from *Alternative Prayer Book 1984*, © 1984 the General Synod of the Church of Ireland, published by Collins, are reproduced with permission.

Collects from *Authorised Services 1973* © 1973 by Charles Mortimer Guilbert as Custodian of the Standard Book of Common Prayer (of the American Episcopal Church) are reproduced with permission.

Rights in Britain and the Commonwealth to the collects of the *Book of Common Prayer,* 1662, are vested in the Crown; they are reproduced by permission of the Crown's patentee, Cambridge University Press.

Collects from *Modern Collects* (1972) and *An Anglican Prayer Book 1989,* © by the Church of the Province of Southern Africa, are reproduced by permission of the Bishop of Bloemfontein.

Collects for Sundays and Seasons from *The Alternative Service Book 1980* are reproduced by permission of the Central Board of Finance of the Church of England. The ASB collects include copyright material from the *Book of Common Prayer* (1662), the Joint Liturgical Group's editions of *The Daily Office,* Southern African *Modern Collects* (1972) and *Liturgy 75* (1975), and *The Book of Common Worship of the Church of South India.*

Original collects in *The Book of Alternative Services of the Anglican Church of Canada,* © 1985 by the General Synod of the Anglican Church of Canada, are reproduced with permission.

Collects from *The Book of Common Worship* of the Church of South India, © Oxford University Press 1963, are reproduced with permission.

Collects from *The Daily Office* and *The Daily Office Revised,* by the Joint Liturgical Group, are reproduced by permission of SPCK.

ABBREVIATIONS
AND SHORT TITLES

1549	*The Book of Common Prayer, 1549*
1662	*The Book of Common Prayer, 1662*
1885Amer	*The Book Annexed*; presented to the General Convention in 1886
1928Amer	*The Book of Common Prayer . . . according to the Use of the Protestant Episcopal Church in the United States of America, 1928*
1928Eng	*The Book of Common Prayer with the Additions and Deviations proposed in 1928*
1929Scot	*The Scottish Book of Common Prayer, 1929*
1959Can	*Draft Prayer Book Canada 1959*
1966Wales	*An Order for the Celebration of the Holy Eucharist and the Administration of the Holy Communion with Collects, Old Testament Lessons, Epistles, Psalms and Gospels,* authorised for experimental use, September 1966
AmerAuthS	*Authorised Services 1973* [USA]
AmerBCP	*The Book of Common Prayer According to the Use of the Episcopal Church* [USA 1979]
ASB	*The Alternative Service Book 1980* [England]
AusPB	*An Australian Prayer Book* [Australia 1978]
AusAC	*Alternative Collects 1985* [Australia]
CanBAS	*The Book of Alternative Services of The Anglican Church of Canada* [1985]

CECal	*The Calendar and Lessons of the Church of England: A Report submitted by the Church of England Liturgical Commission . . . 1968*
CSI	*The Church of South India: The Book of Common Worship* [1963]
Gel	Gelasian Sacramentary; *Liber Sacramentorum Romanae Aeclesiae Ordinis Anni Circuli,* edited by L. C. Mohlberg, Rome 1968.
Greg	Gregorian Sacramentary; *Le Sacramentaire Grégorien,* edited by Jean Deshusses, 3rd ed., Fribourg 1992.
ICEL	International Commission on English in the Liturgy
IrAPB	*Alternative Prayer Book 1984 according to the use of the Church of Ireland*
JLG	*The Daily Office by the Joint Liturgical Group* [1968]
Leo	Leonine Sacramentary, now usually known as the *Sacramentum Veronense;* edited by L. C. Mohlberg, Rome 1968.
NZPB	*A New Zealand Prayer Book* [1989]
RSV	Revised Standard Version
SAAPB	*An Anglican Prayer Book 1989* [Southern Africa]
SAMC	*Modern Collects* [South Africa, 1972]
SM	*The Sarum Missal,* edited by J. Wickham Legg, London 1916. SM with a Roman numeral refers to the Latin collects in chapter one.
WalesBCP	*The Book of Common Prayer for use in The Church of Wales* [1984]
Bright	William Bright, *Ancient Collects and Other Prayers,* 6th ed., Oxford & London 1887
Hatchett	Marion J. Hatchett, *Commentary on the American Book of Common Prayer,* New York 1981
Jasper-Bradshaw	R.C.D. Jasper and Paul F. Bradshaw, *A Companion to the Alternative Service Book,* London 1986
Mackenzie	K. D. Mackenzie, ''Collects, Epistles and Gospels'' in W. K. Lowther Clarke, *Liturgy and Worship,* London 1932
MRR	Joseph A. Jungmann, *The Mass of the Roman Rite,* 2 vols., New York 1950

INTRODUCTION

1. The Roman Orationes

Louis Duchesne divided common prayer into three types : litany prayers, collective prayers, and Eucharistic prayers. As the name suggests, the second type involves the assembly, who are invited to pray by the officiating minister. After this period of silent prayer, the officiant expressed in a short formulary the content of the prayers of the assembly and the congregation responded with *Amen*. [1] These short prayers, or *orationes,* are a peculiarity of the Roman rite. It contains three of them, the *collecta,* the prayer *super oblata,* which became known as the *secreta,* and the *post communio*. [2] The form is already fully developed in the so-called Leonine Sacramentary. It has two other prayers, one probably said at the spreading of the cloth on the table and one *super populum*. The Leonine Sacramentary is not a true sacramentary but a *libellus missarum,* or, more correctly, a collection of *libelli missarum,* small

[1] L. Duchesne, *Christian Worship,* 5th ed., London 1923, 107.

[2] All these prayers have been thoroughly studied by G. G. Willis, 'The Variable Prayers of the Roman Mass' in his *Further Essays in Early Roman Liturgy,* Alcuin Club Collection No 50, London : SPCK 1968, 91–131. This introductory section is largely drawn from Willis. As it is not part of my intention to provide a study of the collects in the sacramentaries but only to indicate aspects of the history of the collect that affect its current use, I have not repeated the detail of Willis' arguments.

booklets containing the *formulae* for one or more Masses,[3] probably transcribed in Verona; hence its new title the *Veronensis* or *Sacramentarium Veronense*.[4] Dating of the *Veronensis* is not easy. The final version was almost certainly compiled between 500 and 590, but the individual sets are up to a hundred years older.[5] The studies that have been undertaken agree that these *libelli* take us back to the earliest prayer forms of the Roman liturgy. The degree of development indicates that these forms were shaped earlier still. Jungmann suggests that they date from the period, beginning in the mid-third century, following the change from Greek to Latin in the Roman liturgy. Certainly there is a specifically Roman quality to the prayers. Greek and Gallican prayers are frequently reflective and expansive, but the early Roman *oratio* is distinguished by its noble simplicity and conciseness of language[6] and by the Roman preference for conciseness and clarity.[7] Willis holds that the three prayers came into the Roman rite during the fifth century. He examines sympathetically Jungmann's 'neat solution' to the relation between them that, parallel in style, structure, and liturgical use, they are also parallel in respect of their position as following a chant, which covers an action.[8] The collect follows and sums up the Introit, which would have been the only text that preceded it in the late fifth-century Mass. By this hypothesis, the chants preceded the prayers, chronologically as well as liturgically. Willis prefers, however, the hypothesis that the collect's position is derived from East-

[3]C. Vogel, *Medieval Liturgy : An Introduction to the Sources,* Washington 1986, 38. See also Pierre-Marie Gy, 'The Different Forms of Liturgical "Libelli" ' in G. Austin, ed., *Fountain of Life,* Washington 1991, 23–34.

[4]This title was given to the 1956 edition by Dom Mohlberg.

[5]Vogel, *Medieval Liturgy* 39–43.

[6]Joseph Lechner and Ludwig Eisenhofer, *The Liturgy of the Roman Rite,* Freiburg 1961, 80.

[7]MRR I:373.

[8]Willis, 'Variable Prayers' 109; he appears to be using the single volume version of MRR.

ern liturgies and is related to the readings that follow it and not to the Introit that precedes it.[9]

The question is not merely academic, for the relation of the collect to what surrounds it affects both the structure of the Eucharist and the content of the collects. Cranmer seems to have held a view similar to Willis's and, in writing new collects, generally related them to the readings, a practice that he found in some instances in the Sarum Missal. An ICEL subcommittee was asked to 'explore the feasibility of providing new presidential prayers that would be related to the three cycles of the Sunday readings, a task which presented questions about how a theme could be appropriately chosen from the diverse and sometimes unrelated readings (as when the second reading is semicontinuous) and how the opening prayer (collect) could 'echo' the Scriptures which had not yet been heard.[10] The logic of this relation is that the collect should follow and conclude the readings, in the way a psalm prayer concludes a psalm.

Orationes are prefaced by the exhortation *Oremus*. In the earlier Roman *ordines* the single word is used,[11] but there are examples of long additions to it which indicate the content of the following prayer.[12] Following the exhortation, the people, standing, prayed in silence, until the leader of the assembly spoke the *oratio*. On penitential occasions and at some other times, at ordinations for example, the faithful knelt for silent prayer at the bidding of the deacon (*Flectamus genua*) and remained kneeling until told to rise (*Levate*).[13]

The *orationes* may be divided into a number of parts. The simplest division is into three : the invocation of God, the rea-

[9]Willis, 'Variable Prayers' 110-12.

[10]Kathleen Hughes, 'Original Texts : Beginnings, Present Projects, Guidelines' in Peter C. Finn and James M. Schellman, eds., *Shaping English Liturgy,* Washington 1990, 236.

[11]E.g., OR I, n.53.

[12]E.g., in the ordination Mass, Gel. 22, and in the Good Friday prayers, Gel. 75.

[13]E.g., OR XI, nn.11, 17, etc.

son why God should hear and answer the prayer (usually joined to the invocation by a relative clause), and the actual petition. Hughes describes these as address, amplification of address, petition, result clause, and adds the conclusion.[14] Willis breaks it down in this way :[15]

(i)   an address to God;
(ii)   a relative or participle clause referring to some attribute of God, or to one of his saving acts;
(iii) the petition;
(iv)   the reason for which we ask;
(v)   the conclusion.

Numbers (ii) and (iv), or one or the other of them, may be dispensed with, reducing the prayer, in its simplest form, to (i), (iii), and (v). The simple form is found in the other prayers rather than in the collect, and the majority of collects include clause (iv).

The earliest liturgical *orationes* were addressed exclusively to the Father, though prayers to the Son were common outside the liturgy. The universal ending, therefore, was *Per Dominum nostrum Jesum Christum Filium tuum.* If the Son was referred to in the body of the prayer, the form *Per eundem . . .* was used; if at the end, . . . *qui tecum vivat et regnat;* and if the Holy Spirit was also named, then we have . . . *in unitate eiusdem.* The prayers generally end with a Trinitarian doxological form. Jungmann shows that 'the collect makes visible to us the grand outlines of that spiritual universe in which our prayer lives and moves and is; it arises in the communion of holy Church and ascends through Christ to God on high'.[16] This is the purpose of its pure structure, a structure necessary in the Church's official prayer uttered by her ordained representa-

---

[14]Kathleen Hughes, R.S.C.J., 'Types of Prayer in the Liturgy' in Peter E. Fink, ed., *The New Dictionary of Sacramental Worship,* Collegeville 1990, 963; see also her 'Original Texts' 243.

[15]Willis, 'Variable Prayers' 118.

[16]MRR I:379.

tives but not in private prayer, the prayer of the people, and in hymns. ICEL's guidelines for new texts hold to these basic principles : 'Christian liturgical prayer is traditionally directed to the Father, through the mediation of the Son, in the power of the Spirit'.[17] The address should be to the First Person of the Trinity, using a variety of forms. The conclusions to prayers should express the mediation of Christ.[18]

Finally, the name 'collect' (*collectio*) is of Gallican origin.[19] It probably means the celebrant's conclusion or summary of the prayers of the faithful.[20] Duchesne, following Bona and Mabillon, holds that the name *collecta* comes from it being the introductory prayer following immediately upon the assembling of the people. He derives his conviction from the use of *colligere plebem* as the ordinary expression for calling the people together to worship and notes that on litany days in the Gregorian Sacramentary the prayer prior to the procession is called *ad collectam*. Willis dismisses this view entirely and holds that the term is purely Gallican. *Collectio,* a word common in Gallican sacramentaries of the seventh and eighth centuries, is supplemented, and ultimately replaced, by *collecta* in the seventh century.[21] The Roman terms *oratio, oratio super oblata,* and *oratio ad complendum* gave way to the Gallican *Collecta, Secreta,* and *Post-communio,* though the Roman Missal continued to call the first prayer *Oratio.*[22]

Although new collects were added to the Roman corpus and some of these from Gallican sources are more verbose and do not adhere to the economy of language and ideas that

[17]Hughes, 'Original Texts' 251.

[18]Hughes, 'Original Texts' 253.

[19]See the Synod of Agde, A.D. 506, can. 30; also OR V, n.25.

[20]*Is, qui orationem collecturus est,* Cassian, *Instit. Coenob.,* II, 7; cf. *Micrologus,* c.4.

[21]Willis, 'Variable Prayers' 106–07.

[22]The missal of Paul VI uses the terms *collecta, super oblata,* and *post communionem.* ICEL uses 'Opening Prayer', 'Prayer over the Gifts', and 'Prayer after Communion', and the French Missal uses *Prière d'ouverture, sur les offrandes,* and *après la communion.*

is characteristic of the Roman collect, the majority of collects in the medieval missal were derived directly from the ancient sacramentaries.

2. The Prayer Books of 1549 and 1662

The English Church knew the historic Latin collects through the Sarum Missal and shared in a common Western liturgical tradition. The collects were translated and adapted by the Lutheran reformers and used in German and Swedish Lutheran services before they appeared in the English translation of 1549. New Lutheran collects were inclined to be rather more Gallican than Roman. Two-thirds of the collects in 1549 were close translations of the terse Latin originals; the remainder were original compositions. New collects had to be written for nearly all saints' days because the Latin collects involved invocation of the saints.[23]

1662 provided a collect for every Sunday (except that the collect of the Circumcision was used until the Epiphany), for Ash Wednesday, for Good Friday and Easter Even, and for feast days of the Lord, the Apostles, the Evangelists, Saint John the Baptist, Saint Michael and All Angels, and All Saints' Day. The collect was said daily at Morning and Evening Prayer and at the Holy Communion. The collect for Advent Sunday was repeated daily until Christmas Eve and that of Ash Wednesday was repeated every day of Lent. When a Sunday or holy day 'hath a Vigil or Eve'—there were sixteen such days—the collect was said at Evening Prayer on that day.

[23]The Prayer Book collects and their sources have been studied in great detail, particularly by Dean E. M. Goulburn, *The Collects of the Day,* 2 vols., London and New York 1880; William Bright, *Ancient Collects,* London 1887, and his article in the *Prayer Book Commentary,* London 1905, and in the Prayer Book commentaries and histories of Palmer, Proctor and Frere, Brightman, and Blunt. The language of the English collect is studied by Stella Brook, *The Language of the Book of Common Prayer,* London and New York 1965.

In a bare translation the Sarum collects were a little too severe for English ears. The collects of 1549 are generally richer than the Latin originals. Those written new in 1661 (Advent 3, Epiphany 5, and Easter Even) and those further expanded are more ornate again. There is also a tendency to relate collects to readings or to general seasonal themes. The new or adapted Advent collects were specially written about subjects and Dearmer thinks them better for it. Certainly they passed swiftly into Anglican consciousness and have frequently provided the basis for Advent sermons.

It has become usual and almost commonplace to praise the matchless perfection of the prayer book collects. With greater perception and frankness Percy Dearmer both lauded them as the finest prayers in the language and stressed they were not equally good. 'The habit of regarding all "Prayer Book Collects" as necessarily perfect,' he wrote in 1919, 'has almost destroyed that faculty of discrimination which it is very important for the Church in these times of change to recover. Some of the original collects show signs of weariness or haste, some fall into a sameness of phrase or idea. Some, following literally their originals in the Sarum Missal, are rather arid'.[24]

No new collects were added to the offices of *The Book of Common Prayer* and such new collects as came into use were intended for days and occasions for which 1662 made no provision. The 1885 draft of the American book shows that late-nineteenth-century collects were frequently verbose and overloaded with ideas and images. In a period of much collect making, Dearmer holds up those of Bishop John Wordsworth as worthy of special respect, as fine modern examples of the art of collect making, and he draws special attention to the collect for Saint George. Dearmer offers us a perfect example of how inculturated forms of prayer can be and how unaware of it we can be :

> O Lord God of hosts, who didst give grace to thy servant George to lay aside the fear of man and to confess thee even

[24]Percy Dearmer, *The Art of Public Worship*, Milwaukee 1919, 159.

in death; Grant that we, and all our countrymen who bear office in the world, may think lightly of earthly place and honour, and seek rather to please the Captain of our salvation, who hath chosen us to be his soldiers; to whom with thee and the Holy Ghost be thanks and praise from all the armies of thy saints now and for evermore.[25]

A collect for Saint George tests the ingenuity of the most accomplished liturgical artisan. The Wordsworth collect did not gain the favour of Bishop Gore's committee (though it got into *The Cuddesdon Office Book*) and the Oxford book has this :

Visit us, we beseech thee, O Lord, with thy loving-kindness, and grant that the people of this land after the example of thy servant Saint George, may boldly confess the faith of Christ crucified, and manfully fight under his banner against sin, the world, and the devil, and continue thy faithful soldiers and servants unto their lives' end; through the merits of the same thy Son, Jesus Christ our Lord.[26]

Little progress with the Patron Saint of England has been made. David Silk uses the collect from the Roman Missal in his 1980 collection, *Prayers for use at the Alternative Services*. George Timms wrote this collect, published in 1982 :

Almighty God, who called your holy martyr George to bear before men the banner of the cross, and to serve you even unto death : Grant that, following his fortitude, we may be strong in the Christian warfare, and with him attain the crown of eternal life; through Jesus Christ our Lord.[27]

Certainly, Wordsworth's collect is a remarkable piece. The Oxford collect relies too heavily and obviously on the baptism service. Timms's collect is too much the all purpose saint's day prayer : 'Almighty God, who called N. to . . . : Grant that . . . ' ending in a stock phrase. Wordsworth acknowl-

[25]Dearmer, *Public Worship* 173.

[26]*The Diocesan Service Book authorised for Use in the Diocese of Oxford*, London and Oxford 1920, 32.

[27]*The Cloud of Witnesses*, London 1982, 72.

edges that George is both martyr and patron saint and uses the image of Christians as 'soldiers of Christ' popularised by Wesley's 'Soldiers of Christ, arise', Baring-Gould's 'Onward, Christian Soldiers', Walsham How's 'Soldiers of the Cross, arise!' and J. H. Clark's translation of the Latin hymn *Pugnate, Christi milites* (from the Bourges Breviary of 1734 and included in Newman's *Hymni Ecclesiae* of 1838) as 'Soldiers, who are Christ's below'. His is not a timeless collect, nor a modern one, but may well be considered both right and admirable for its time and place.

3. The Prayer Books of 1928 and 1929

The invaluable volume *Liturgy and Worship : A Companion to the Prayer Books of the Anglican Communion,* edited by W. K. Lowther Clarke, appeared in 1932, when America and Scotland had definitive new prayer books and England had an unlawful book. In the chapter entitled 'Collects, Epistles and Gospels' K. D. Mackenzie examined the collect form and indicated the source, in general terms, of all the collects. He also added delightful, pithy, and incisive comments about many of them. No new collects were added to the Sunday cycle during these revisions. A number of additional collects for second celebrations on major feasts were added (recovered in part from 1549) and so was a significant collection of collects for feast days and the commons of various saints. Collects for Corpus Christi, the Transfiguration, and Mary Magdalene appear and are of particular interest, but otherwise there was little development shown by these books.

4. The Period of Transition 1930–1972

In this period Anglican liturgy passes from traditional to contemporary language, and the full effect of the liturgical movements can be observed. The transition does not begin at once, indeed its effect will not be noted for more than thirty years after the revisions of the late 1920s. But the highly influential liturgical texts produced by the Church of South India and the Anglican Province of South Africa did not appear spontaneously and the renewed interest in liturgy, its creation as well as its history, began early in the period.

Official Anglican liturgy has always been supplemented by private endeavour. Two strands contributed to collect writing : collections of private prayers and the provision of supplementary offices. From the beginnings of Anglicanism collections such as Richard Daye's *Christian Prayers* (1578), John Cosin's *Collection of Private Devotions* (1627), and Lancelot Andrewes's *Preces Privatae* (published posthumously in 1648 and in a revised edition by F. E. Brightman in 1903) not only nourished the spirituality of clergy and educated laity but created a private devotion that paralleled the liturgy. There was renewed interest in books of prayers in the late-nineteenth century and among the more influential collections were Dean Charles Vaughan's *Family Prayers,* W. H. Draper's *A Harvest of Myrrh and Spices* (1898), and, from the Anglo-Catholic wing, T. T. Carter's *The Guide to Heaven : A Book of Prayers for Every Want* (1891). William Bright's influential *Ancient Collects and Other Prayers* (6th ed. 1887) began as a supplementary prayer manual but introduced the English Church to the riches of liturgical prayer, Eastern and Western. The Anglo-Catholic movement also initiated the recovery of medieval offices. The best known version was *The Priest's Book of Private Devotion* which contained Prime and the Hours with other devotions. It added to its calendar names that did not appear in 1662 'for the purposes of devotion' and provided collects for them. There was an inevitable crossing over from the supplementary devotional texts to the official liturgy and with the failure of the 1928Eng this was tacitly accepted if not actively encouraged.

Among the more influential books were *The Cuddesdon Office Book* prepared for use at the theological college at Cuddesdon, near Oxford, and the collections of F. B. Macnutt and Eric Milner-White. Macnutt gathered prayers from many sources, and they were published in *The War Primer* (prepared hastily in 1939 at Archbishop Lang's suggestion) and, more fully, in *The Prayer Manual* (published posthumously in 1951). Milner-White was a prolific writer of prayers and a diligent compiler;[28] his collections include *Cambridge Offices and Oraisons* (with B.T.D. Smith, 1921; new ed. 1949), *The Kingdom, the Power and the Glory* (4th ed. 1934), *Daily Prayer* (with G. W. Briggs, 1941), *After the Third Collect,* and *A Procession of Passion Prayers* (1962). These were supplemented in 1967 by Frank Colquhoun's first collection, *Parish Prayers.* All exercised, in different degrees, an influence on the collects of the current books. The relation between official and unofficial texts requires further investigation, but it seems likely that the proliferation of additional forms, widely accepted within the Church though still unofficial, reduces the urgency of liturgical change. The freedom allowed in England, as a result of the failure of the 1928 book, contrasts very strongly with the reassertion by the American bishops of the normative nature of *The Book of Common Prayer,* meaning, in the American context, the book so designated at the present time by the General Convention. In 1928 the Americans had one book and the English had two. Although the American Episcopal Church supplements its Prayer Book with volumes such as *Lesser Feasts and Fasts* and *The Book of Occasional Services* (and with study texts that will lead to the next revision), it does not have the plethora of texts, authorised and commended, that is found in the Church of England.

The Supplement to the Book of Common Prayer, published by the Indian SPCK in 1961, and the product of an earlier proposed revision, provides a number of saints' days collects but

---

[28]His prayers were not universally admired. Professor E. L. Mascall wrote of Milner-White : 'He had acquired the reputation of being a great liturgical expert, but I think he knew very little about either the history or the theology of liturgy. He produced several manuals of prayers and was much in demand as a writer of collects for special occasions. But, beautiful as these undoubtedly are, they have always seemed to me to be badly lacking in strength and drive'. *Sarabande : The Memoirs of E. L. Mascall,* Leominster 1992, 70.

only adds Whitsun Eve to the general calendar. The Canadian *Draft Book of Common Prayer* of 1959 (1959Can) maintained the standard 1662 structure for the liturgical year and made only slight additions to it, for example, by adding the octave days of Christmas and Easter. The 1662 collects were very slightly modified and a very few new ones were added. The 1966 Welsh Eucharist (1966Wales) also follows the traditional calendar structure and maintains Sundays after Trinity. With the dominant perception that collects are linked to readings, lectionary changes give rise to concern about the appropriateness of collects. There are no changes in the 1959Can lections, but 1966Wales introduces an Old Testament lesson in Advent and from Septuagesima to Good Friday.

The main changes take place between Advent Sunday and the Sundays after the Epiphany. 1959Can changes the collect for Advent 4 to 'Raise up, we beseech thee, O Lord, thy power, and come among us . . . ' and also changes the ending, omitting the words 'through the satisfaction of thy Son our Lord'. 1966Wales adopts the changes of 1928Amer. For Christmas Day, 1959Can uses the 1662 collect with a modernised version of 1549 as an alternative, following the practice of 1928Amer. It also give January 1 the main title of 'The Octave Day of Christmas' and provides the Christmas collect, together with additional collects for the Circumcision and New Year's Day. This is a reversion to earlier liturgical practice. Brightman writes that the change from the Octave Day to the Circumcision 'has altered the proportion of things, and in fact turned the day into a commemoration of circumcision rather than of the Circumcision of our Lord; not to edification'.[29] 1959Can follows 1928Eng in giving a New Year's collect (no 177). The Christmas Day collect is then used until the Epiphany and there is no provision for the Second Sunday after Christmas Day; 1966Wales uses the provision of 1928Eng. The 1662 Epiphany collect is expanded in 1959Can (no 178) and it also specifically provides for the Baptism of

[29]Brightman, *The English Rite* xcv, London, 1915.

our Lord with a collect that can be used at a second service on the Epiphany or on any weekday in the Octave (no 179).

This latter collect is heavily dependent on the Christmas collect. 1959Can also has a collect for the missionary work of the Church overseas (no 180) that may be used throughout the Epiphany season on weekdays. 1966Wales made slight amendment to the 1662 Epiphany collect, changing 'which' to 'who' and concluding 'may after this life enjoy the vision of thy glorious Godhead'. On the Second Sunday after the Epiphany, 1966Wales has a baptism collect dependent on nos 8 and 179 (no 181). As a result, each of the 1662 Epiphany collects is moved on a Sunday and that for Epiphany 6 is omitted entirely. It has a modified collect for Lent 5 which picks up the theme of Passion Sunday, the subtitle given in the book (no 182). The opening line and the conclusion are from 1662.

On Maundy Thursday both 1959Can and 1966Wales add a eucharistic collect; the two forms, though related, and derived from the medieval collect for Corpus Christi, attributed to Saint Thomas Aquinas, are different (nos 183–84). Versions of this collect had previously been provided for 'Commemoration of' or 'Thanksgiving for' the institution of the Holy Eucharist (no 49). The Oxford *Diocesan Service Book* (1920) has the 1966Wales version, though it begins, as the Roman Missal does, 'O God, who in this wonderful Sacrament . . . .' 1929Scot begins 'O Lord Jesus Christ, who in a wonderful Sacrament . . . ' and includes 'we beseech thee'. 1959Can has the 1928Eng version but beginning 'O Lord'. *The Cuddesdon Office Book* (new ed. 1940) has the Canadian version but with 'perceive' rather than 'know'. We must conclude that there have been two versions in circulation since very early this century.

Table 1 indicates the various texts used in the versions cited above, together with the supplement to the Indian BCP and the *English Missal* (3rd ed. 1958).

These may be compared with nos 455–59 in which the address is uniformly to the Father and the reference to Christ's passion in one way or another. There is, it seems, a contem-

1	God, who in a wonderful Sacrament O God, who in this wonderful Sacrament O God, who under a wonderful sacrament O Lord Jesus Christ, who in a wonderful sacrament O Lord, who in a wonderful Sacrament	India/Canada/Cuddesdon Oxford English Missal 1929Scot 1928Eng
2	hast left unto us a memorial of thy passion hast left us a memorial of thy passion	1929Scot/India/Canada/ Oxford 1928Eng/Cuddesdon/English Missal
3	Grant us, we beseech thee, so to venerate Grant us so to reverence Grant us so to venerate	1929Scot/India/Oxford/ English Missal 1928Eng/Canada Cuddesdon
4	the sacred mysteries of thy Body and Blood the holy mysteries of thy Body and Blood	1929Scot/India/Cuddesdon/ Oxford/English Missal 1928Eng/Canada

Table 1

porary difficulty about the address which comes from the way in which the original is addressed to God but refers to *passionis tuae memoriam*. Anglican liturgists have become wary, it seems, of addressing Christ as God!

Both 1959Can and 1966Wales have followed the example of the 1928 revisions in changing the third Good Friday collect, though neither follow exactly the provisions of those books. The first line is the same in both. Canada follows and slightly modifies 1928Eng : 'Have mercy upon the Jews, thine ancient people, and upon all who reject and deny thy Son; take from them . . . '. The Welsh revision is more extensive (no 185).[30]

There are other minor variations : the omission of 'preventing us' from the 1662 Easter collect in 1959Can, which also has a second collect based on 1929Scot; Wales second Easter collect drawn from 1928Amer/Eng; the return to 'example' in Easter 2. On Whitsunday, 1959Can has another new collect in the 'yearly remembrance' shape, with the petition drawn from the words for the administration of confirmation (no 187). For the rest of the year both books use the 1662 provision of collects.

The Book of Common Worship of the Church of South India, authorised by the Synod in 1962, is less tied to the Prayer Book tradition. It has a restructured calendar. It has four Sundays before Christmas (also termed Sundays in Advent) followed by Christmas Eve and Christmas Day and up to seven Sundays after Christmas. There are nine Sundays before Easter (six to three before being also called Sundays in Lent, two before being Passion Sunday, then Palm Sunday), Holy Week and Easter itself, and six Sundays after Easter, leading to Pentecost and Trinity Sunday, Sundays 2–27 after Pentecost and the Sunday next before Advent. The Sundays all carry thematic and lections appropriate to the theme. For many Sundays CSI uses 1662 collects but changes their places.

---

[30]See my 'The Jews in the Good Friday Liturgy', *Anglican Theological Review*, vol. LXXVI, no. 1 (Winter 1994) 61–70.

It also has numerous new collects. The CSI provision was extensively used by the Joint Liturgical Group (JLG) in its 1968 volume *The Daily Office*. It followed the general shape of the Church's year in the CSI book but the themes were very different and this, inevitably, influenced the choice of collects. JLG chose to retain a number of existing collects 'in their traditional Anglican form' both because of their great beauty 'both in their Latin form and in Cranmerian English' and because of their wide use in non-Anglican churches.[31] The style of the collects was a problem, however, but one which could not be addressed with any seriousness until the liturgy was put into more modern English, then, the Group thought, the use of the collect itself would have to be reconsidered.[32]

The JLG collects passed largely without amendment into the November 1968 report of the Church of England Liturgical Commission *The Calendar and Lessons for the Church's Year*.[33] It concluded that a new lectionary required new collects and, though some people questioned the necessity for a collect for every Sunday and special occasion, the Commission decided to adopt the JLG collects. But the Commission's chairman, R.C.D. Jasper, found that he had to defend them when addressing the February 1969 Liturgical Conference of the Church Assembly. His speech sets out the principle problems faced by the churches as they moved towards a modern liturgy without being able or perhaps even wanting to abandon traditional and well-loved forms.

> Some comment has already been raised about the collects. Here, quite frankly, we regard the proposals as an interim measure pure and simple. We know perfectly well that this set of collects cannot be regarded as ideal, but the whole ques-

[31]R.C.D. Jasper, ed., *The Daily Office by the Joint Liturgical Group,* London 1968, 78.

[32]Jasper, *The Daily Office* 79.

[33]D.E.W. Harrison, Dean of Bristol, was chairman of JLG and vice-chairman of the Commission; R.C.D. Jasper was secretary of JLG and chairman of the Commission.

tion of the collects is, at the moment, exercising the minds of virtually every church, both here in this country and on the Continent, and no one is finding it an easy one to resolve. It is not simply a question of asking what form a collect should take if you are wishing to phrase it in contemporary language. This in itself is an extremely difficult problem; but there are far deeper questions, and questions which, quite frankly, we have all tended to ignore in days gone by. What is the function of a collect? And is the function of a collect necessarily the same in the Office as it is in the Eucharist? What sort of prayer should a collect be? What should a collect say? What should its content be? It seemed that such important questions of principle as these are involved. It would be very wrong, before any sort of answers to those questions are clear, to ask any one man or one small group of men to devote considerable time and energy in producing a set of collects for an entire Christian year, which might prove either to be on the wrong basis or even unacceptable. This would be a wanton waste of time and energy. Far better to produce some pilot scheme, setting out the whole of the problem as clearly as one can, trying to reduce the thing to basic principles, and then suggesting a possible solution and, with the solution, some examples.

If the Church could see these and decide whether they were on the right lines or not, one could then approach the whole question of a revision of the entire set of collects and do the job properly. I should hope that, so far as this set of collects is concerned, which is at present in the [JLG] Daily Office, it would be regarded as a purely temporary, stop-gap arrangement, which can stand until something much worthier can be evolved and, I hope, evolved on ecumenical lines.[34]

They were also one of the starting points for the first attempt at true modernization in *Modern Collects* (SAMC) published by the Church of the Province of South Africa in 1972. At that time South Africa used the JLG calendar and lectionary. These were subsequently abandoned with the result that few SAMC collects passed unamended into SAAPB. These

---

[34] *The Liturgical Conference 1969 : Report of Proceedings* 6.

three sets of collects provided models for a number of other churches and provinces, including *The Alternative Service Book 1980* (ASB) and the *Alternative Collects 1985* of the Anglican Church in Australia (AusAC). The Church of England Liturgical Commission began work on contemporary collects in 1970, and worked closely with JLG and the Province of South Africa. It took note of American developments (see below), of SAMC, and of an unofficial stopgap collection, *Collects with the New Lectionary* by Peter Akehurst and Anthony Bishop published by Grove Books in 1972. The Commission's proposals were published in 1975, went through the General Synod without significant change, and were authorised from 1 February 1977. In due course they became the ASB collects.

Another path towards a new liturgy was taken by the American Episcopal Church. A series of *Prayer Book Studies* was begun to pave the way for liturgical revision at a future, unspecified time. The first of these, in 1958, was concerned with baptism and confirmation and the second, published with it, dealt with the liturgical lectionary. In 1967 the General convention entrusted the Standing Liturgical commission with the task of preparing a revision of the 1928 *The Book of Common Prayer* (1928Amer). *Prayer Book Studies 19,* published in 1970, was concerned with the Church Year, including the calendar and the propers. It enables us to follow the Commission's thinking. The primary question was that of the continued viability of the classic form of the collect for use by congregations who are not used to its style and structure. The study was undertaken after the Roman Missal had been translated and this added a new perspective. ICEL frequently broke the Latin collect into two or three sentences and so avoided subordinate clauses. In particular, the Commission noted, the relative clause of the opening address was changed into a declarative statement which made it an acclamation. Two examples will demonstrate this approach :

The 22nd Sunday in Ordinary Time

Deus, virtutem, cuius est totum quod est optimum, insere pectoribus nostris tui nominis amorem, et praesta, ut in nobis, religionis augmento, quae sunt bona nutrias, ac, vigilanti studio, quae sunt nutrita custodias.

Almighty God, every good thing comes from you. Fill our hearts with love for you, increase our faith, and by your constant care protect the good you have given us.[35]

The 23rd Sunday in Ordinary Time

Deus, per quem nobis et redemptio venit et præstatur adoptio, filios dilectionis tuæ benignus intende, ut in Christo credentibus et vera tribuatur libertas, et hereditas æterna.

God our Father, you redeem us and make us your children in Christ. Look upon us, give us true freedom and bring us to the inheritance you promised.

After much discussion and consideration of alternative forms, the Standing Liturgical Commission decided to keep the classic structure and to modernize grammatical forms and vocabulary.[36] (SAMC, under the influence of Professor Leonard Lanham, used a relative clause introduced by 'who' rather than by 'you' and retained the second person throughout the rest of the prayer.) Every collect in 1928Amer was studied. Some were discarded. Others were changed and shortened; clutter was removed. Many new collects were provided, drawn from ancient and modern sources or newly composed. Familiar collects were moved in order to relate them more directly to the new lections, though the Commission's guiding principle was that a good collect should not be tied to those lections but be useful at a variety of types of service on a given day or for

[35]The French translation, closer in style to the Latin, deserves comparison : *Dieu puissant, de qui vient tout don parfait, enracine en nos coeurs l'amour de ton nom; resserre nos liens avec toi, pour développer ce qui est bon en nous; veille sur nous avec sollicitude pour protéger ce que tu as fait grandir.*

[36]*Prayer Book Studies 19,* New York 1970, 42.

a given season. The result, in that volume, was the text of
the Sunday and holy day propers, together with those for the
Common of Saints and Special Occasions. These passed into
Authorised Services 1973 and, after further revision, into *The
Book of Common Prayer* of 1979.

5. The Anglican Collect from 1979

The majority of the collects in this collection are modern,
drawn from those currently in use in a number of provinces
of the Anglican Communion. They come from the prayer
books of the American Episcopal Church, the Anglican
Church in Australia, the Anglican Church of Canada, the
Church of England, the Church of Ireland, the Church of
the Province of Southern Africa, and the Church in Wales.
In general, the collects are given in modern language and in
English. The Welsh liturgy is still in traditional language and
only a few of its collects are used. The American *The Book
of Common Prayer,* 1979, provides traditional and contemporary
versions of the collects, and the Church of England eventually issued the collects of *The Alternative Service Book 1980* in
language suitable for Rite B, the traditional language rite.
In both cases only modern language versions are given here.
Modern Anglican collects appear in a number of languages.
The Welsh prayer book is bilingual. The American book has
been translated into Spanish, French, and other languages.
Translation and the creation of collects in another language
raise issues which cannot be dealt with here.

The Anglican Church of Australia provided two collects
for each Sunday in its 1978 prayer book : a modernised but
unamended version of 1662 and, as an alternative, the first
collect for each Sunday from the English translation of the
Prayers from the Roman Missal produced by the International
Commission on English in the Liturgy (ICEL). The Collects
used in the Missal of Paul VI translated by ICEL have clearly
influenced the development of Anglican forms, but they are

not included in this collection because they are, at least until the new English translation is published, readily available.

SOURCES OF TEXTS

1972 *Modern Collects,* Church of the Province of South Africa [SAMC]

1973 *Authorized Services 1973,* Episcopal Church in the United States of America [AmerAuthS]

1978 *An Australian Prayer Book,* The Church of England in Australia [AusPB]

1979 *The Book of Common Prayer and Administration of the Sacraments and Other Rites and Ceremonies of the Church . . . According to the Use of the Episcopal Church,* Episcopal Church in the United States of America [AmerBCP]

1980 *The Alternative Service Book 1980,* Church of England [ASB]

1984 *Alternative Prayer Book 1984 according to the use of The Church of Ireland* [IrAPB]

1984 *The Book of Common Prayer for use in The Church in Wales* [WalesBCP]

1985 *The Book of Alternative Services of the Anglican Church of Canada* [CanBAS]

1985 *Alternative Collects 1985,* The Anglican Church of Australia [AusAC]

1989 *An Anglican Prayer Book 1989,* Church of the Province of Southern Africa [SAAPB]

1989 *A New Zealand Prayer Book,* Church of the Province of New Zealand [NZPB]

The appearance and significance of *Modern Collects* has already been noted. It was not a printed text but a typed and duplicated manuscript in a flimsy card cover. Its influence was greater than this ephemeral format suggests. *Authorized Services* appeared the next year and used the collects proposed in *Prayer Book Studies 19.* There is no borrowing between AmerAuthS and SAMC and the developments operate in parallel.

The American one remains largely internal. The English one, for CSI, JLG, and SAMC lead eventually to the ASB collects, draws from a wider field. Both have roots in 1662 and the 1928 revisions. *An Australian Prayer Book* retains 1662 in modernized form for the first collect and uses ICEL texts for the alternative. This ultimately proved to be unsatisfactory and the *Alternative Collects* appeared in 1985. The immediate sources of these were indicated and we can see that the Liturgical Commission drew on 1662, 1928Eng, AmerAuthS, AmerBCP, JLG (by way of *The Calendar and Lessons for the Church's Year*), the short-lived English Series 3 collects, SAMC, and other sources. The Series 3 collects prepared the way for those of *The Alternative Service Book 1980.* Ireland had produced revised services in parallel with England in 1973; the *Alternative Prayer Book 1984* uses a large number of ASB collects, though it often makes slight amendments and changes the punctuation and endings. The Welsh *The Book of Common Prayer* is the most disappointing of the modern books. Wales had been well ahead liturgically with Arthur Couratin's 1966 rite for the Holy Eucharist, but it eschewed modern language and so has very few instances of new collects. The Canadian *The Book of Alternative Services* uses a form of the Common Lectionary, as does AmerBCP. ASB and IrAPB use the JLG two-year lectionary with Sunday themes. The CanBAS collects are generally American in derivation, though there are a number of new ones. The Southern African *An Anglican Prayer Book* also uses the Common Lectionary; the SAMC collects were produced in line with the JLG lectionary and in consequence SAAPB draws on American and Canadian prayers. The 1989 *A New Zealand Prayer Book* requires separate consideration (see below).

DEVELOPING NEW COLLECTS : THE GOOD SHEPHERD

One set of collects is particularly illuminating. In the Missal of 1570, the Second Sunday after Easter took up the theme of the Good Shepherd. This had been the Mass of the week but not the Sunday in the Sarum Missal. Pius Parsch points out that practically all the units comprising the Mass formulary mention the Good Shepherd thus giving the Mass a remarkable unity.[37] John 10:11-16, 'I am the good shepherd', is the Gospel; 1 Peter 2:21-25 is the Epistle. The Alleluia combines Luke 24:35, Jesus made known in the breaking of bread, with John 10:14, and so combines the story of the road to Emmaus with the good shepherd. John 10:14 is used for the Communion. The collect *Deus, qui in Filii tui humilitate* (no xxvi) has no reference to the good shepherd, but the Roman stational church was Saint Peter's, judged by Parsch to be particularly apt given the Lord's command to Peter 'feed my sheep'. The Prayer Books of 1549, 1552, and 1662 had the same lections; the collect (no 66), composed for the 1549 book, speaks of Christ as both 'a sacrifice for sin and also an ensample of godly life'.

'Good Shepherd Sunday', as it came to be known, has kept a place in the Anglican and Roman calendars. It is kept on the Second Sunday after Easter in Wales, New Zealand, Ireland, and England. In England, only Year 2 uses John 10 as the Gospel. Year 1 uses the Emmaus readings but keeps the same collect (no 502). Ireland also has the Emmaus road in Year 1 and the Good Shepherd in Year 2, but it has collects proper for each year. The Fourth Sunday of Easter (Third after) has Good Shepherd lections in the United States of America, Canada, Australia, and in *The Lutheran Book of Worship*.

The ASB collect *God of peace, who brought again from the dead* (no 502) derives from SAMC but was revised by the Liturgical Commission. It is also used in CanBAS, SAAPB, and AusAC. AmerBCP has its own collect, drafted by Massey Shepherd, which has not been used by other provinces. The ASB collect derives from Hebrews 13:20-21 :

> Now may the God of peace, who brought again from the dead our Lord Jesus, the great shepherd of the sheep by the blood

[37]Pius Parsch, *The Church's Year of Grace*, vol. 3, Collegeville 1954, 74.

of the eternal covenant, make you complete in everything good
so that you may do his will, working among us that which
is pleasing in his sight, through Jesus Christ, to whom be glory
forever and ever. Amen.

The collect begins by addressing God as 'God of peace' but
thereafter it follows the Hebrews passage word for word in
the RSV translation. NZPB revises this collect and puts it
into a more traditional form (no 501); it is still not entirely
satisfactory in the way it repeats 'work' in the fifth and sixth
lines and in the very weak 'good' at the end of the line six.
These lines might be rewritten as

> . . . make us perfect in everything good
> and work in us what is pleasing in your sight.

NZPB also has a splendid prayer addressed to the Good Shepherd :

> Good Shepherd of the sheep,
> by whom the lost are sought
> and guided into the fold;
> feed us and we shall be satisfied,
> heal us and we shall be whole,
> and lead us that we may be with you,
> with the Father and the Holy Spirit.[38]

The Lutheran collect for the Fourth Sunday of Easter, after
addressing God, draws on Hebrews before continuing with
the petition and ending in doxological form :

> God of all power,
> you called from death our Lord Jesus,
> the great shepherd of the sheep.
> Send us as shepherds to rescue the lost,
> to heal the injured,
> and to feed one another with knowledge and understanding.

AusPB uses 1662 Easter 4 together with a rather weak Good

[38]NZPB 596.

Shepherd collect, and Ireland, Year 2, also has a weak one (no 503).

ASB shows how slavish adherence to the biblical text creates a poor collect. In NZPB, the Lutheran book, and AmerBCP (no 504) the basic image of Christ as Good Shepherd has been united with other images of shepherding to create a richer collect that resonates with Scripture rather than repeating it. A wrong word can destroy the power of a collect, and IrAPB often falls into that trap; here it used a stock phrase 'grace to follow in his steps', but sheep don't follow in the shepherd's step; they follow where he leads, as Massey Shepherd says.

A NEW ZEALAND PRAYER BOOK

For every Sunday NZPB provides three prayer texts described as collects. In general, one of them fulfils the criteria for being a collect in the traditional sense employed here. This is the set for the Fifth Sunday after the Epiphany :

> Merciful God,
> in Christ you make all things new;
> transform the poverty of our nature
> by the riches of your grace,
> and in the renewal of our lives
> make known your heavenly glory;
> through Jesus Christ our Redeemer.

> Jesus our Lord,
> you have taught us that judgment begins at the house of God;
> save us from our self-satisfaction, rigidity and corruption,
> so that we may stand ready to do your will.

> Jesus, when you call us to challenge authority,
> help us to follow closely your example,
> that we may be ready to suffer for the truth,
> and to give whatever glory there may be to God.

It is no part of my argument that prayers like the second and third ones here are invalid or inappropriate but only that they are not collects as such because they do not belong to this particular liturgical literary genre. It may be that, in due time, they will be counted as collects because NZPB follows a path already taken by ICEL in the preparation of the first English version of the Roman Sacramentary. Kathleen Hughes tells how ICEL turned, in 1971, to the Trappist monk Robert Morhous for alternative Opening Prayers.[39] There was 'something refreshingly new about the style and content' of some initial prayers that he wrote, and these encouraged ICEL to take a more creative approach.[40] This prayer, given as an example by Hughes, was inspired by the Latin collect for Passion Sunday :

> Eternal Father
> by his birth as man
> and his death on a tree
> your Son Jesus Christ
> came as a servant
> and emptied himself
> of divine prestige.
>
> Grant us the blessing
> to follow him now
> in love and humility
> through the way of his emptiness
> to the sharing
> of his glory.[41]

Morhous, together with Peter Scagnelli, provided the majority of the alternative prayers, though they were subsequently revised by the ICEL secretariat. These were not intended to be collects in the Latin tradition but to initiate an appropriate liturgical form for a contemporary English liturgy. A few examples must suffice to illustrate this :

> Father in heaven,
> our hearts desire the warmth of your love
> and our minds are searching for the light of your Word.

[39]Hughes, 'Original Texts'.
[40]Ibid., 'Original Texts' 227.
[41]Ibid., 'Original Texts' 228.

Increase our longing for Christ our Saviour
and give us the strength to grow in love
that the dawn of his coming
may find us rejoicing in his presence
and welcoming the light of his truth.[42]

Almighty God and Father of light,
a child is born for us and a son is given to us.
Your eternal Word leaped down from heaven
in the silent watches of the night,
and now your Church is filled with wonder
at the nearness of her God.

Open our hearts to receive his life
and increase our vision with the rising of dawn,
that our lives may be filled with his glory and his peace,
who lives and reigns for ever and ever.[43]

God and Father of our Lord Jesus Christ,
though your people walk in the valley of darkness,
no evil should they fear;
for they follow in faith the call of the shepherd
whom you have sent for their hope and strength.

Attune our minds to the sound of his voice,
lead our steps in the path he has shown,
that we may know the strength of his outstretched arm
and enjoy the light of your presence for ever.[44]

God our Father,
gifts without measure flow from your goodness
to bring us your peace.
Our life is your gift.
Guide our life's journey,
for only your love makes us whole.
Keep us strong in your love.[45]

---

[42]Roman Missal, 1st Sunday of Advent.
[43]Ibid., The Nativity of our Lord—Dawn Mass.
[44]Ibid., 4th Sunday of Easter.
[45]Ibid., 18th Sunday in Ordinary Time.

The ICEL text of the Roman Missal appeared in 1974 and came into use on the First Sunday of Advent of that year. That is to say, it appeared before any of the Anglican liturgical texts we are now considering and makes it the more remarkable that none of the collections of collects were influenced by these original texts until NZPB fifteen years later.

Not all original texts cling rigidly to traditional forms, as most of the collects marked 'new' in this collection do, or depart from it in the way that Morhous does. Janet Morley attempted to write alternatives to the weekly ASB collects using inclusive and woman-centred language.[46] Morley found the collect 'a fascinating and economic literary genre, combining a recognizable form with considerable flexibility of use'.[47] The main areas requiring revision were the 'trinitarian padding' which she describes as 'words that by their familiarity go in one ear and out the other' and 'the constantly irritating presence of the superfluous "men" '. Of the twenty-nine references to men noted in the index, only twelve come from contemporary collects, and of those ten come from ASB, which also uses 'man' and 'mankind'. Morley also notes that the direct address to God 'seems to be routine in a way that paralyses fresh thought or perception'. The index of first lines reveals very few collects that do not begin with direct address and few addresses other than 'Almighty God', 'Almighty and . . . God', 'God our Father', 'Heavenly Father', and the like. Whereas Kathleen Hughes can offer a number of new titles in *Opening Prayers for Experimental Use at Mass* (1986)—

> God of majesty and power
> God whose will is justice for the poor and peace for the afflicted
> God of glory and splendour
> Guardian of our homes and source of all blessings
> Lord God of the nations
> God of the covenant

[46]Janet Morley, 'Liturgy and Danger' in Monica Furlong, ed., *Mirror to the Church : Reflections on Sexism,* London 1988, 28f.

[47]Morley, 'Liturgy and Danger' 28.

God of light and life
God of all mystery, all wisdom, all truth

—the index of first-lines lists only

Eternal Giver of life and light
God of peace
God of power and life
Holy God and Lord of Life

and a series of SAAPB collects beginning 'Sovereign Lord'.[48]
Morley used titles such as deliverer, disturber, healer, friend,
beloved, hidden God, vulnerable God, God of the dispos-
sessed.[49] Janet Schaffran and Pat Kozak list 102 alternative
titles of God.[50] NZPB includes the following :

God of hope
God of Israel old and new
God for whom we wait and watch
God faithful and true
God in Trinity, Creator, Saviour, Giver of life and truth
Creator God
God of compassion
God of the desert
God of the unexpected
God of the hungry
Infinite, intimate God
Crucified saviour, naked God
Lord of the passover
God our friend
Lord of the Church
Servant God
God of all delight
Gentle God
God, the mother and father of us all

[48]Hughes, 'Original Texts' 252.

[49]Her collection of collects was published in *All Desires Known,* London
1988 and later editions.

[50]Janet Schaffran and Pat Kozak, *More Than Words : Prayer and Ritual
for Inclusive Communities,* 2nd ed., Oak Park, Ill., 1988.

Morley has demonstrated flexibility within the traditional collect form; NZPB pushes beyond those traditional boundaries. It is unlikely that either form will prevail to the exclusion of the other, but that both will find a place in the liturgy. We may wish to keep 'collect' as a term for a quite specific literary genre and use 'prayer', qualified or not by 'opening', 'entry', 'proper', or some other term, to cover all forms. NZPB continues to use the term 'collect', and that certainly means that we must redefine the meaning of the word.

COLLECTS AND COMPILATIONS

The collect is, in general, a discrete unit. It could be said to be free-floating. Compilers of new prayer books have been able to choose from three options : using an already existing collect, modifying an existing collect, and writing a new collect. In setting a collect as proper to a certain Sunday or feast day, another set of options is available. Some collects belong self-evidently to certain days because they celebrate so obviously some aspect of the mystery of creation and redemption. Some have been inspired by particular lections or themes and they tend to move with them and to be displaced if they are abandoned. Others are detached, free-floating, and available for use in any suitable position. Proper collects are not established first. The calendar determining the nature of the day or season comes first; then the lections; then the collect. Collect and lections together form the propers for a given day.

As the different liturgical commissions have employed the options available to them in widely different ways, it has been difficult to present the collects in an orderly way. Three methods have been employed to introduce a degree of order and to facilitate comparison between texts. In the first, the collects are presented in order according to the time and season; so, all the collects for the Sundays of Advent are gathered together, Sunday by Sunday. This immediately presents difficulties. The 1662 collect for Advent 2—'Blessed Lord, who caused all holy Scriptures to be written for our learning'—

is used in three books on the same Sunday, but in the American and Canadian books it is used in the propers between Pentecost and Advent. The same scattering is found for other prayers. The second method involves grouping collects derived from a common original; so, all the collects deriving from the 1662 collect for Saint Philip and Saint James's Day have been put together.

The third method involves the grouping of collects that have a common theme; so, most of the collects concerned with the Eucharist, whether for Maundy Thursday or a feast of thanksgiving for its institution, have been gathered together. The current use of a collect and its immediate and remote sources are indicated. Charts and indexes should aid cross referencing and comparison. There is an index of first lines, though its effectiveness is reduced by a marked tendency to change the form of address when a collect is reused. There is also an index of key words. It is not an exhaustive concordance, but it should make it possible to track down a collect when only a few words are known or remembered.

PUNCTUATION AND LAYOUT

Even when collects appear to be identical, significant differences in punctuation and presentation may occur. ASB and IrAPB frequently use the same collect but print it with different punctuation. Where ASB divides the collect into two sentences, using a full stop, IrAPB uses a colon followed by a capital letter, as in the collect for Trinity Sunday :

> . . . live and reign in the perfect unity of love :
> Keep us in this faith, . . .

This use was adopted in SAMC; the opening address to God ends with a colon and the petition begins with a capital letter. A semicolon marks the end of the petition and is followed by the conclusion.

On Pentecost 3, ASB has this :

Lord God, our Father,
through our Saviour Jesus Christ
you have assured mankind of eternal life
and in baptism have made us one with him.
Deliver us from the death of sin
and raise us to new life in your love,
in the fellowship of the Holy Spirit,
by the grace of our Lord Jesus Christ.

IrAPB punctuates it differently :

Lord God our Father
through our Saviour Jesus Christ
you have assured mankind of eternal life,
and in baptism have made us one with him :
Deliver us from the death of sin
and raise us to new life in your love,
in the fellowship of the Holy Spirit,
by the grace of our Lord Jesus Christ.

Modern usage has tended to move away from the colon. *The Oxford Guide to English Usage* says that a colon 'links two grammatically complete clauses, but marks a step forward, from introduction to main theme, from cause to effect, or from premise to conclusion'.[51] For this reason it is ideal as the punctuation mark in a collect. The two parts are grammatically complete clauses, but the latter is the main theme or effect or, at least, the petition whose effectiveness derives from the former clause. A full stop is used at the end of sentences that are neither questions nor exclamations. The next word after a full stop normally has a capital letter. *The Chicago Manual of Style* notes that in contemporary usage clauses are separated more frequently by a semicolon than by a colon or are treated as separate sentences with the employment of a full stop.[52] Despite this, AmerBCP also favours the colon, followed, as in IrAPB, by a capital letter. AusAPB, WalesBCP, and SAAPB use colons followed by a lower-case letter.

[51] *The Oxford Guide to English Usage,* Oxford 1983, 193.
[52] *The Chicago Manual of Style,* 13th ed., Chicago and London 1982, 148.

Punctuation provides a guide to reading. Variations in punctuation may change the sense or flow of a prayer. There are significant differences between American punctuation, which, in this context, tends to be more traditional, and that employed by the Canadians. The same collect appears as AmerBCP Proper 12 and CanBAS Proper 17; it is, therefore, used on the same day throughout North America. AmerBCP prints it like this :

> O God, the protector of all who trust in you, without whom nothing is strong, nothing is holy: Increase and multiply upon us your mercy; that, with you as our ruler and guide, we may so pass through things temporal, that we lose not the things eternal; through Jesus Christ our Lord, . . .

This is almost word for word the 1662 collect for Trinity 4 and it keeps the original punctuation. In CanBAS it appears like this :

> O God,
> the protector of all who trust in you,
> without whom nothing is strong, nothing is holy,
> increase and multiply upon us your mercy,
> that with you as our ruler and guide,
> we may so pass through things temporal,
> that we lose not the things eternal;
> through Jesus Christ our Lord, . . .

ASB punctuates it in a third way :

> Lord God,
> the protector of all who trust in you,
> without whom nothing is strong, nothing is holy :
> increase and multiply upon us your mercy,
> that you being our ruler and guide
> we may so pass through things temporal
> that we lose not the things eternal.
> Grant this, heavenly Father,
> for the sake of Jesus Christ our Lord.

In both the Canadian and English versions the sense has been lost. The reason for receiving mercy—that we may pass through things temporal in such a way that we do not lose the things eternal—follows from the petition for mercy. The 'with you as our ruler and guide' is parenthetical and so is placed between commas. There are other examples of this changed punctuation in CanBAS, e.g., Lent 2.

SAMC and SAAPB use layout as an alternative to some punctuation and as a guide to reading. The initial address to God, followed in other books by a comma, has no punctuation; the full address concludes, as already noted, with a colon :

> Merciful Lord
> you have taught us through your Son
>   that love is the fulfilling of the law :

This method is used for the first collect in each set through SAAPB. SAMC also introduced the hanging indentation. The introduction to the book explains why :

> The end of a line and a comma within a line mark a pause, at which the intonation may rise or fall. An indented line indicates that a falling intonation must be avoided at the end of the preceding line (a falling intonation signals a major grammatical boundary). There should either be no pause at the end of the line or, alternatively, pause and a rising intonation.[53]

A good example of this method is provided by the collect used throughout the Triduum :

> Holy and Everliving God
> who revealed the glory of your Son
>   when he was exalted on the Cross :
> Accept our praise and thanksgiving
>   for the power of his victory
> and grant us never to be afraid
>   to suffer or to die with him;
>   our crucified King who lives and reigns
>   in all eternity

[53]SAMC 2.

with you and the Holy Spirit
one God for ever and ever.

The collects in this collection have been printed in continu-
ous form and punctuation has been added when necessary
to those from SAMC and SAAPB.

ENDINGS

In some liturgical books collects are printed with their full
endings; in others additional endings are provided for in a
rubric or note. All AmerBCP, AusAC, CanBAS, and
WalesBCP collects are printed in full. ASB provides that when
a collects ends with the words 'Christ our Lord', the minister may add the longer ending 'who is alive and reigns with
you and the Holy Spirit, one God, now and for ever'.[54]
SAAPB allows this longer ending—in the form 'who lives and
reigns with you . . . '—for collects that end 'through Jesus
Christ our Lord . . . ', 'through our Lord and Saviour Jesus
Christ . . . ', and 'for Jesus Christ's sake . . . '.[55] IrAPB has
the same rules as ASB and uses the same form of the longer
ending as SAAPB.

The following forms of Trinitarian endings are in general
use :

1a who lives and reigns with you and the Holy Spirit, one
God, now and for ever.

1b who lives and reigns with you and the Holy Spirit, one
God, for ever and ever.

2 to whom, with you and the Holy Spirit, be honor and
glory, now and for ever.

3 who lives and reigns with you, in the unity of the Holy
Spirit, one God, now and for ever.

4a where with you and the Holy Spirit he lives and reigns,
one God, in glory everlasting. *(Used when there has been
a reference to life in heaven or in the kingdom.)*

[54]ASB 32 n.8.
[55]SAAPB 128 n.6.

4b   where he lives and reigns with you and the Holy Spirit, one God, now and for ever.

5a   who lives and reigns with you and the Holy Spirit, one God, in glory everlasting.

5b   who with you and the Holy Spirit lives and reigns, one God, in glory everlasting.

5c   who with you and the Holy Spirit lives and reigns, one God, now and for ever.

THE USE OF THE COLLECT IN THE REVISED LITURGIES

The compilers of *The Promise of His Glory* pointed out that, historically, the collect has been a succinct prayer, prayed by the president. In the Eucharist it concludes the introduction and need not be linked thematically to the readings. The collect is also used in other places, in the office, for example, and to conclude intercessions, a litany, or the silence after reading and psalmody in a vigil. Here, say the compilers, the collect relates more closely to whatever precedes it. Certainly the revised liturgies use a greatly increased number of collects and collect-type prayers.

1. *At the Eucharist.* In AmerBCP the Eucharistic liturgy may begin immediately with 'The Word of God' or it may have a penitential introduction. In the former case, it has the following structure :

Hymn, psalm or anthem (optional)
Introductory dialogue
'Collect for Purity' (optional)
Gloria in excelsis or other song of praise
or the *Kyrie* or *Trisagion*
The Collect of the Day

The minimum requirement is, therefore, the introductory dialogue, *Gloria, Kyrie,* or *Trisagion,* and the Collect. The ASB begins with a section entitled 'The Preparation' but allows the introductory welcome to be followed immediately by the collect. The rest of the material is either optional or may be used in another position. Most other Eucharistic rites also allow this short form, but we must recognise that in sung celebrations the collect usually comes after a good deal of preparatory material, perhaps including a penitential rite, and concludes one part of the Eucharist. Only NZPB suggests that the collect might be used elsewhere; it suggests before or after the sermon, a position that implies close relation to the readings, and the New Zealand prayers are closely linked to the lections.

AmerBCP has the celebrant greet the people before the collect. After they reply, the celebrant says 'Let us pray', the collect is said, and the people respond 'Amen'. WalesBCP has the greeting but not the call to prayer. AusPB and CanBAS provide for the celebrant to say 'Let us pray'.[56] The Canadian rubric says that the community may pray silently before the celebrant sings or says the collect and the people respond 'Amen'. IrAPB, the Scottish Liturgy of 1982, and NZPB lack an introductory invitation to prayer. An ASB note says that the collect 'may be introduced by the words "Let us pray" and a brief bidding, after which silence may be kept'.[57] Its absence from the main text means that congregations are rarely aware of it.

2. *At the Office.* The collect was not an original part of the Daily Office and probably only found a place there in the eighth century, borrowed from the Mass to provide a conclusion at Vespers.[58] In the Sarum Breviary it was used at Lauds and Vespers on Sundays, station days, and festivals. Cranmer introduced it into Morning and Evening Prayer. The 1662 Offices had three collects; four in Lent and Advent. The first of them was always the collect for the day. Many offices are self-contained and the first collect is one appropriate to the time (morning, midday, evening, night) or the day

[56]SAAPB also has 'Let us pray' and the final 'Amen'.
[57]ASB 116 n.9.
[58]Jasper-Bradshaw 123.

(Friday, Saturday, Sunday) rather than to the overall liturgical season. Compline has never used the collect for the day.

There is a good deal of variation in current use, but the main tendency is that use of the collect at the offices is encouraged if not actually required. In AmerBCP, the collect of the day may be used at the offices but is not mandatory. CanBAS is also permissive allowing the use of the collect for the day or another collect appropriate to the time of day. In ASB Morning and Evening Prayer the use of the Collect of the Day is mandatory. It is also mandatory in the shorter form of Morning Prayer but not of Evening Prayer. IrAPB follows ASB. SAAPB includes the collect but allows for its omission if the Eucharist is to follow. NZPB requires one of the collects of the day to be used at both Morning and Evening Worship and at Daily Services.

CHOICE AND NUMBER OF COLLECTS

In the Anglo-Catholic manual *Anglican Services* (1953) it takes more than two pages to set out how many collects should be said on a given day : one on major festivals, two when there are commemorations and on the Sunday in an octave, three on ordinary Sundays, on all days of semi-double or simple rank, and at Votive Masses, five or even seven at Masses of simple rite, and so on.[59] Today it is much simpler and there are two general principles. Only one collect is used. On weekdays, it is the collect of the previous Sunday unless other provision is made. Such divergences as there are spring from different ideas about the calendar and the nature and extent of feast days (e.g., whether they have one proper evening prayer or two) and some residual rules about seasons and octaves.

In his guide to Eucharistic celebration in the American Church, Howard Galley lays down that 'only one collect is used at a given service'.[60] The rule applies to *The Collect of the*

[59]*Anglican Services,* London 1953, 101–04.
[60]Howard E. Galley, *The Ceremonies of the Eucharist,* Cambridge, Mass., 1989, 81; the only exceptions, he writes, are ordinations and funerals.

Day; an additional collect may be said to conclude the Prayers (Intercessions). Galley suggests that on the Sundays in Lent and in the Easter season, one of the seasonal collects given in *Lesser Feasts and Fasts* may appropriately be used. *Lesser Feasts and Fasts* also suggests that, when Lenten weekdays displace Lesser feasts, the saint's name should be mentioned in the prayers and the Collect might be used to conclude them.[61] AmerBCP allows the collect 'appointed for any Sunday or other Feast' to be used at the evening service of the day before.[62] ASB does not rule out the use of two or more collects, but simply rules that when more than one collect is provided only one need be used.[63] ASB and IrAPB allow for one evening prayer of a Festival or Greater Holy Day (IrAPB : Holy Day); it is usually celebrated on the day itself but may be celebrated on the evening before. SAAPB holds to the general rule of using only one collect',[64] but it allows for the repetition, after the collect of the day, of the collect for Advent 1 throughout Advent and the collect for Ash Wednesday throughout Lent, as in 1662. An extra collect is also allowed on a Rogation Day, an Ember Day, and Harvest Thanksgiving, and on the feasts of Stephen, John, and the Holy Innocents when they occur on the Sunday after Christmas.[65] It also allows for the Sunday collect to be used at evening prayer on Saturday (except at Easter) and provides a first evening prayer for Christmas, the Epiphany, Ascension Day, Pentecost, Corpus Christi, and All Saints.[66] WalesBCP allows for more than one collect and for use of Sunday collects and of those of principal feasts at evening prayer on the previous day, and so provides for the order in which collects are to be said.[67]

[61]*Lesser Feasts and Fasts,* New York 1988, 20.
[62]AmerBCP 158.
[63]ASB 32 n.7.
[64]SAAPB 29.
[65]SAAPB 147 n.5.
[66]SAAPB 28.
[67]WalesBCP 1:xxv.

SOURCES OF THE COLLECTS

The source has been indicated for the majority of collects. The commentary on ASB produced by the liturgical commission lists the immediate source of each of its collects. The list is no more detailed than giving "CSI, 1662, New" or some other very brief statement. The commentary claims that 'to trace all of them back to their origin, either in their first appearance in writing or to the individuals who composed them, would be an immense task and in most cases impossible'.[68] It is certainly an immense task but, if a significant part of liturgical history is not to be lost, it is a necessary one. Every collect will have been amended in varying degrees since having first been written. Many are translations. Not only does the translation often involve amendment, as shown by the ICEL texts, but the translations, by Bright for example, have been further amended. Following each collect, I have endeavoured to provide some indication of the collect's ancestry. In some cases information is lacking, and I have opted for 'new' or, at most, a reference to another similar collect.

There is not a set of normative liturgical texts and, to my knowledge, this is the first attempt to gather texts of a particular sort and to provide some sort of concordance and cross referencing. A starting point for the current ICEL project of revising the English translation of the Roman Missal is textual criticism. At least in an elementary form it is a necessary part of the *creative* process, because of the need to know what the original text is saying before the central thought can be conveyed by translation.[69] Though Anglicans do not have to translate and adapt from an *editio typica,* a little research will show that many prayers derive directly from Greek and Latin originals and, of greater significance, translation is today an essential part of liturgical activity. The Anglican litur-

---

[68] *The Alternative Service Book 1980 : A Commentary by the Liturgical Commission,* London 1980, 51.

[69] ICEL, *Progress Report on the Revision of the Roman Missal,* Washington 1988, 12.

gist, used to operating in English, sometimes forgets that
Anglican liturgies are celebrated in diverse languages. Some,
like Welsh, have an ancient store of religious idioms; others
have been shaped by pre-Christian belief systems.

Many African Provinces are now preparing new liturgies,
and in doing so they want to be true to their Anglican inheritance.[70] To do this their liturgists must be able to ascer-
tain the original meaning of key words and phrases and to
understand how this fundamental meaning can be conveyed
and developed. This is particularly true when using apparently familiar terms. It is no less important for English-
speaking liturgists to do this. It is too easy to combine liturgical *tesserae* together in a mosaic without having given proper
consideration to the terms. The full process involves careful
research into the origin of a text, including its scriptural references and its historical formation. Its place in the liturgy must
be considered. The key words in the text need more careful
exploration and comparison with existing translations. A lex-
icon of such words would go beyond the mere listing of oc-
currences to explore the meaning in different contexts, and
such a tool would aid theology as well as liturgy.

Among words occurring very frequently in these collects
we must note the extensive use of the words church, death,
glory, life, light, and love, and wonder if there is, for example,
a clearly recognisable Anglican theology of glory (which seems
assumed by the collects). This sort of textual criticism is necessary for translation, but it should not be shunned by compilers of liturgies or writers of new material.

It is impossible to speak of a logic in ordering contemporary
collects; identical or similar collects sharing a common source
are used by provinces *that share a lectionary* on completely different days, and changes to texts are frequently arbitrary and
inconsistent. A province that insists on saying 'Almighty God,

---

[70]The writer was an observer and consultant at the 1993 Consultation
on African Culture and Anglican Liturgy in Mombasa, called by the Coun-
cil of Anglican Provinces in Africa.

you . . . ' will suddenly switch to 'who' without apparent reason, and some of the examples given above show how changing words can change theology. Textual criticism reduces the likelihood of inappropriate couplings and inadvertent heresies.

The writer of new collects does not begin from a *tabula rasa*. The most frequently employed method of writing is the 'mosaic' method in which the writer gathers the liturgical *tesserae* and pieces them together to form a text. When the origin of a collect has eluded me, I usually discover that it is a new prayer put together from bits that sound like a number of old prayers. This method is sometimes effective, but many modern collects are weak and ineffective. Imitation, especially when it does little more than combine fragments, does not produce strong and memorable collects that have grown organically from the tradition. As it is necessary to prune the calendar, removing persons who are not heroes or exemplars of the faith for modern Christians, so the liturgical corpus must, from time to time, be rigorously edited. It is extraordinary that some collects (such as 396) are included in the liturgy at all!

CONCLUSION

Twenty-five years ago R.C.D. Jasper enunciated the questions asked in liturgical commissions of every denomination across the Christian world. What is the function of a collect? Is the function of a collect necessarily the same in the Office as it is in the Eucharist? What sort of prayer should a collect be? What should a collect say? What should its content be? There has been no comprehensive answer, and it is not entirely clear that we need one.

What we need to say about the collect is fairly simple. I believe that we must begin with the collect's role in expressing, to use Jungmann's phrase, 'the spiritual universe in which our prayer lives and moves and is', and in representing, in worship, our approach to God. It is because of this that, except for a limited number of special occasions, it is a general prayer expressing general truths and making petition for such gifts and graces as are needed for daily living. We could have prayers that related strongly to the readings, but these would be in addition to and not instead of the traditional collects. The writing of new collects depends upon a grasp of that spiritual universe, and it will surely lead us to a different mode of expression and different petitions from those found in the ancient sacramentaries and the earlier prayer books. The collect will continue to reveal itself as a prayer form of great flexibility if we will allow it to be governed by these greater principles and not by arbitrary and limited themes.

For generations, Anglicans have learned the essential truths of the faith—that God created us in his image, that he hates nothing that he has made, that he gave his Son as a sacrifice for sin and an example of godly life, and that he is the strength of all who put their trust in him—from the collects in their annual repetition. It is a fundamental Anglican principle that the language of our worship provides the language with which we talk about God. There is not a divorce in Anglicanism between the language of liturgical prayer and private devotion, between liturgy and theology. The relationship is dynamic. There will be a gap, inevitably, between the ideal and the reality, but the dynamic relationship should ensure that the language in which individual faith is expressed does not go far from the liturgy nor the liturgy fail to express the community's understanding of its faith. The collects are the pivot for the Anglican conception of *lex orandi, lex credendi,* expressing in prayer that which binds together the Creator and the creature, the Redeemer and the redeemed.[71]

[71]See Louis Weil, *Gathered To Pray,* Cambridge, Mass., 1986.

Chapter One

LATIN COLLECTS OF THE SARUM MISSAL

Advent 1

i   Excita, quaesumus, Domine, potentiam tuam, et veni : ut ab imminentibus peccatorum nostrorum periculis te mereamur protegente eripi, te liberante salvari. Qui vivis.

Advent 2

ii   Excita, Domine, corda nostra ad praeparandas unigeniti tui vias : ut per ejus adventum purificatis tibi mentibus servire mereamur. Qui tecum.

Advent 3

iii   Aurem tuam, quaesumus, Domine, precibus nostris accommoda : et mentis nostrae tenebras gratia tuae visitationis illustra. Qui vivis.

Advent 4

iv   Excita, quaesumus, Domine, potentiam tuam, et veni : et magna nobis virtute succurre : ut per auxilium gratiae tuae quod nostra peccata praepediunt, indulgentia tuae propitiationis acceleret. Qui vivis.

Christmas : Mass *In vigilia*

v   Deus qui nos redemptionis nostrae annua expectatione laetificas; praesta ut unigentium tuum, quem redemptorem laeti suscipimus venientem quoque judicem securi videamus.

Missa in gallicantu

vi   Deus qui hanc sacratissimam noctem veri luminis fecisti illustratione clarescere; da, quaesumus; ut cujus lucis mysteria in terra cognovimus, ejus quoque gaudiis in caelo perfruamur : Qui tecum.

Missa in mane

vii   Da nobis, quaesumus omnipotens Deus : ut qui nova incarnati Verbi tui luce perfundimur; hoc in nostro resplendeat opere, quod per fidem fulget in mente. Per eundem.

Ad magnam missam

viii   Concede, quaesumus, omnipotens Deus; ut nos Unigeniti tui nova per carnem Nativitas liberet : quos sub peccati jugo vetusta servitus tenet. Per eundem.

The Epiphany

ix   Deus, qui hodierna die Unigenitum tuum gentibus stella duce revelasti : concede propitius, ut qui jam te ex fide cognovimus, usque ad contemplandam speciem tuae celsitudinis perducamur.

Epiphany 2 (prima post octabas epiphanie)

x   Vota, quaesumus, Domine, supplicantis populi coelesti pietate prosequere : ut et quae agenda sunt videant, et ad implenda quae viderint convalescant.

Epiphany 3

xi   Omnipotens sempiterne Deus, qui coelestia simul et terrena moderaris : supplicationes populi tui clementer exaudi, et pacem tuam nostris concede temporibus.

Epiphany 4

xii Omnipotens sempiterne Deus, infirmitatem nostram propitius respice; atque ad protegendum nos dexteram tuae majestatis ostende.

Epiphany 5

xiii Deus, qui nos in tantis periculis constitutos pro humana scis fragilitate non posse subsistere : da nobis salutem mentis et corporis; ut ea quae pro peccatis nostris patimur, te adjuvante, vincamus.

Epiphany 6

xiv Familiam tuam, quaesumus, Domine, continue pietate custodi; ut quae in sola spe gratiae coelestis innititur, tua semper protectione muniatur.

Septuagesima

xv Preces populi tui, quaesumus, Domine, clementer exaudi; ut qui juste pro peccatis nostris affligimur, pro tui nominis gloria misericorditer liberemur.

Sexagesima

xvi Deus qui conspicis quia ex nulla nostra actione confidimus : concede propitius, ut contra adversa omnia doctoris gentium protectione muniamur.

Quinquagesima

xvii Preces nostras, quaesumus, Domine, clementer exaudi; atque a peccatorum vinculis absolutos ab omnia nos adversitate custodi.

Lent 1

xviii Deus qui ecclesiam tuam annua quadragesimali observatione purificas : praesta familiae tuae, ut quod a te obtinere abstinendo nititur, hoc bonis operibus exequatur.

Lent 2

xix   Deus qui conspicis omni nos virtute destitui, interius exteriusque custodi, ut ab omnibus adversitatibus muniamur in corpore et a pravis cogitationibus mundemur in mente.

Lent 3

xx   Quaesumus, omnipotens Deus, vota humilium respice; atque ad defensionem nostram dexteram tuae majestatis extende.

Lent 4

xxi   Concede, quaesumus, omnipotens Deus, ut qui ex merito nostrae actionis affligimur, tuae gratiae consolatione respiremus.

Passion Sunday

xxii   Quaesumus, omnipotens Deus, familiam tuam propitius respice; ut te largiente regatur in corpore, et te servante custodiatur in mente.

Palm Sunday

xxiii   Omnipotens sempiterne Deus qui humano generi ad imitandum humilitatis exemplum salvatorem nostrum carnem sumere et crucem subire fecisti : concede propitius ut et patientiae ipsius habere documenta et resurrectionis consortia mereamur.

Easter Day

xxiv   Deus qui hodierna die per Unigenitum tuum aeternitatis nobis aditum devicta morte reserasti : vota nostra quae praeveniendo aspiras etiam adjuvando prosequere.

Easter 1

xxv   Praesta, quasumus, omnipotens Deus : ut, qui pas-
chalia festa peregimus, haec, te largiente, moribus et
vita teneamus. Per.

Easter 2

xxvi   Deus, qui in Filii tui humilitate jacentem mundum
erexisti : fidelibus tuis perpetuam concede laetitiam;
ut, quos perpetuae mortis eripuisiti casibus gaudiis
facias perfrui sempiternis. Per eundem.

Easter 3

xxvii   Deus qui errantibus, ut in viam possint redire jus-
titiae, veritatis tuae lumen ostendis : da cunctis, qui
christiana professione censentur, et illa respuere quae
huic inimica sunt nomini, et ea quae sunt apta sectari.

Easter 4

xxviii   Deus qui fidelium mentes unius efficis voluntatis : da
populis tuis id amare quod praecipis, id desiderare
quod promittis, ut inter mundanas varietates ibi nostra fixa sint corda, ubi vera sunt gaudia.

Easter 5

xxix   Deus a quo cuncta bona procedunt, largire supplici-
bus tuis ut cogitemus te inspirante quae recta sunt,
et te gubernante eadem faciamus.

Ascension Day

xxx   Concede, quaesumus, omnipotens Deus, ut qui hodierna die Unigenitum tuum redemptorem nostrum
ad coelos ascendisse credimus, ipsi quoque mente in
coelestibus habitemus.

The Sunday after the Ascension

xxxi   Omnipotens sempiterne Deus : fac nos tibi semper
et devotam gerere voluntatem; et majestati tuae sin-
cero corde servire. Per Dominum.

Pentecost : Whitsunday

xxxii   Deus, qui hodierna die corda fidelium Sancti Spiri-
tus illustratione docuisti : da nobis in eodem Spiritu
recta sapere, et de ejus semper consolatione gaudere.

Trinity Sunday

xxxiii   Omnipotens sempiterne Deus, qui dedisti famulis tuis
in confessione verae fidei aeterne Trinitatis gloriam
agnoscere, et in potentia majestatis adorare Unita-
tem : quaesumus ut ejusdem fidei firmitate ab omnibus semper muniamur adversis.

Trinity 1

xxxiv   Deus, in te sperantium fortitudo adesto propitius in-
vocationibus nostris; et quia sine te nihil potest mor-
talis infirmatas, praesta auxilium gratiae tuae, ut in
exequendis mandatis tuis et voluntate tibi et actione
placeamus.

Trinity 2

xxxv   Sancti nominis tui, Domine, timorem pariter et
amorem fac nos habere perpetuum : quia nunquam
tua gubernatione destituis, quos in soliditate tuae
dilectionis instituis. Per Dominum.

Trinity 3

xxxvi   Deprecationem nostram, quaesumus, Domine, benignus exaudi; et quibus supplicandi praestas affectum, tribue defensionis auxilium.

Trinity 4

xxxvii Protector in te sperantium Deus, sine quo nihil est validum, nihil sanctum; multiplica super nos misericordiam tuam, ut te rectore, te duce, sic transeamus per bona temporalia ut non amittamus aeterna.

Trinity 5

xxxviii Da nobis, quaesumus, Domine, ut et mundi cursus pacifice nobis tuo ordine dirigatur, et ecclesia tua tranquilla devotione laetetur.

Trinity 6

xxxix Deus, qui diligentibus te bona invisibilia praeparasti; infunde cordibus nostris tui amoris affectum, ut te in omnibus et super omnia diligentes promissiones tuas, quae omne desiderium superant, consequamur.

Trinity 7

xl Deus virtutum, cujus est totum quod est optimum; insere pectoribus nostris amorem tui nominis, et praesta in nobis religionis augmentum : ut quae sunt bona nutrias ac pietatis studio quae sunt nutrita custodias.

Trinity 8

xli Deus, cujus providentia in sui dispositione non fallitur, te supplices exoramus, ut noxia cuncta submoveas, et omnia nobis profutura concedas.

Trinity 9

xlii Largire nobis, quaesumus, Domine, semper spiritum cogitandi quae recta sunt propitius, et agendi; ut qui sine te esse non possumus, secundum te vivere valeamus.

Trinity 10

xliii   Pateant aures misericordiae tuae, Domine, precibus supplicantium; et ut petentibus desiderata concedas, fac eos quae tibi sunt placita postulare.

Trinity 11

xliv   Deus, qui omnipotentiam tuam parcendo maxime et miserando manifestas; multiplica super nos misericordiam tuam, ut ad tua promissa currentes coelestium bonorum facias esse consortes.

Trinity 12

xlv   Omnipotens sempiterne Deus, qui abundantia pietatis tuae et merita supplicum excedis et vota; effunde super nos misericordiam tuam, ut dimittas quae conscientia metuit, et adjicias quod oratio non praesumit.

Trinity 13

xlvi   Omnipotens et misericors Deus, de cujus munere venit ut tibi a fidelibus tuis digne et laudabiliter serviatur; tribue nobis, quaesumus, ut ad promissiones tuas sine offensione curramus.

Trinity 14

xlvii   Omnipotens sempiterne Deus, da nobis fidei spei et caritatis augmentum; et ut mereamur assequi quod promittis, fac nos amare quod praecipis.

Trinity 15

xlviii   Custodi, Domine, quaesumus, ecclesiam tuam propitiatione perpetua : et quia sine te labitur humana mortalitas, tuis semper auxiliis et abstrahatur a noxiis, et ad salutaria dirigatur.

Trinity 16

xlix   Ecclesiam tuam, quaesumus, Domine, miseratio continuata mundet et muniat; et quia sine te non potest salva consistere, tuo semper munere gubernetur.

Trinity 17

l   Tua nos, Domine, quaesumus, gratia semper et praeveniat et sequatur; ac bonis operibus jugitur praestet esse intentos.

Trinity 18

li   Da quaesumus, Domine, populo tuo diabolica vitare contagia, et te solum Deum pura mente sectari.

Trinity 19

lii   Dirigat corda nostra, quaesumus, Domine, tuae miserationis operatio, quia tibi sine te placere non possumus.

Trinity 20

liii   Omnipotens et misericors Deus, universa nobis adversantia propitiatus exclude; ut mente et corpore pariter expediti, quae tua sunt liberis mentibus exequamur.

Trinity 21

liv   Largire, quaesumus, Domine, fidelibus tuis indulgentiam placatus et pacem; ut pariter ab omnibus mundentur offensis, et secura tibi mente deserviant.

Trinity 22

lv   Familiam tuam, quaesumus, Domine, continua pietate custodi; ut a cunctis adversitatibus te protegente sit libera, et in bonis actibus tuo nomini sit devota.

Trinity 23

lvi   Deus, refugium nostrum et virtus, adesto piis eccle-
           siae tuae precibus, auctor ipse pietatis; et praesta ut
           quod fideliter petimus efficaciter consequamur.

Trinity 24

lvii   Absolve, quaesumus, Domine, tuorum delicta populo-
           rum; et a peccatorum nostrorum nexibus quae pro
           nostra fragilitate contraximus tua benignitate
           liberemur.

Dominica proxima ante adventum or *ultima ante adventum Domini*

lviii   Excita, quaesumus, Domine, tuorum fidelium volun-
           tates; ut divina operis fructum propensius exequentes
           pietatis tuae remedia majora percipiant.

Chapter Two

ANGLICAN COLLECTS
1549–1929

This collection of collects is from *The Book of Common Prayer,* 1549 and 1662, the English and American books of 1928, and the Scottish book of 1929. Titles of Sundays and other days are taken from 1662, with additions from 1928. The *Current Use* note attached to a collect indicates contemporary collects derived from it.

First Sunday in Advent

1 Almighty God, give us grace that we may cast away the works of darkness and put upon us the armour of light, now in the time of this mortal life, in which thy Son Jesus Christ came to visit us in great humility; that in the last day, when he shall come again in his glorious Majesty to judge both the quick and the dead, we may rise to the life immortal, through him who liveth and reigneth with thee and the Holy Ghost, now and ever.

1549 has 'in which thy Son . . . humility;' in parentheses.

Source : new in 1549
Current Use : no 309

Second Sunday in Advent

2   Blessed Lord, who hast caused all holy Scriptures to be written for our learning; Grant that we may in such wise hear them, read, mark, learn, and inwardly digest them, that by patience, and comfort of thy holy Word, we may embrace, and ever hold fast the blessed hope of everlasting life, which thou hast given us in our Saviour Jesus Christ.

Source : new in 1549
Current Use : no 312

Third Sunday in Advent

1549 has this short collect.

3   Lord, we beseech thee, give ear to our prayers, and by thy gracious visitation lighten the darkness of our heart, by our Lord Jesus Christ.

Source : SM iii

In 1662 it was replaced by this collect written by John Cosin.

4   O Lord Jesu Christ, who at thy first coming didst send thy messenger to prepare thy way before thee; Grant that the ministers and stewards of thy mysteries may likewise so prepare and make ready thy way, by turning the hearts of the disobedient to the wisdom of the just, that at thy second coming to judge the world we may be found an acceptable people in thy sight, who livest and reignest with the Father and the Holy Spirit, ever one God, world without end.

[1928Amer begins 'O Lord Jesus Christ . . . '.]

1929Scot has a collect for Advent Ember Days to be said after the collect of the day.

5   Almighty God, the giver of all good gifts, who of thy divine providence hast appointed divers Orders in thy

Church : Give thy grace, we humbly beseech thee, to all those who are to be called to any office and administration in the same; and so replenish them with innocency of life, that they may faithfully serve before thee, to the glory of thy great Name, and the benefit of thy holy Church; through Jesus Christ our Lord.

Source : the second of the 1662 Prayers and Thanksgivings for the Ember Weeks derived originally from the Scottish book of 1637

Fourth Sunday in Advent

The 1549 collect (no 6) was expanded in 1662 (no 7).

6   Lord raise up (we pray thee) thy power, and come among us, and with great might succour us; that whereas, through our sins and wickedness, we be sore let and hindered, thy bountiful grace and mercy, through the satisfaction of thy son our Lord, may speedily deliver us; to whom with thee and the Holy Ghost be honour and glory, world without end.

7   O Lord, raise up (we pray thee) thy power, and come among us, and with great might succour us; that whereas, through our sins and wickedness, we are sore let and hindered in running the race that is set before us, thy bountiful grace and mercy may speedily help and deliver us; through the satisfaction of thy Son our Lord, to whom with thee and the Holy Ghost be honour and glory, world without end.

[1928Amer begins 'O Lord, raise up, we pray thee, thy power . . .'; 1959Can begins 'Raise up, we beseech thee, O Lord, thy power' and omits 'through the satisfaction . . .'.]

Source : SM iv
Current Use : no 319

Nativity of our Lord, or the Birthday of Christ [commonly called Christmas Day]

1662 has one collect; it was the one for use at a second celebration in 1549.

8　　　Almighty God, who hast given us thy only-begotten Son
　　　to take our nature upon him, and as at this time to be
　　　born of a pure Virgin; Grant that we being regener-
　　　ate, and made thy children by adoption and grace, may
　　　daily be renewed by the Holy Spirit; through the same
　　　our Lord Jesus Christ, who liveth and reigneth with thee
　　　and the same Spirit, ever one God, world without end.

Source : new in 1549 and probably suggested by a Greg. collect (58)
Current Use : no 338

1928Amer provides a collect, which was proposed in the 1885
draft revision, for the first celebration of the Holy Communion if there are two on Christmas Day; in 1928Eng it is the
Christmas Eve collect and in 1929Scot it is given as 'an additional Collect for Christmastide'; it is, in fact, the first 1549
collect.

9　　　O God, who makest us glad with the yearly remem-
　　　brance of the birth of thine [1549 and Scot : thy] only
　　　Son Jesus Christ; Grant that as we joyfully receive him
　　　for our Redeemer, so we may with sure confidence be-
　　　hold him when he shall come to be our Judge, who liveth
　　　and reigneth with thee and the Holy Ghost, one God,
　　　world without end.

Source : 1549; derived from SM v, the Vigil Mass
Current Use : nos 328–32

Saint Stephen's Day

The 1549 collect (no 10) was replaced in 1662 (no 11).

10   Grant us, O Lord, to learn to love our enemies, by the example of thy martyr saint Stephen, who prayed to thee for his persecutors; which livest and reignest . . . .

Source: SM; Greg (62)

11   Grant, O Lord, that, in all our sufferings here upon earth for the testimony of thy truth, we may stedfastly look up to heaven, and by faith behold the glory that shall be revealed; and, being filled with the holy Ghost, may learn to love and bless our persecutors by the example of thy first Martyr Saint Stephen, who prayed for his murderers to thee, O blessed Jesus, who standest at the right hand of God to succour all those that suffer for thee, our only Mediator and Advocate.

[1928Amer/Eng and 1929Scot have 'Holy Ghost'; 1959Can has 'Holy Spirit'.]

Source : an amplification by Cosin of 1549

Saint John the Evangelist's Day

The 1662 collect (no 13) develops that given in 1549 (no 12).

12   Merciful Lord, we beseech thee to cast thy bright beams of light upon thy Church : that it being lightened by the doctrine of thy blessed Apostle and evangelist John may attain to thy everlasting gifts; through Jesus Christ our Lord.

13   Merciful Lord, we beseech thee to cast thy bright beams of light upon thy Church, that it being enlightened [1928Amer : illumined] by the doctrine of thy blessed Apostle and Evangelist Saint John may so walk in the light of thy truth, that it may at length attain to the light of everlasting life [1928Amer : attain to life everlasting]; through Jesus Christ our Lord.

Source : SM; Greg (67)

The Innocents' Day

The 1662 collect (no 15) takes a different approach to that of 1549 (no 14).

14   Almighty God, whose praise this day the young innocents thy witnesses hath confessed and shewed forth, not in speaking but in dying; Mortify and kill all vices in us, that in our conversation our life may express thy faith, which with our tongues we do confess; through Jesus Christ our Lord.

Source : SM; Greg (75)

15   O Almighty God, who out of the mouths of babes and sucklings hast ordained strength, and madest infants to glorify thee by their deaths; Mortify and kill all vices in us, and so strengthen us by thy grace, that by innocency of our lives, and constancy of our faith even unto death, we may glorify thy holy Name [1928Eng : holy name]; through Jesus Christ our Lord.

Source : new in 1662

Sunday after Christmas Day, originally the Sunday in the octave, uses the Christmas Day collect.

Circumcision of Christ

16   Almighty God, who madest thy blessed Son to be circumcised, and obedient to the law for man; Grant us the true Circumcision [1928Amer/Eng and 1929Scot : circumcision] of the Spirit; that, our hearts and all our members, being mortified from all worldly and carnal lusts, we may in all things obey thy blessed will; through the same thy Son Jesus Christ our Lord.

Source : 1549; adapted from a benediction in Greg.
Current Use : no 354

1928Eng provided a New Year collect.

17   O Eternal Lord God, who hast brought thy servants to the beginning of another year : Pardon, we humbly beseech thee, our transgressions in the past, and graciously abide with us all the days of our life; through Jesus Christ our Lord.

Source : new in 1928

1662 provides that the collect of the Circumcision 'shall serve for every day after unto the Epiphany'. 1928Amer has the following collect for the Second Sunday after Christmas Day.

18   Almighty God, who hast poured upon us the new light of thine incarnate Word; Grant that the same light enkindled in our hearts may shine forth in our lives; through Jesus Christ our Lord.

Mackenzie calls it 'a free translation' of the Roman daybreak collect no vii.

1928Eng provides a collect which 'shall be used on any day after the Circumcision unto the Epiphany' and which derives from the Leonine Sacramentary.

19   Almighty God, who didst wonderfully create man in thine own image, and didst yet more wonderfully restore him : Grant, we beseech thee, that as thy Son our Lord Jesus Christ was made in the likeness of men, so we may be made partakers of the divine nature; through the same thy Son, who with thee and the Holy Ghost liveth and reigneth, one God, world without end.

Source : Leo (1239); Greg (59)
Current Use : nos 345–49

1929Scot gives another version of the same original Collect.

20   O God, whose blessed Son Jesus Christ became man that we might become the sons of God : Grant, we be-

seech thee, that, being made partakers of the divine nature of thy Son, we may be conformed to his likeness;
who liveth and reigneth with thee and the Holy Ghost,
now and ever.

Epiphany [1928Amer/Eng and 1929Scot : The Manifesta-
tion of Christ to the Gentiles]

21   O God, who by the leading of a star didst manifest thy
only-begotten Son to the Gentiles; Mercifully grant, that
we, which know thee now by faith, may after this life
have the fruition of thy glorious Godhead; through Jesus
Christ our Lord.

1928Amer has 'Mercifully grant that we, who know thee now
by faith, may . . . '.

Source : SM ix
Current Use : nos 362–68

First Sunday after Epiphany

22   O Lord, we beseech thee mercifully to receive the
prayers of thy people which [1928Amer : who] call upon
thee; and grant that they may both perceive and know
what things they ought to do, and also may have grace
and power faithfully to fulfil the same; through Jesus
Christ our Lord.

Source : SM x
Current Use : no 555

Second Sunday after Epiphany

23   Almighty and everlasting God, who dost govern all
things in heaven and earth; Mercifully hear the supplications of thy people, and grant us thy peace all the
days of our life; through Jesus Christ our Lord.

Source : SM xi
Current Use : no 378

Third Sunday after Epiphany

24   Almighty and everlasting God, mercifully look upon our
      infirmities, and in all our dangers and necessities stretch
      forth thy right hand to help and defend us; through Jesus
      Christ our Lord.

Source : SM xii

Fourth Sunday after Epiphany

1662 again develops the themes begun in 1549.

25   God, which knowest us to be set in the midst of so many
      and great dangers, that for man's frailness we cannot
      always stand upright; Grant us the health of body and
      soul that all those things which we suffer for our sin,
      by thy help we may well pass and overcome; through
      Jesus Christ our Lord.

26   O God, who knowest us to be set in the midst of so many
      and great dangers, that by reason of the frailty of our
      nature we cannot always stand upright; Grant to us such
      strength and protection, as may support us in all dan-
      gers, and carry us through all temptations; through
      Jesus Christ our Lord.

Source : SM xiii

Fifth Sunday after Epiphany

27   O Lord, we beseech thee to keep thy Church and house-
      hold continually in thy true religion; that they who do
      lean only upon the hope of thy heavenly grace may ever-
      more be defended by thy mighty power; through Jesus
      Christ our Lord.

Source : SM xiv

Sixth Sunday after Epiphany

1549 has no provision for the Sixth Sunday and repeats the Fifth Sunday. 1662 provides a new collect probably written by John Cosin.

28   O God, whose blessed Son was manifested that he might destroy the works of the devil, and make us the sons of God and heirs of eternal life; Grant us, we beseech thee, that, having this hope, we may purify ourselves, even as he is pure; that when he shall appear again with power and great glory, we may be made like unto him in his eternal and glorious kingdom; where with thee, O Father, and thee, O Holy Ghost, he liveth and reigneth, ever one God, world without end.

Current Use : no 394

Sunday called Septuagesima

29   O Lord, we beseech thee favourably to hear the prayers of thy people; that we, who are justly punished for our offences, may be mercifully delivered by thy goodness, for the glory of thy Name; through Jesus Christ our Saviour, who liveth and reigneth with thee and the Holy Ghost, ever one God, world without end.

Source : SM xv

Sunday called Sexagesima

30   O Lord God, who [1549 : which] seest that we put not our trust in any thing that we do; Mercifully grant that by thy power we may be defended against all adversity; through Jesus Christ our Lord.

Source : SM xvi
Current Use : SAAPB : Lent 4 [second collect] modernised

Sunday called Quinquagesima

31 O Lord, who hast taught [1549 : which dost teach] us
    that all our doings without charity are nothing worth;
    Send thy Holy Ghost, and pour into our hearts that most
    excellent gift of charity, the very bond of peace and of
    all virtues, without which whosoever liveth is counted
    dead before thee : Grant this for thine only Son Jesus
    Christ's sake.

1929Scot offers 'love' as an alternative to 'charity' in this
collect.

Source : new in 1549
Current Use : no 381

First Day of Lent [commonly called Ash Wednesday]

32 Almighty and everlasting God, who [1549 : which]
    hatest nothing that thou hast made, and dost forgive
    the sins of all them that are penitent; Create and make
    in us new and contrite hearts, that we worthily lament-
    ing our sins, and acknowledging our wretchedness, may
    obtain of thee, the God of all mercy, perfect remission
    and forgiveness; through Jesus Christ our Lord.

Source : new in 1549
Current Use : no 402

First Sunday in Lent

33 O Lord, who [1549 : which] for our sake didst fast forty
    days and forty nights; Give us grace to use such absti-
    nence, that, our flesh being subdued to the Spirit, we
    may ever obey thy godly motions in righteousness, and
    true holiness, to thy honour and glory, who livest and
    reignest with the Father and the Holy Ghost, one God,
    world without end.

Source : new in 1549
Current Use : no 407

1929Scot inserts the Ember collect here.

Second Sunday in Lent

34   Almighty God, who seest [1549 : which dost see] that we have no power of ourselves to help ourselves; Keep us both outwardly in our bodies and inwardly in our souls; that we may be defended from all adversities which may happen to the body, and from all evil thoughts which may assault and hurt the soul; through Jesus Christ our Lord.

Source : SM xix
Current Use : no 418

Third Sunday in Lent

35   We beseech thee, Almighty God, look upon the hearty desires of thy humble servants, and stretch forth the right hand of thy Majesty, to be our defence against all our enemies; through Jesus Christ our Lord.

Source : SM xx

Fourth Sunday in Lent

36   Grant, we beseech thee, Almighty God, that we, who [1549 : which] for our evil deeds do worthily deserve to be punished [1549 : are worthily punished], by the comfort of thy grace may mercifully be relieved; through our Lord and Saviour Jesus Christ.

Source : SM xxi

Fifth Sunday in Lent [1928Amer/Eng and 1929Scot : commonly called Passion Sunday]

37   We beseech thee, Almighty God, mercifully to look upon thy people; that by thy great goodness they may

be governed and preserved evermore, both in body and soul; through Jesus Christ our Lord.

Source : SM xxii

1929Scot has six additional collects 'which may be said at any Service from Passion Sunday to Good Friday inclusive'.

38   O Lord God our heavenly Father, regard we beseech thee, with thy divine pity the pains of all thy children, and grant that the passion of our Lord and his infinite merits may make fruitful for good the miseries of the innocent, the sufferings of the sick, and the sorrows of the bereaved; through him who suffered in our flesh and died for our sake, thy Son our Saviour Jesus Christ.

39   O God, who by the cross and passion of thy Son Jesus Christ didst save and deliver mankind : Grant that by stedfast faith in the merits of that holy sacrifice we may find help and salvation, and may triumph in the power of his victory; through the same Jesus Christ our Lord.

40   O God, who didst will that thy Son should suffer death upon the cross, that thou mightest deliver us from the snares of the enemy : Grant that by the merits of his death we may know the power of his resurrection; through the same Jesus Christ our Lord.

41   O God, whose blessed Son did overcome death for our salvation : Mercifully grant that we who have his glorious passion in remembrance may take up our cross daily and follow him; through the same thy Son Jesus Christ our Lord.

42   O Lord God, whose blessed Son did bear our sins in his own body on the tree : Give us, we pray thee, such true repentance and amendment of life, that we may never crucify him afresh, and put him to an open shame by conscious and wilful sin; through the same Jesus Christ our Lord.

43 O God, whose blessed Son did suffer for all mankind : Grant unto us that, rightly observing this holy season, we may learn to know thee better, to love thee more, and to serve thee with a more perfect will; through the same Jesus Christ our Lord.

Sunday next before Easter [1928Amer/Eng and 1929Scot : commonly called Palm Sunday]

44 Almighty and everlasting God, who of thy tender love towards mankind, hast sent thy Son, our Saviour Jesus Christ, to take upon him our flesh, and to suffer death upon the cross, that all mankind should follow the example of his great humility; Mercifully grant, that we may both follow the example of his patience, and also be made partakers of his resurrection; through the same Jesus Christ our Lord.

Source : SM xxiii
Current Use : nos 437–43

In 1662 and 1928Eng this collect together with that of Ash Wednesday is used for every day until Good Friday; 1928Amer provides a new collect for the days of Holy Week, and the Palm Sunday collect is used after that appointed for the day.

Monday before Easter

45 Almighty God, whose most dear Son went not up to joy but first he suffered pain, and entered not into glory before he was crucified; Mercifully grant that we, walking in the way of the cross, may find it none other than the way of life and peace; through the same thy Son Jesus Christ our Lord.

Source : Written by William Reed Huntington and included in his *Materia Ritualis* of 1882; it was proposed for inclusion in the 1892 revision of the American Prayer Book but found its place here on the Monday of Holy Week in the 1928 revision. The preamble is taken from the exhortation in the 1662 order for the Visitation of the Sick. In the modern prayer books it keeps its place in AmerBCP and is also used as a Friday collect at morning prayer; it is used for Lent 3 in ASB.

Tuesday before Easter

46   O Lord God, whose blessed Son, our Saviour, gave his back to the smiters and hid not his face from shame; Grant us grace to take joyfully the suffering of the present time, in full assurance of the glory that shall be revealed; through the same thy Son Jesus Christ our Lord.

Source : The author of this collect, proposed for inclusion in the American 1892 book, is unknown. It was placed here in 1928Amer but moved to the Wednesday in Holy Week in AmerBCP.

Wednesday before Easter

47   Assist us mercifully with thy help, O Lord God of our salvation; that we may enter with joy upon the meditation of those mighty acts, whereby thou hast given us life and immortality; through Jesus Christ our Lord.

Source : This collect has a long and interesting history which is given by Marion Hatchett : 'It is based upon one used in the Sarum Missal as a *super populum* . . . on the Monday of Holy Week. It was similarly used in the Gregorian Sacramentary (no 318). The Gelasian Sacramentary has it as the second collect for Sexagesima (no 74) . . . ' (Hatchett p. 226). It came into the American liturgy in 1928 and is now the collect at the beginning of the Liturgy of the Palms on the Sunday of the Passion : Palm Sunday [AmerBCP p. 270].

Thursday before Easter [1928Amer/Eng : commonly called Maundy Thursday]

1662 and 1928Eng use the Palm Sunday collect. This collect is provided in 1928Amer.

48   Almighty Father, whose dear Son, on the night before he suffered, did institute the Sacrament of his Body and Blood; mercifully grant that we may thankfully receive the same in remembrance of him, who in these holy mysteries giveth us a pledge of life eternal; the same thy Son Jesus Christ our Lord, who now liveth and reigneth with thee and the Holy Spirit ever, one God, world without end.

Source : This collect, with its echoes of the Communion exhortations of 1662, was written by the 1928Amer revision committee, following on from a collect proposed for the 1882 book. It keeps the same place in AmerBCP (cp the 1928Eng collect [i] for 'Thanksgiving for the Institution of Holy Communion'). See no 454.

Scot1929 has this 'additional collect'.

49   O Lord Jesus Christ, who in a wonderful sacrament hast left unto us a memorial of thy passion : Grant us, we beseech thee, so to venerate the Sacred Mysteries of thy Body and Blood, that we may ever perceive within ourselves the fruit of thy redemption; who livest and reignest with the Father in the unity of the Holy Spirit, God, for ever and ever.

Source : See the discussion of these collects in the Introduction.

Good Friday

50   Almighty God, we beseech thee graciously to behold this thy family, for which our Lord Jesus Christ was contented to be betrayed, and given up into the hands of wicked men, and to suffer death upon the cross, who

now liveth and reigneth with thee and the Holy Ghost, ever one God, world without end.

Source : a translation of the *Oratio super populum* in the Roman Mass for Wednesday of Holy Week

51   Almighty and everlasting God, by whose Spirit the whole body of the Church is governed and sanctified; Receive our supplications and prayers, which we offer before thee for all estates of men in thy holy Church, that every member of the same, in his vocation and ministry, may truly and godly serve thee; through our Lord and Saviour Jesus Christ.

Source : a translation of the third of the Good Friday Solemn Prayers

52   O merciful God, who hast made all men, and hatest nothing that thou hast made, nor wouldest the death of a sinner, but rather that he should be converted and live; Have mercy upon all Jews, Turks, Infidels, and Hereticks, and take from them all ignorance, hardness of heart, and contempt of thy Word; and so fetch them home, blessed Lord, to thy flock, that they may be saved among the remnant of the true Israelites, and be made one fold under one shepherd, Jesus Christ our Lord, who liveth and reigneth with thee and the Holy Spirit, one God, world without end.

Source : new in 1549; see the discussion in the Introduction

1928Amer has an extensively revised version, removing all reference to the Jews.

53   O merciful God, who hast made all men, and hatest nothing that thou hast made, nor desirest the death of a sinner, but rather that he should be converted and live; Have mercy upon all who know thee not as thou art revealed in the Gospel of thy Son. Take from them all ignorance, hardness of heart, and contempt of thy

Word; and so fetch them home, blessed Lord, to thy
fold, that they may be made one flock under one shepherd, Jesus Christ our Lord, who liveth and reigneth
with thee and the Holy Spirit, one God, world without
end.

1928Eng and 1929Scot have a very similar collect amended
in accordance with the suggestion of Dr. Brightman. It keeps
'wouldest' in the opening sentence. It has a petition for the
Jews.

Have mercy upon thine ancient people the Jews, and
upon all who have not known thee, or who deny the
faith of Christ crucified; take from them . . . .

It continues as 1928Amer. 1929Scot allows the use of a further prayer for the Jews here.

54   O God, the God of Abraham, look upon thine ever-
lasting covenant, and cause the captivity of Judah and
Israel to return. They are thy people; O be thou their
Saviour, that all who love Jerusalem and mourn for her
may rejoice with her; for Jesus Christ's sake, their
Saviour and ours.

It is described as 'a prayer of Bishop Wilson' and is, presum-
ably, from the *Sacra Privata* (published posthumously in 1781)
of Thomas Wilson, Bishop of Sodor and Man.

Easter Even

No collect is provided in 1549.

55   Grant, O Lord, that as we are baptized into the death
of thy blessed Son our Saviour Jesus Christ, so by continual mortifying our corrupt affections we may be buried with him; and that through the grave, and gate of
death, we may pass to our joyful resurrection; for his
merits, who died, and was buried, and rose again for
us, thy Son Jesus Christ our Lord.

Source : new in 1662; from the Scottish prayer book, 1637

Easter Day

This, the sole collect in 1662, was the first collect in 1549, also used on the Monday in Easter Week.

56   Almighty God, who through thine only-begotten Son Jesus Christ hast overcome death and opened unto us the gate of everlasting life; We humbly beseech thee, that, as by thy special grace preventing us thou dost put into our minds good desires, so by thy continual help we may bring the same to good effect; through Jesus Christ our Lord, who liveth and reigneth with thee and the Holy Ghost, ever one God, world without end.

1928Amer has an additional collect, which first appeared as an alternative provision in 1885, to be used at the first celebration of the Eucharist if there were two celebrations on Easter Day; it is also given as an additional collect for Eastertide in 1929Scot.

57   O God, who for our redemption didst give thine only-begotten Son to the death of [Scot : to suffer death upon] the Cross, and by his glorious resurrection hast delivered us from the power of our enemy; Grant us so to die daily from sin, that we may evermore live with him in the joy of his resurrection; through the same thy Son Christ our Lord.

1928Eng also has this collect but with 'to die daily unto sin'.

Source : Greg (324); found in the Sarum *Processionale;* used before Easter Mattins in 1549.
Current Use : no 474

The Easter Day collect is used throughout Easter Week in 1662. 1928Amer has special provisions for Monday and Tuesday in Easter Week.

58   O God, whose blessed Son did manifest himself to his
        disciples in the breaking of bread; Open, we pray thee,
        the eyes of our faith, that we may behold thee in all thy
        works; through the same thy Son Jesus Christ our Lord.

Source : new; written by John W. Suter, Sr.
Current Use : no 490

59   Grant, we beseech thee, Almighty God, that we who
        celebrate with reverence the Paschal feast, may be found
        worthy to attain to everlasting joys; through Jesus Christ
        our Lord.

Source : Hatchett writes, 'This collect dates to the old Gallican books, the Missale Gallicanum vetus (no 226), where it
is an alternative collect for the Friday after Easter, and the
Missale Gothicum (no 285) and Bobbio missal (no 285), where
it is used at the exchange of the peace. A variant version is
in the Gregorian Sacramentary (no 429) and in the Sarum
Missal for the Saturday in Easter Week' (Hatchett p. 179).
Current Use : no 488

First Sunday after Easter [1928Eng and 1929Scot : commonly called Low Sunday]

This is the collect for a second celebration of the Communion on Easter Day in 1549. It was also used for the Tuesday
in Easter Week and the First Sunday.

60   Almighty Father, who hast given thine only Son to die
        for our sins, and to rise again for our justification; Grant
        us so to put away the leaven of malice and wickedness,
        that we may always serve thee in pureness of living and
        truth; through the merits of the same thy Son Jesus
        Christ our Lord.

Source : new in 1549
Current Use : no 495

Second Sunday after Easter

61   Almighty God, who [1549 : which] hast given thine only
[1549 : thy holy] Son to be unto us both a sacrifice for
sin, and also an ensample of godly life; Give us grace
that we may always most thankfully receive that his in-
estimable benefit, and also daily endeavour ourselves
to follow the blessed steps of his most holy life; through
the same Jesus Christ our Lord.

Source : new in 1549
Current Use : no 561

Third Sunday after Easter

62   Almighty God, who [1549 : which] shewest [1928Amer :
showest] to them that be in error the light of thy truth,
to the intent that they may return into the way of righteousness; Grant unto all them that are admitted into
the fellowship of Christ's Religion, that they may es-
chew [1928Amer : avoid] those things that are contrary
to their profession, and follow all such things as are
agreeable to the same; through our Lord Jesus Christ.

Source : SM xxvii; from a Leonine April Mass
See no 579.

Fourth Sunday after Easter

63   O Almighty God, who alone canst order the unruly wills
and affections of sinful men; Grant unto thy people,
that they may love the thing which thou commandest,
and desire that which thou dost promise; that so, among
the sundry and manifold changes of the world, our
hearts may surely there be fixed, where true joys are
to be found; through Jesus Christ our Lord.

1549 had a completely different first line : 'Almighty God,

which dost make the minds of all faithful men to be of one
will; grant . . . '.

Source : SM xxviii
Current Use : nos 426–30

Fifth Sunday after Easter [1928Amer/Eng and 1929Scot :
commonly called Rogation Sunday]

64   O Lord [1549 : Lord], from whom all good things do
come; Grant to [1549 : omits 'to'] us thy humble servants, that by thy holy inspiration we may think those
things that be good, and by thy merciful guiding may
perform the same; through our Lord Jesus Christ.

Source : SM xxix
Current Use : no 547

Ascension Day

65   Grant, we beseech thee, Almighty God, that like as we
do believe thy only-begotten Son our Lord Jesus Christ
to have ascended into the heavens; so we may also in
heart and mind thither ascend, and with him continually dwell, who liveth and reigneth with thee and the
Holy Ghost, one God, world without end.

Source : SM xxx
Current Use : nos 521–22

1928Amer has this collect said daily throughout the Octave.
1928Eng provides that it shall be used except when the book
has other provision.

Sunday after Ascension Day [1928Amer : The Sunday . . .]

66   O God the King of glory, who hast exalted thine only
Son Jesus Christ with great triumph unto thy kingdom
in heaven; We beseech thee, leave us not comfortless;
but send to us thine Holy Ghost to comfort us, and ex-

alt us unto the same place whither our Saviour Christ
is gone before, who liveth and reigneth with thee and
the Holy Ghost, one God, world without end.

Source : new in 1549
Current Use : no 527

Whitsunday [1928Amer : Pentecost, commonly called Whitsunday; 1928Eng : Whitsunday]

67   God [1928Amer : O God], who as at this time didst
teach [1549 : which as upon this day hast taught] the
hearts of thy faithful people, by the sending [1928Amer :
by sending] to them the light of thy Holy Spirit; Grant
us by the same Spirit to have a right judgement in all
things, and evermore to rejoice in his holy comfort;
through the merits of Christ Jesus our Saviour, who
liveth and reigneth with thee, in the unity of the same
Spirit, one God, world without end.

Source : SM xxxii
Current Use : no 533

1928Amer has the collect said daily throughout Whitsunday
Week. As at Easter, it also has provision for the first Communion if there are two.

68   Almighty and most merciful God, grant, we beseech
thee, that by the indwelling of thy Holy Spirit, we may
be enlightened and strengthened for thy service; through
Jesus Christ our Lord, who liveth and reigneth with thee
in the unity of the same Spirit ever, one God, world
without end.

Source : new

Monday in Whitsunday Week [1928Amer]

69   Send, we beseech thee, Almighty God, thy Holy Spirit
into our hearts, that he may direct and rule us accord-

ing to thy will, comfort us in all our afflictions, defend
us from all error, and lead us into all truth; through
Jesus Christ our Lord, who with thee and the same Holy
Spirit liveth and reigneth, one God, world without end.

Source : new

Tuesday in Whitsunday Week [1928Amer]

70   Grant, we beseech thee, merciful God, that thy Church,
being gathered together in unity by thy Holy Spirit, may
manifest thy power among all peoples, to the glory of
thy Name; through Jesus Christ our Lord, who with
thee and the same Holy Spirit liveth and reigneth, one
God, world without end.

Source : new
Current Use : no 563

Trinity Sunday

71   Almighty and everlasting God, who hast given us thy
servants grace by the confession of a true faith to acknowledge the glory of the eternal Trinity, and in the
power of the Divine Majesty to worship the Unity; We
beseech thee, that thou wouldest keep us stedfast in
this faith, and evermore defend us from all adversities
[1549 : we beseech thee, that through the stedfastness
of this faith, we may evermore be defended from all ad-
versity], who livest and reignest, one God, world without end.

Source : SM xxxiii
Current Use : no 540

First Sunday after Trinity

72   O God, the strength of all them that put their trust in
thee, mercifully accept our prayers; and because through

the weakness of our mortal nature we can do no good thing without thee, grant us the help of thy grace, that in keeping of thy commandments we may please thee, both in will and deed; through Jesus Christ our Lord.

Source : SM xxxiv
Current Use : no 380

Second Sunday after Trinity

The 1662 collect keeps a few words from that of 1549.

73 Lord, make us to have a perpetual fear and love of thy holy name : for thou never failest to help and govern them whom thou dost bring up in thy stedfast love. Grant this . . . .

74 O Lord, who never failest to help and govern them who thou dost bring up in thy stedfast fear and love; Keep us, we beseech thee, under the protection of thy good providence, and make us to have a perpetual fear and love of thy holy Name; through Jesus Christ our Lord.

Source : SM xxxv
Current Use : no 549

Third Sunday after Trinity

75 O Lord, we beseech thee mercifully to hear us; and grant that we, to whom thou hast given a hearty desire to pray, may by thy mighty aid be defended and comforted in all dangers and adversities; through Jesus Christ our Lord.

Source : SM xxxvi

Fourth Sunday after Trinity

76 O God, the protector of all that trust in thee, without whom nothing is strong, nothing is holy; Increase and multiply upon us thy mercy; that, thou being our ruler

and guide, we may so pass through things temporal,
that we finally lose not the things eternal : Grant this,
O heavenly Father, for Jesus Christ's sake our Lord.

Source : SM xxxvii
Current Use : no 557

Fifth Sunday after Trinity

77   Grant, O Lord, we beseech thee, that the course of this
world may be so peaceably ordered by thy governance,
that thy Church may joyfully serve thee in all godly
quietness; through Jesus Christ our Lord.

Source : SM xxxviii
Current Use : no 545

Sixth Sunday after Trinity

78   O God, who hast prepared for them that love thee such
good things as pass man's understanding; Pour into our
hearts such love toward thee, that we, loving thee above
all things [1549 : loving thee in all things], may obtain
thy promises which exceed all that we can desire;
through Jesus Christ our Lord.

Source : SM xxxix
Current Use : no 515

Seventh Sunday after Trinity

79   Lord of all power and might, who art the author and
giver of all good things; Graft in our hearts the love of
thy Name, increase in us true religion, nourish us with
all goodness, and of thy great mercy keep us in the same;
through Jesus Christ our Lord.

Source : SM xl
Current Use : no 564

Eighth Sunday after Trinity

80   O God, whose never-failing providence ordereth all things both in heaven and earth; We humbly beseech thee to put away from us all hurtful things, and to give us those things which be profitable for us; through Jesus Christ our Lord.

1549 had a different first line : 'God, whose providence is never deceived, we humbly beseech . . . .'.

Source : SM xli
Current Use : no 546

Ninth Sunday after Trinity

81   Grant to us, Lord, we beseech thee, the spirit to think and do always such things as be rightful; that we, who cannot do any thing that is good without thee, may by thee be enabled to live according to thy will; through Jesus Christ our Lord.

Source : SM xlii
Current Use : nos 254, 393, 559, 608

Tenth Sunday after Trinity

82   Let thy merciful ears, O Lord, be open to the prayers of thy humble servants; and that they may obtain their petitions make them to ask such things as shall please thee; through Jesus Christ our Lord.

Source : SM xliii

Eleventh Sunday after Trinity

1662 again develops the ideas embodied in 1549.

83   God, which declarest thy almighty power most chiefly in shewing mercy and pity; Give unto us abundantly thy grace that we, running to thy promises, may be

made partakers of thy heavenly treasure; through Jesus Christ our Lord.

84   O God, who declarest thy almighty power most chiefly in shewing mercy and pity; mercifully grant unto us such a measure of thy grace, that we, running the way of thy commandments, may obtain thy gracious promises, and be made partakers of thy heavenly treasure; through Jesus Christ our Lord.

Source : SM xliv
Current Use : no 568

Twelfth Sunday after Trinity

85   Almighty and everlasting God, who art always more ready to hear than we to pray, and art wont to give more than either we desire or deserve; Pour upon us the abundance of thy mercy; forgiving us those things whereof our conscience is afraid, and giving us those good things which we are not worthy to ask, but through the merits and mediation of Jesus Christ, thy Son, our Lord.

Source : SM xlv
Current Use : no 569

Thirteenth Sunday after Trinity

86   Almighty and merciful God, of whose only gift it cometh that thy faithful people do unto thee true and laudable service; Grant, we beseech thee, that we may so faithfully serve thee in this life, that we fail not finally to attain thy heavenly promises; through the merits of Jesus Christ our Lord.

Here 1549 had a different second line : 'grant we beseech thee, that we may so run to thy heavenly promises, that we fail not finally to attain the same'.

Source : SM xlvi
Current Use : no 573

Fourteenth Sunday after Trinity

87 Almighty and everlasting God, give unto us the increase of faith, hope, and charity; and, that we may obtain that which thou dost promise, make us to love that which thou dost command; through Jesus Christ our Lord.

1929Scot gives 'love' as an alternative to 'charity'.

Source : SM xlvii
Current Use : no 572

Fifteenth Sunday after Trinity

88 Keep, we beseech thee, O Lord, thy Church with thy perpetual mercy : and, because the frailty of man without thee cannot but fall, keep us ever by thy help from all things hurtful, and lead us to all things profitable to our salvation; through Jesus Christ our Lord.

Source : SM xlviii

Sixteenth Sunday after Trinity

89 O Lord, we beseech thee, let thy continual pity cleanse and defend thy Church; and, because it cannot continue in safety without thy succour, preserve it evermore by thy help and goodness; through Jesus Christ our Lord.

Source : SM xlix
Current Use : no 558

Seventeenth Sunday after Trinity

90 Lord, we pray thee that thy grace may always prevent and follow us, and make us continually to be given to all good works; through Jesus Christ our Lord.

Source : SM 1
Current Use : no 570

Eighteenth Sunday after Trinity

1662 again develops 1549.

91   Lord we beseech thee, grant thy people grace to avoid the infections of the devil, and with pure heart and mind to follow thee the only God; through Jesus Christ our Lord.

92   Lord, we beseech thee, grant thy people grace to withstand the temptations of the world, the flesh, and the devil, and with pure hearts and minds to follow thee the only God; through Jesus Christ our Lord.

Source : SM li
Current Use : nos 409–10

Nineteenth Sunday after Trinity

93   O God, forasmuch as without thee we are not able to please thee; Mercifully grant, that thy Holy Spirit may in all things direct and rule our hearts; through Jesus Christ our Lord.

Source : SM lii
Current Use : no 566

Twentieth Sunday after Trinity

1549 and 1662 are close parallels here but not identical.

94   Almighty and merciful God, of thy bountiful goodness, keep us from all things that may hurt us; that we, being ready both in body and soul, may with free hearts accomplish those things that thou wouldest have done; through Jesus Christ our Lord.

95   O Almighty and most merciful God, of thy bountiful goodness keep us, we beseech thee, from all things that

may hurt us; that we, being ready both in body and soul, may cheerfully accomplish those things that thou wouldest have done; through Jesus Christ our Lord.

Source : SM liii
Current Use : no 544

Twenty-First Sunday after Trinity

96   Grant, we beseech thee, merciful Lord, to thy faithful people pardon and peace, that they may be cleansed from all their sins, and serve thee with a quiet mind; through Jesus Christ our Lord.

Source : SM liv
Current Use : no 391

Twenty-Second Sunday after Trinity

97   Lord, we beseech thee to keep thy household the Church in continual godliness; that through thy protection it may be free from all adversities, and devoutly given to serve thee in good works, to the glory of thy Name; through Jesus Christ our Lord.

Source : SM lv
Current Use : no 307

Twenty-Third Sunday after Trinity

98   O God [1549 : God], our refuge and strength, who [1549 : which] art the author of all godliness; Be ready, we beseech thee [1549 : omits 'we beseech thee'], to hear the devout prayers of thy Church; and grant that those things which we ask faithfully we may obtain effectually; through Jesus Christ our Lord.

Source : SM lvi

Twenty-Fourth Sunday after Trinity

99   O Lord, we beseech thee, absolve thy people from their offences; that through thy bountiful goodness we may all be delivered from the bands of those sins, which by our frailty we have committed : Grant this, O heavenly Father, for Jesus Christ's sake, our blessed Lord and Saviour.

Source : SM lvii

Twenty-Fifth Sunday after Trinity [1928Amer/Eng and 1929Scot : The Sunday next before Advent]

100   Stir up, we beseech thee, O Lord, the wills of thy faithful people; that they, plenteously bringing forth the fruit of good works, may of thee be plenteously rewarded; through Jesus Christ our Lord.

Source : SM lviii
Current Use : no 597

Saint Andrew's Day

1549

101   Almighty God, which hast given such grace to thy Apostle saint Andrew, that he counted the sharp and painful death of the cross to be a high honour, and a great glory; Grant us to take and esteem all troubles and adversities which shall come unto us for thy sake, as things profitable for us toward the obtaining of everlasting life.

Source : new in 1549

1662

102   Almighty God, who didst give such grace unto thy holy Apostle saint Andrew, that he readily obeyed the calling of thy Son Jesus Christ, and followed him without delay; Grant unto us all, that we, being called by thy

holy Word, may forthwith give up ourselves obediently to fulfil thy holy commandments; through the same Jesus Christ our Lord.

Source : new in 1552

Saint Thomas the Apostle

103 Almighty and everliving God, who [1549 : Almighty everliving God, which] for the more confirmation of the faith didst suffer thy holy Apostle Thomas to be doubtful in thy Son's resurrection; Grant us so perfectly, and without all doubt, to believe in thy Son Jesus Christ, that our faith in thy sight may never be reproved. Hear us, O Lord, through the same Jesus Christ, to whom, with thee and the Holy Ghost, be all honour and glory, now and for evermore.

Source : new in 1549

Conversion of Saint Paul

1549

104 God, which hast taught all the world, through the preaching of thy blessed apostle Saint Paul; grant, we beseech thee, that we which have his wonderful conversion in remembrance, may follow and fulfil the holy doctrine that he taught; through Jesus Christ our Lord.

1662

105 O God, who, through the preaching of the blessed Apostle Saint Paul, hast caused the light of the Gospel to shine throughout the world; Grant, we beseech thee, that we, having his wonderful conversion in remembrance, may shew forth our thankfulness unto thee for the same, by following the holy doctrine which he taught; through Jesus Christ our Lord.

Source : SM

Presentation of Christ in the Temple [commonly called The Purification of Saint Mary the Virgin]

106   Almighty and everliving God, we humbly beseech thy Majesty, that, as thy only-begotten Son was this day presented in the Temple in substance of our flesh, so we may be presented unto thee with pure and clean hearts [1549 : minds], by the same thy Son Jesus Christ our Lord.

Source : SM; Greg (124)
Current Use : no 350

Saint Matthias's Day

107   O Almighty God, who into [1549 : which in] the place of the traitor Judas didst choose thy faithful servant Matthias to be of the number of the [1549 : thy] twelve Apostles; Grant that thy Church, being alway preserved from false apostles, may be ordered and guided by faithful and true pastors; through Jesus Christ our Lord.

Source : new in 1549

Annunciation of the Blesssed Virgin Mary

108   We beseech thee, O Lord, pour thy grace into our hearts; that, as we have known the incarnation of thy Son Jesus Christ [1549 : Christ, thy Son's incarnation,] by the message of an angel, so by his cross and passion we may be brought unto the glory of his resurrection; through the same Jesus Christ our Lord.

Source : new in 1549; from a Greg. post-communion (143)

Saint Mark's Day

109   O [1549 : omits 'O'] Almighty God, who hast instructed thy holy Church with the heavenly doctrine of thy Evangelist Saint Mark; Give us grace, that, being not like

children carried away with every blast of vain doctrine, we may be established in the truth of thy holy Gospel; through Jesus Christ our Lord.

1549 gives the petition a different order : 'Give us grace so to be established by thy holy Gospel, that we be not, like children, carried away with every blast of vain Doctrine'.

Source : new in 1549; revised during Elizabeth's reign

Saint Philip and Saint James's Day

110　O [1549 : omits 'O'] Almighty God, whom truly to know is everlasting life; Grant us perfectly to know thy Son Jesus Christ to be the way, the truth, and the life; that, following the steps of thy holy Apostles, Saint Philip and Saint James, we may stedfastly walk in the way that leadeth to eternal life; through the same thy Son Jesus Christ our Lord.

1549 has a very short conclusion : ' . . . and the life, as thou hast taught Saint Philip and the other Apostles; through Jesus Christ our Lord'.

Source : new in 1549

Saint Barnabas the Apostle

111　O Lord God Almighty [1549 : Lord Almighty], who didst endue [1549 : hast endued] thy holy Apostle Barnabas with singular gifts of the [1549 : thy] Holy Ghost; Leave us not, we beseech thee, destitute of thy manifold gifts, nor yet of grace to use them always to thy honour and glory; through Jesus Christ our Lord.

1549 omits 'Leave us not, we beseech thee' and has 'let us not be'.

Source : new in 1549

Saint John Baptist's Day

112   Almighty God, by whose providence thy servant John
Baptist was wonderfully born, and sent to prepare the
way of thy Son our Saviour, by preaching of repentance
[1549 : penance]; Make us so to follow his doctrine and
holy life, that we may truly repent according to his
preaching; and after his example constantly speak the
truth, boldly rebuke vice, and patiently suffer for the
truth's sake; through Jesus Christ our Lord.

Source : new in 1549

Saint Peter's Day

113   O [1549 : omits 'O'] Almighty God, who [1549 : which]
by thy Son Jesus Christ didst give [1549 : hast given]
to thy Apostle Saint Peter many excellent gifts, and commandest him earnestly to feed thy flock; Make, we beseech thee, all Bishops and Pastors diligently to preach
thy holy Word, and the people obediently to follow the
same, that they may receive the crown of everlasting
glory; through Jesus Christ our Lord.

Source : new in 1549

Saint James the Apostle

114   Grant, O merciful God, that as thine holy Apostle Saint
James, leaving his father and all that he had, without
delay was obedient unto the calling of thy Son Jesus
Christ, and followed him; so we, forsaking all worldly
and carnal affections, may be evermore ready to follow thy holy [1549 : omits 'holy'] commandments;
through Jesus Christ our Lord.

Source : new in 1549

Saint Bartholomew the Apostle

115   O Almighty and everlasting God, which hast given grace to thy apostle Bartholomew truly to believe and to preach thy word; grant, we beseech thee, unto thy Church, both to love that he believed, and to preach that he taught; through Christ our Lord.

116   O Almighty and everlasting God, who didst give thine Apostle Bartholomew grace truly to believe and to preach thy Word; Grant we beseech thee, unto thy Church to love that Word which he believed, and both to preach and receive the same; through Jesus Christ our Lord.

Source : SM
Current Use : nos 294, 603

Saint Matthew the Apostle

117   O [1549 : omits 'O'] Almighty God, who [1549 : which] by thy blessed Son didst call Matthew from the receipt of custom to be an Apostle and Evangelist : Grant us grace to forsake all covetous desires, and inordinate love of riches, and to follow the same thy Son [1549 : follow thy said Son] Jesus Christ, who liveth and reigneth with thee and the Holy Ghost, one God, world without end.

Source : new in 1549

Saint Michael and All Angels

118   O [1549 : omits 'O'] Everlasting God, who [1549 : which] hast ordained and constituted the services of [1549 : inserts 'all'] Angels and men in a wonderful order; Mercifully grant, that as thy holy Angels always [1549 : that they which always] do thee service in heaven, so [1549 : may] by thy appointment they may

[1549 : omits 'they may'] succour and defend us on
[1549 : in] earth; through Jesus Christ our Lord.

Source : SM

Saint Luke the Evangelist

119   Almighty God which calledst Luke the physician, whose
praise is in the gospel, to be a physician of the soul;
it may please thee, by the wholesome medicines of his
doctrine, to heal all the diseases of our souls; through
thy Son Jesus Christ our Lord.

120   Almighty God, who calledst Luke the Physician, whose
praise is in the Gospel, to be an Evangelist, and Physician of the soul; May it please thee, that, by the wholesome medicines of the doctrine delivered by him, all
the diseases of our souls may be healed; through the
merits of thy Son Jesus Christ our Lord.

Source : new in 1549

1928Amer has a different version of this collect.

121   Almighty God, who didst inspire thy servant Saint Luke
the Physician, to set forth in the Gospel the love and
healing power of thy Son; Manifest in thy Church the
like power and love, to the healing of our bodies and
souls; through the same thy Son Jesus Christ our Lord.

Source : new in 1928Amer; composed by Charles Morris
Addison

Saint Simon and Saint Jude, Apostles

122   O Almighty God, who hast built thy Church upon the
foundation of the Apostles and Prophets, Jesus Christ
himself being the head corner-stone; Grant us so to be
joined together in unity of spirit by their doctrine, that
we may be made an holy temple acceptable unto thee;
through Jesus Christ our Lord.

In 1549 the opening line is 'Almighty God, which hast builded the congregation . . . '.

Source : new in 1549
Current Use : no 550

All Saints' Day

123   O [1549 : omits 'O'] Almighty God, who [1549 : which] hast knit together thine [1549 : thy] elect in one communion and fellowship in the mystical body of thy Son Christ our Lord; Grant us grace so to follow thy blessed Saints in all virtuous [1549 : virtues] and godly living, that we may come to those unspeakable joys, which thou hast prepared for them that unfeignedly love thee; through Jesus Christ our Lord.

Source : new in 1549

Saint Mary Magdalene and the Transfiguration

Two feast days have a more complex history than these Red Letter Days. The first is the Feast of Saint Mary Magdalene which, included in 1549, was omitted from 1552 and 1662. It reappears in 1928Eng but not 1928Amer. It is included in 1929Scot among a group of lesser feasts, including the Marian feasts of the Conception, Nativity, Visitation, and Falling Asleep of the Blessed Virgin Mary. This collect, described by Mackenzie as 'very poor', was used in 1549 but not used thereafter.

124   Merciful Father, give us grace, that we never presume to sin through the example of any creature; but if it shall chance us at any time to offend thy divine majesty; that we may truly repent, and lament the same, after the example of Mary Magdalene, and by lively faith obtain remission of all our sins; through the only merits of thy Son our Saviour Christ.

It did, however, appear with some modification in 1885Amer for the Wednesday before Easter (see no 170).

The Priest's Book of Private Devotion (1902) has this collect.

125   Grant, we beseech Thee, O risen Lord, that we who commemorate the blessed Mary Magdalene may be healed by Thee of all our diseases, and taught to worship Thee, our Master and our God; Who livest and reignest . . . .

The Oxford book (1920) provides a modern collect which also appears in 1928Eng and, in a slightly modified form, in 1929Scot.

126   O Almighty God, whose blessed Son did call and sanctify Mary Magdalene [1928Eng : Magdalen] [1929Scot : did sanctify Mary Magdalene, and did call her] to be a witness to his resurrection; Mercifully grant that by thy grace we may be healed of all our infirmities, and always serve thee in the power of his endless life, who with thee and the Holy Ghost liveth and reigneth, one God, world without end.

In the Scottish book it does not appear among the Red Letter Days but in a collection 'For Various Occasions' which includes the Conception, Nativity, Visitation, and Falling Asleep of the Blessed Virgin Mary.

The Transfiguration was omitted from 1549 and hence from 1662. The option of drawing on ancient sources was not possible here because, though the Feast of the Transfiguration was widely adopted in the West before A.D. 1000, it only achieved general observance in 1457. *The Priest's Book of Private Devotion* uses a version of the collect credited by Hatchett to Huntington and used in the American 1892, 1928, and 1979 books.

127   O God, who on the mount didst reveal to chosen witnesses thine only-begotten Son wonderfully transfigured, in raiment white and glistering; Mercifully grant that we, being delivered from the disquietude of this

world [*PBPD :* turmoil of this world], may be permit-
ted to behold the King in his beauty, who with thee,
O Father, and thee, O Holy Ghost, liveth and reigneth,
one God, world without end.

1928Eng had another collect.

128   O God, who before the passion of thine only-begotten
Son didst reveal his glory upon the holy mount : Grant
unto us thy servants, that in faith beholding the light
of his countenance, we may be strengthened to bear the
cross, and be changed into his likeness from glory to
glory.

The Diocesan Service Book of the Diocese of Oxford (1920) had
another collect, of unknown origin, that is also found in
1929Scot.

129   Almighty and everlasting God, whose blessed Son was
revealed to the three Apostles when he was transfigured
on the holy mount, and in the excellent glory spake with
Moses and Elijah of his decease which he should accomplish at Jerusalem; Grant to us thy servants that
though now we see him not, yet in faith beholding the
light of his countenance, we may be strengthened to bear
the cross; through the same Jesus Christ our Lord.

It is tempting to think that both the English and Oxford/
Scottish collects have a common but as yet undetermined origin, perhaps the original collect of Callistus III. It is clear that
they did not derive from the *Roman Missal* of 1570.

OTHER FEASTS FOR WHICH PROPERS
WERE PROVIDED IN 1928–1929

Whereas the 1549 book had only Red Letter Days, the Calendar of 1561, incorporated into later issues of the Elizabethan
book, contained a list of Black Letter Saints almost the same
as that found in 1662. *The Book of Common Prayer,* 1662, had

sixty-seven Black Letter Days. Lowther Clarke subscribes to Wheatly's view that these dates were included not for any religious reason, but for secular convenience.

> The Courts of Justice used them for reckoning; trades would have been displeased had they lost their tutelary saint; for example, Crispin, patron of Shoemakers. The patronal festival of a church had a wake or fair associated with it, and for convenience' sake the date was given; history books referred to periods as Lammastide or Martinmas, and it was well that such references should not become unintelligible. . . . The bishops' answer to the Puritans in 1661 shows their motives. The names were left not to be kept as holy-days, but for secular purposes and for the preservation of memories. So little interest was taken in Christian antiquity that even exceptionally well-informed writers some fifty years later, such as Wheatly and Nichols, remembered only the secular motive.

The calendar published in *The Priest's Book of Private Devotion* is that of the 1662 book supplemented by other traditional observances 'suggested for use for purposes of devotion'. Through the Catholic revival of the nineteenth century, devotional purposes replaced secular ones. *The Priest's Book* contained proper collects for a large number of saints and commons for all others. There can be no doubt that these unofficial developments affected the official liturgical provision (Lowther Clark points to the contributions of John Wordsworth in *The Ministry of Grace* and Frere in *Some Principles of Liturgical Reform*).

1928Eng has a collection of propers for 'The Lesser Feasts' right at the back of the book, followed by provisions for the Common of Saints and some other collects. 1929Scot does something very similar. Oxford (1920) provided for the Transfiguration, the Name of Jesus, Holy Cross Day, Conception BVM, Nativity BVM, Visitation BVM, Saint Mary Magdalene; national observances of Saint George, Saints Columba, Patrick, and David; and local observances of Saint

Birinus, Saint Hugh of Lincoln, and Saint Frideswide. 1929Scot counts Saints Kentigern, Patrick, Columba, and Ninian (one collect for all four), and Margaret of Scotland as Red Letter Days.

Saints Kentigern, Patrick, Columba, and Ninian

130   O God, who by the preaching of thy blessed servant Saint *N.* didst cause the light of the Gospel to shine in this our land [*or :* in these islands] : Grant, we beseech thee that, having his life and labours in remembrance, we may shew forth our thankfulness unto thee for the same by following the example of his zeal and patience; through Jesus Christ our Lord [1929Scot].

Saint Margaret of Scotland

131   O God, who didst call thy servant Queen Margaret to an earthly throne that she might advance thy heavenly kingdom, and didst endue her with zeal for thy Church and charity towards thy people : Mercifully grant that we who commemorate her example may be fruitful in good works, and attain to the glorious fellowship of thy Saints; through Jesus Christ our Lord [1929Scot].

Visitation of the Blessed Virgin Mary

132   O God, who didst lead the Blessed Virgin Mary to visit Elisabeth, to their exceeding joy and comfort : Grant unto thy people [1929Scot : us thy people], that as Mary did rejoice to be called the Mother of the Lord, so they [1929Scot : we] may ever rejoice to believe the incarnation of thine only-begotten Son; to whom with thee and the Holy Ghost be all honour and glory, world without end [1928Eng and 1929Scot].

Lammas Day

133   O God, who didst cause thy holy Apostle Peter to be loosed from his chains and to depart without hurt : Break, we beseech thee, the chains of our sins, and mercifully put away all evil from us; through Jesus Christ our Lord [1929Scot].

Name of Jesus

134   Almighty God, who has taught us that in the Name of Jesus Christ alone is salvation : Mercifully grant that thy faithful people, ever glorying in his Name, may make thy salvation known to all the world; through the same Jesus Christ our Lord [1928Eng].

135   O Almighty God, who hast given unto thy Son Jesus Christ the Name which is above every name, and has taught us that there is none other whereby we may be saved : Mercifully grant that as thy faithful people have comfort and peace in his Name, so thy may ever labour to proclaim it unto all nations; through the same Jesus Christ our Lord [1929Scot].

Beheading of Saint John Baptist

136   O God, who didst vouchsafe to thy servant John Baptist to be in birth and death the forerunner of thy Son : Grant that as he was slain for truth and righteousness, so we may contend for the same unto the end; for the love of thy Son Jesus Christ our Lord [1928Eng and 1929Scot].

Nativity of the Blessed Virgin Mary

137   O Merciful God, hear the prayers of thy servants who commemorate the Nativity of the Mother of the Lord; and grant that by the incarnation of thy dear Son we

may indeed be made nigh unto him; who liveth and reigneth . . . [1928Eng].

138   O Almighty God, who didst endue with singular grace the Blessed Virgin Mary, the Mother of our Lord : Vouchsafe, we beseech thee, to hallow our bodies in purity, and our souls in humility and love; through the same our Lord and Saviour Jesus Christ [1929Scot].

The Scottish collect is also used for August 15 and December 8.

Holy Cross Day

The Scottish book uses the collect for Palm Sunday. England has a modern collect which Mackenzie describes as 'far from satisfactory'!

139   O God, who by the passion of thy blessed Son hast made the instrument of shameful death to be unto us the means of life and peace : Grant us so to glory in the Cross of Christ, that we may gladly suffer shame and loss; for the same thy Son our Lord [1928Eng].

Current Use : nos 446–48

Commemoration of All Souls

140   O Lord, the maker and redeemer of all believers : Grant to the faithful departed all the unsearchable benefits of thy Son's passion; that in the day of his appearing they may be manifested as thy true children; through the same thy Son Jesus Christ our Lord [1928Eng].

Source : the Manual of the Society (Community) of the Resurrection, probably by Dr. Brightman

141   O Eternal Lord God, who holdest all souls in life : We beseech thee to shed forth upon thy whole Church in Paradise and on earth the bright beams of thy light and heavenly comfort; and grant that we, following the good example of those who have loved and served thee here

and are now at rest, may at the last enter with them into the fulness of thine unending joy; through Jesus Christ our Lord [1928Eng : from Occasional Prayers §32].

142   O Eternal God, who holdest all souls in life : We beseech thee to shed forth upon all the faithful departed the bright beams of thy light and heavenly comfort; and grant that they, and we with them, may at length attain to the joys of thine eternal kingdom; through Jesus Christ our Lord [1929Scot].

Saints, Martyrs, Missionaries, and Doctors of the Church of England

143   We beseech thee, O Lord, to multiply thy grace upon us who commemorate the saints of our nation; that as we rejoice to be their fellow-citizens on earth, so we may have fellowship also with them in heaven; through Jesus Christ our Lord [1928Eng].

Conception of the Blessed Virgin Mary

144   O Merciful God, hear the prayers of thy servants who commemorate the Conception of the Mother of our Lord; and grant that by the incarnation of thy dear Son we may indeed be made nigh unto him; who liveth and reigneth . . . [1928Eng].

COMMON OF SAINTS

1928Eng provided common collects under six specific categories—martyr, doctor or confessor, bishop, abbot or abbess, missionary, virgin or virgin-martyr, matron—together with one for any saint. 1929Scot provided for martyrs, confessors and doctors, virgins, and other saint's days. Mackenzie says that all the collects appear to be modern; he praises that of a bishop in 1928Eng as 'possessing all the qualities of a good Collect' and condemns the same rite's provision for a matron as being 'of almost incredible banality' and 'the probably worst which has ever been admitted to an Anglican rite!' (p. 409). By contrast, 1928Amer only added the Transfiguration to the Church's feasts and had no lesser feasts in the Prayer Book calendar. Though it anticipated, with the provision of readings, the celebration of patronal festivals of saints who are bishops, confessors, martyrs, virgins, and matrons, no specific collects were provided other than two for any saint's day, one of which is non-specific.

Of a Martyr or Martyrs

145 Almighty God, by whose grace and power thy holy Martyr N. or M. triumphed over suffering, and despised death; Grant, we beseech thee, that enduring hardness, and waxing valiant in fight, we may with the noble army of martyrs receive the crown of everlasting life; through Jesus Christ our Lord [1928Eng].

The Oxford version is of holy martyrs in general, without space to include a name, and concludes : 'Inspire us, we beseech thee, with the same faith, that enduring affliction and waxing valiant in fight, we may with them receive the crown of everlasting life'. The Scottish version is different again.

146 Almighty God, by whose grace and power thy holy Martyr, Saint N., triumphed over suffering and death : Endue us, we beseech thee, with the same power, that we may finish our course in faith, and with *him* receive the crown of everlasting life; through Jesus Christ our Lord [1929Scot].

Of a Doctor or Confessor

147 O God, who has enlightened thy Church by the teaching of thy servant N. [1929Scot : by the example of thy Confessor or Doctor, Saint N.] : Enrich it evermore,

we beseech thee, with thy heavenly grace, and raise up faithful witnesses, who by their life and doctrine may set forth to all men the truth of thy salvation; through Jesus Christ our Lord [1928Eng/1929Scot].

Of a Bishop

148   O God, the light of the faithful, and shepherd of souls, who didst set blessed N. to be a Bishop in the Church, that he might feed thy sheep by his word and guide them by his example : Grant us, we pray thee, to keep the faith which he taught, and to follow in his footsteps; through Jesus Christ our Lord [1928Eng/1929Scot].

The same collect appears in *The Priest's Manual of Private Devotion*. Mackenzie says that it is the best of the modern collects among the commons, 'possessing all the qualities of a good Collect'. The collect in the Oxford book is different.

149   O Lord God Almighty, who didst endue thy servant N. with singular gifts of the Holy Ghost; Grant that thy Church, being always preserved from false teachers, may be ordered and guided by faithful and true pastors; through Jesus Christ our Lord.

Of an Abbot or Abbess

150   O God, by whose grace the blessed Abbot (Abbess) N., enkindled with the fire of thy love, became a burning and a shining light in thy Church : Grant that we may be inflamed with the same spirit of discipline and love, and ever walk before thee as children of light; through Jesus Christ our Lord [1928Eng].

Of Missionaries

151   O Lord Jesus Christ, who callest to thee whom thou willest and sendest them whither thou dost choose : We thank thee for calling thy servant N. to preach thy

Gospel to the nations; and we humbly pray thee to raise up among us those who shall be heralds and evangelists of thy kingdom, and shall build up thy Church in every land; who livest and reignest with the Father and the Holy Spirit, one God world without end [1928Eng].

Of a Virgin or Virgin Martyr

152   O God, who didst endue thy holy Virgin N. with grace to witness a good confession (and to suffer gladly for thy sake) : Grant that we, after her example, [1929Scot : Grant that after her example we] may be found ready when the Bridegroom cometh, and enter with him to the marriage feast; through the same thy Son Jesus Christ our Lord [1928Eng and 1929Scot].

Of a Matron

153   O God, who hast built up thy Church through the divers gifts and graces of thy saints : We give thee humble thanks for the example of holy women, and especially this day for thy servant N.; and we beseech thee to maintain among us the shelter of a mother's love and the protection of a mother's prayer, in the grace of thy Son, Jesus Christ our Lord [1928Eng].

An earlier form of this collect, entitled 'Holy Women', is found in the Oxford book. It offers thanks for 'all good women' and concludes 'Help us, we beseech thee, to follow in their steps, and fill our hearts with love of thee, and of others for thy sake; through Jesus Christ our Lord'.

Of Any Saint

154   O Almighty God, who willest to be glorified in thy Saints and didst raise up thy servant N. to shine as a light in the world : Shine, we pray thee, in our hearts, that we also in our generation may shew forth thy praises, who

hast called us out of darkness into thy marvellous light;
through Jesus Christ our Lord [1928Eng].

155   Almighty God, who dost choose thine elect out of every
nation, and dost shew forth thy glory in their lives :
Grant, we pray thee, that following the example of thy
servant Saint N., we may be fruitful in good works to
the praise of thy holy Name; through Jesus Christ our
Lord [1929Scot].

Ember Days

156   Almighty God, our heavenly Father, who hast pur-
chased to thyself an universal Church by the precious
blood of thy dear Son : Mercifully look upon the same,
and so guide and govern the minds of thy servants the
Bishops and Pastors of thy flock, that they may lay hands
suddenly on no man, but faithfully and wisely make
choice of fit persons to serve in the sacred ministry of
thy Church. And to those which shall be ordained to
any holy function give thy grace and heavenly benediction; that both by their life and doctrine they may set
forth thy glory, and set forward the salvation of all men;
through Jesus Christ our Lord [1662 Prayers and
Thanksgivings; 1928Eng].

157   O Almighty God, who hast committed to the hands of
men the ministry of reconciliation; We humbly beseech
thee, by the inspiration of thy holy Spirit, to put it into
the hearts of many to offer themselves for this ministry; that thereby mankind may be drawn to thy blessed
kingdom; through Jesus Christ our Lord [1928Amer].

Dedication Festival

158   O God, by whose providence we celebrate again the con-
secration [*or* : dedication] of this church : Send down
upon us, we beseech thee, thy heavenly blessing; and,

because holiness becometh thine house for ever, make us living temples, holy and acceptable unto thee; through Jesus Christ our Lord [1928Eng].

159   Almighty God, whom year by year we praise for the dedication of this church, and who hast preserved us in safety to worship therein : Hear, we beseech thee, the prayers of thy people, and grant that whosoever in this place shall make his supplications before thee, may by the granting of his petitions be filled with joy to the glory of thy holy Name; through Jesus Christ our Lord [1929Scot].

1928Amer has a much shortened version of this prayer (p. 259).

Harvest Thanksgiving

160   Almighty and everlasting God, who hast graciously given us the fruits of the earth in their season : We yield thee humble and hearty thanks for these thy bounties, beseeching thee to give us grace rightly to use them to thy glory and the relief of those that need; through Jesus Christ our Lord [1928Eng].

161   O Almighty and everlasting God, who hast given unto us the fruits of the earth in their season, and hast crowned the year with thy goodness : Give us grateful hearts, that we may unfeignedly thank thee for all thy loving kindness, and worthily magnify thy holy Name; through Jesus Christ our Lord [1929Scot].

162   Stir up, we beseech thee, O Lord, the wills of thy faithful people; that they who have freely received of thy bounty may, of thy bounty, freely give; through Jesus Christ our Lord [1929Scot].

163   O Lord Jesus Christ, who hast taught us that man doth not live by bread alone : Feed us, we humbly beseech thee, with the true Bread that cometh down from

heaven, even thyself, O blessed Saviour; who livest and
reignest . . . [1929Scot].

Synods and Councils

164   O Eternal God, the fountain of all wisdom, who didst
send thy Holy Spirit to lead the disciples into all the
truth : Vouchsafe that he, being present with thy servants now assembled in [Synod], may so rule their hearts
and guide their counsels that in all things they may seek
only thy glory and the good of thy holy Church; through
Jesus Christ our Lord.

Thanksgiving for the Institution of Holy Baptism

165   Almighty God, our heavenly Father, who has given us
the Sacrament of Holy Baptism that souls thereby being born again may be made heirs of everlasting salvation : We yield thee hearty thanks for this thy gift, and
humbly we beseech thee to grant that we who have thus
been made partakers of the death of thy Son may also
be partakers of his resurrection; through the same Jesus
Christ, our Lord [1928Eng].

166   O God who hast united men of every nation in the confession of thy Name, and dost continually multiply thy
Church with new offspring : Grant that those who have
been born again of water and of the Spirit may be one
both in inward faith and in outward devotion, and with
thankful hearts may shew forth in their lives the grace
of that Sacrament which they have received; through
Jesus Christ our Lord [1929Scot].

Thanksgiving for the Institution of Holy Communion

167   O Lord Jesus Christ, who hast ordained this Holy Sacrament to be a pledge of thy love, and a continual remembrance of thy passion : Grant that we, who partake

thereof by faith with thanksgiving, may grow up into
thee in all things, until we come to thy eternal joy; who
with the Father and the Holy Ghost livest and reignest,
one God, world without end [1928Eng (first collect)].

Overseas Missions

168   O God, our heavenly Father, who didst manifest thy
love by sending thine only-begotten Son into the world
that all might live through him : Pour thy Spirit upon
thy Church that it may fulfil his command to make disciples of all the nations; send forth, we beseech thee,
labourers into thy harvest; and hasten the time when
the fulness of the Gentiles shall be gathered in, and all
Israel shall be saved; through the same Jesus Christ our
Lord [1929Scot].

Eight collects which appear in 1885Amer did not find a place
in the 1892 revision and were not subsequently used. The provide an excellent example of verbose late-nineteenth-century
collects.

169   Almighty and everlasting God; grant us so to celebrate
the mysteries of our Lord's Passion, that we, obtaining pardon through his precious Blood, may come with
joy to the commemoration of that sacrifice by which thou
hast been pleased to redeem us; through the same thy
Son our Saviour Jesus Christ.

1885Amer : Monday before Easter

170   Merciful Father, give us grace that we never presume
to sin through the example of a fellow creature; but if
we be led at any time to offend thy Divine Majesty,
vouchsafe us to repent with Peter, rather than to despair with Judas, so that by a godly sorrow and a lively
faith we may obtain remission of our sins; through the
only merits of thy Son, Christ our Lord.

Source : See no 124.

1885Amer : Wednesday before Easter

---

171   Almighty Father, whose dear Son did in the Garden
of Gethsemane accept the cup thou gavest him to drink,
that so he might taste death for every man; Mercifully
grant that we to whom he ministers the cup of blessing
may thankfully receive it in remembrance of him, and
show our Lord's death till he come; who liveth and
reigneth with thee and the Holy Ghost, one God, world
without end.

1885Amer : Thursday before Easter

---

172   O God, who hast called us to be children of the resurrection, and hast made us citizens of the Jerusalem
which is above; Grant that whensover in the dimness
of this life present our eyes are holden that we see thee
not, our hearts may be always attentive to thy holy
Word, and burn within us, as it is opened by the Son,
our Saviour Jesus Christ.

1885Amer : Monday in Easter Week

---

173   O Holy Jesus, who by the travail of thy soul, hast made
a people to be born out of every kindred and nation
and tongue; Grant that all those who are called into the
unity of thy Church to be the children of God by the
washing of regeneration, may have one faith in their
hearts, and one law of holiness in their lives; through
thy merits who livest and reignest with the Father and
the Holy Ghost, one God, world without end.

1885Amer : Tuesday in Easter Week

---

174   O God, Holy Ghost, who, as on this day, didst descend
       in the likeness of fiery tongues, bringing to the Church
       the promise of the Father in the gift of power; Take away
       all vices from our hearts, and fill us with all wisdom
       and spiritual understanding. Grant this, O blessed
       Spirit, who with the Father and the Son, livest and
       reignest, ever one God, world without end.

1885Amer : Whitsunday [alternative collect]

---

175   O Lord Jesus Christ, who didst send from the Father
       the Comforter, even the Spirit of Truth; Grant that he
       may enlighten our minds with the teaching of thy truth,
       and sanctify our hearts with the power of thy grace, so
       that evermore abiding in thee we may be found stead-
       fast in faith and holy in life, being conformed unto thine
       image, who art with the Father and the Holy Ghost,
       ever one God, world without end.

1885Amer : Monday in Whitsunday Week

---

176   O God, the light and life of all believers; Grant that
       they whom the Holy Ghost hath made thy children by
       adoption and grace, loving thee without lukewarmness,
       and confessing thy faith without dissension, may ob-
       tain that peace which our Lord Jesus Christ promised
       to all those who truly follow him; through the same Jesus
       Christ our Lord.

1885Amer : Tuesday in Whitsunday Week

Chapter Three

COLLECTS IN TRANSITION
1930–1972

Few changes were made in the Anglican books before the publication of *Modern Collects* in 1972. 1959Can follows 1928Eng in having a New Year collect.

177   O Immortal Lord God, who inhabitest eternity, and hast brought thy servants to the beginning of another year : Pardon, we humbly beseech thee, our transgressions in the past, bless to us this New Year, and graciously abide with us all the days of our life; through Jesus Christ our Lord.

Source : no 17

The Christmas Day collect is then used until Epiphany, and there is no provision for the Second Sunday after Christmas Day; 1966Wales uses the provision from 1928Eng. The 1662 Epiphany collect is expanded in 1959Can, and it also specifically provides for the Baptism of our Lord with a collect that may be used at a second service on the Epiphany or on any weekday in the Octave. The second collect is heavily dependent on the Christmas collect.

178   O God, who by the leading of a star didst manifest thy only-begotten Son to the Gentiles : Mercifully grant,

that we, who know thee now by faith, may be led onward through this earthly life, until we see the vision
of thy heavenly glory; through the same thy Son . . . .

Source : no 21

---

179 O Heavenly Father, whose blessed Son Jesus Christ did
take our nature upon him, and was baptized for our
sake in the river Jordan : Mercifully grant that we being regenerate, and made thy children by adoption and
grace, may also be partakers of thy Holy Spirit; through
him whom thou didst send to be our Saviour and
Redeemer, even the same thy Son Jesus Christ our
Lord.

Source : no 8

It also has a collect for the missionary work of the Church
overseas that may be used throughout the Epiphany season
on weekdays.

180 Almighty and everlasting God, who desirest not the
death of sinners, but rather that they may turn unto
thee and live : Deliver the nations of the world from
superstition and unbelief, and gather them all into thy
holy Church, to the praise and glory of thy Name;
through Jesus Christ our Lord.

1966Wales has made slight alterations to the 1662 Epiphany
collect, changing 'which' to 'who' and concluding 'may after
this life enjoy the vision of thy glorious Godhead'. On the
Second Sunday after the Epiphany, 1966Wales has a baptism
collect dependent on, like 1959Can, no 8.

181 Almighty God, our heavenly Father, who at the baptism of Christ our Lord in Jordan didst declare him to
be thy beloved Son : Mercifully grant that we, being
regenerate, and made thy children by adoption and

grace, may daily be renewed by thy Holy Spirit; through him whom thou didst send to be our Saviour and Redeemer, even the same thy Son, Jesus Christ our Lord.

As a result, each of the Epiphany collects is moved on a Sunday, and 1662 : Epiphany 6 is omitted entirely.

---

182   We beseech thee, Almighty God, mercifully to look upon thy people; that by the glorious Passion of thy Son, our Saviour, they may be preserved evermore both in body and soul; through the same Jesus Christ our Lord.

Source : new; opening line and conclusion from 1662
Use : 1966Wales : Lent 5

On Maunday Thursday both 1959Can and 1966Wales add a Eucharistic collect.

183   O God, who in a wonderful sacrament hast left unto us a memorial of thy passion : Grant us so to reverence the holy mysteries of thy Body and Blood, that we may ever know within ourselves the fruit of thy redemption; who livest and reignest . . . .

Source : See Introduction.
Use : 1959Can : Maundy Thursday

184   Blessed Lord, who in a wonderful Sacrament hast left us a memorial of thy Passion : Grant us, we beseech thee, so to venerate the sacred mysteries of thy Body and Blood, that we may ever perceive within ourselves the fruit of thy redemption, who livest and reignest

. . . .

Source : See Introduction.
Use : 1966Wales : Maundy Thursday

Both 1959Can and 1966Wales have followed the example of the 1928 revisions in changing the third Good Friday collect, though neither follow exactly the provisions of those books. The first line is the same in both. 1959Can follows and slightly modifies 1928Eng : 'Have mercy upon the Jews, thine ancient people, and upon all who reject and deny thy Son; take from them . . . '. The Welsh revision is more extensive.

185   Have mercy we beseech thee, upon all who do not confess the faith of Christ crucified. Take from them all ignorance, hardness of heart, and contempt of thy Word; and so bring them home to thy fold, that they with us may be one flock under One Shepherd, Jesus Christ . . . .

On Easter Day 1959Can has removed 'preventing us' from the 1662 collect and provides an additional collect.

186   O God, who makest us glad with the yearly remembrance of the resurrection from the dead of thy only Son Jesus Christ : Grant that we who celebrate this Paschal feast may die daily unto sin, and live with him evermore in the glory of his endless life; through the same Jesus Christ our Lord.

Source : no 9 : 'O God, who . . . '; no 59 : 'Grant that . . . feast'; no 57 : 'die daily . . . '.

1966Wales uses the additional provision found in 1928Amer/ Eng. On the Second Sunday after Easter both books have reverted to the 1549 'example'.

On Whitsunday, 1959Can has another new collect in the 'yearly remembrance' shape. The petition draws on the words of administration from the rite of confirmation.

187   O God, who makest us glad with the yearly remembrance of the coming of the Holy Spirit upon thy dis-

ciples in Jerusalem : Grant that we who celebrate before thee the feast of Pentecost may continue thine for ever, and daily increase in thy Holy Spirit, until we come to thine eternal kingdom; through Jesus Christ our Lord.

THE COLLECTS OF *THE BOOK OF COMMON WORSHIP* OF THE CHURCH OF SOUTH INDIA

Fourth Sunday before Christmas :
The Beginning of Advent [The Coming of the Lord]

1662 : Advent 1

Third Sunday before Christmas :
Second Sunday in Advent

188 Almighty God, who in many and various ways didst speak to thy chosen people by the prophets, and hast given us, in thy Son our Saviour Jesus Christ, the fulfilment of the hope of Israel : Hasten, we beseech thee, the coming of the day when all things shall be subject to him, who liveth and reigneth with thee and the Holy Spirit, ever one God, world without end.

Second Sunday before Christmas :
Third Sunday in Advent

The first line is taken from the 1662 collect for Advent 3.

189 O Lord Jesus Christ, who at thy first coming didst send thy messenger to prepare thy way before thee : Grant that we, paying urgent heed to the message of repentance, may with hearts prepared await thy final coming to judge the world; who with the Father and the Holy Spirit ever livest and reignest, one God, world without end.

Next Sunday before Christmas :
Fourth Sunday in Advent

The 1928Amer version of 1662 : Advent 4 is used.

Christmas Eve

The 1928Amer alternative collect for Christmas Day, 'O God, who makest us glad', is given as the first collect for the Eve, and there is an additional and entirely new one.

190   O God, who before all others didst call shepherds to the cradle of thy Son : Grant that by the preaching of the gospel the poor, the humble, and the forgotten, may know that they are at home with thee; through Jesus Christ our Lord.

Christmas Day

1662 but with 'regenerate' replaced by 'born again'

Next Sunday after Christmas

1928Eng : Second Sunday after Christmas

Second Sunday after Christmas

191   O God, who by a star didst guide the Wise Men to the worship of thy Son : Lead, we pray thee, to thyself the wise and the great in every land, that unto thee every knee may bow, and every thought be brought into captivity; through Jesus Christ our Lord.

Third Sunday after Christmas

192   O Lord Jesus Christ, who as a child wast presented in the Temple and received with joy by Simeon and Anna as the Redeemer of Israel : Mercifully grant that we, like them, may be guided by the Holy Spirit to acknowl-

edge and love thee unto our lives' end; who with God
the Father, in the unity of the Holy Spirit, livest and
reignest God, world without end.

Fourth Sunday after Christmas

193   O Lord Jesus Christ, who didst humble thyself to take
the baptism of sinful men, and wast forthwith declared
to be the Son of God : Grant that we who have been
baptized into thee may rejoice to be the sons of God
and servants of all; for thy name's sake, who with the
Father and the Holy Spirit livest and reignest ever one
God, world without end.

Fifth Sunday after Christmas

194   Almighty God, whose blessed Son did call the apostles
and send them forth to preach his name in all the world :
Grant us like grace, that obeying his call we may be
faithful disciples and witnesses to him, who with thee
and the Holy Spirit liveth and reigneth, ever one God,
world without end.

Sixth Sunday after Christmas

195   Almighty God, the Giver of strength and joy : Change,
we beseech thee, our bondage into liberty, and the poverty of our nature into the riches of thy grace; that by
the transformation of our lives thy glory may be revealed; through Jesus Christ, our Lord.

Seventh Sunday after Christmas

1662 : Trinity 12

Ninth Sunday before Easter

196 O Almighty God, who hast created the heavens and the
earth, and hast made man in thine own image : Give
us grace so to meditate on thy power, wisdom, and love,
that we may glorify thee in thy works; through Jesus
Christ our Lord.

Eighth Sunday before Easter

197 O God of love, who in a world estranged from thee didst
send forth thy Son to turn mankind from darkness to
light, and from the power of Satan to thyself the living
God : Overcome in us, we pray thee, all pride and self-
will, and remake us a people in whom thou art well
pleased; through Jesus Christ our Lord.

Seventh Sunday before Easter

1662 : Trinity 1

Ash Wednesday

1662

Sixth Sunday before Easter : First Sunday in Lent

1662 : Easter 4

Fifth Sunday before Easter : Second Sunday in Lent

1662 : Trinity 19

Fourth Sunday before Easter : Third Sunday in Lent

198 Grant, O Lord, that as thy Son our Saviour Jesus Christ
prayed for his enemies on the cross, so we may have
grace to forgive those that wrongfully or scornfully use

us; that we ourselves may be able to receive thy forgiveness; through the same Jesus Christ our Lord.

Third Sunday before Easter : Fourth Sunday in Lent

199   O Almighty and everlasting God, whose blessed Son
revealed himself to his chosen apostles when he was
transfigured on the holy mount, and amidst the excellent glory spake with Moses and Elijah of his depar-
ture which he should accomplish at Jerusalem : Grant
to us thy servants, that, beholding the brightness of his
countenance, we may be strengthened to bear the cross,
and be changed into his likeness from glory to glory;
through the same Jesus Christ our Lord.

Source : no 129

Second Sunday before Easter : Passion Sunday

200   O Blessed Saviour, who by thy cross and passion didst
give life to the world : We pray thee to enlighten, visit,
and comfort, all thy servants who bear the cross and
glory in thy name; whom with the Father and the Holy
Spirit we worship and glorify, one God, for ever and
ever.

Next Sunday before Easter : Palm Sunday

1662 collect with this additional collect

201   O Christ, the King of glory, who didst enter the holy
city in meekness to be made perfect through the suffering of death : Give us grace, we beseech thee, in all our
life here to take up our cross daily and follow thee, that
hereafter we may rejoice with thee in thy heavenly kingdom; who livest and reignest with the Father and the
Holy Spirit, God, world without end.

Thursday (of Holy Week)

1928Eng collect for Thanksgiving for the Institution of Holy Communion from the provision for Lesser Feasts and Fasts

---

Good Friday

The first collect is the first of those provided in 1662; the second is the alternative third collect provided in 1928Eng.

Saturday (of Holy Week)

202 O Lord Jesus Christ, who after thy death on the cross wast laid in the tomb : Grant that we, having been buried with thee by baptism into thy death, may also be made partakers of thy resurrection; so that, serving thee here in newness of life, we may finally inherit thine everlasting kingdom; who livest and reignest with the Father and the Holy Spirit, ever one God, world without end.

Easter Day

Altered version of 1662

Next Sunday after Easter

The first line comes from 1662 Easter 1 (no 60) and the reference to doubt from Saint Thomas (no 103).

203 Almighty Father, who hast given thine only Son to die for our sins, and to rise again for our justification : Grant us so perfectly, and without all doubt, to believe in his resurrection, that in thy sight our faith may never be reproved; through the same Jesus Christ our Lord.

Second Sunday after Easter

1662 : Easter 2 with 'example'

Third Sunday after Easter

204   O Thou who are the Light of the minds that know thee, the Life of the souls that love thee, and the Strength of the wills that serve thee : Help us to know thee that we may truly love thee, so to love thee that we may fully serve thee, whose service is perfect freedom; through Jesus Christ our Lord.

This is a prayer of Saint Augustine. It is given by Milner-White and Briggs in *Daily Prayer* (p. 28) and in Colquhoun (1592).

Fourth Sunday after Easter

205   O Lord Jesus Christ, who art the Way, the Truth, and the Life : Suffer us not, we pray thee, to wander from thee, who art the Way; nor to distrust thee, who art the Truth; nor to look for strength anywhere but in thee, who art the Life; ever living and reigning with the Father and the Holy Spirit, one God, world without end.

Fifth Sunday after Easter

206   O Lord Jesus Christ, who hast gone to the Father to prepare a place for us : Grant us so to live in communion with thee here on earth, that hereafter we may enjoy the fullness of thy presence; who livest and reignest with the Father and the Holy Spirit, ever one God, world without end.

Ascension Day

1662

Sixth Sunday after Easter : Sunday after the Ascension

207   O God, whose blessed Son, our great High Priest, has entered once for all into the holy place, and ever liveth

to intercede on our behalf : Grant that we, sanctified by the offering of his body, may draw near with full assurance of faith by the way which he has dedicated for us, and evermore serve thee, the living God; through the same our Lord Jesus Christ, who liveth and reigneth with thee, O Father, and the Holy Spirit, one God, world without end.

Pentecost

208 O God, who according to thy promise hast given thy Holy Spirit to us thy people, that we might know the freedom of thy children and taste on earth our heavenly inheritance : Grant that we may ever hold fast the unity which he gives, and, living in his power, may be thy witnesses to all men; through Jesus Christ our Lord.

Next Sunday after Pentecost : Trinity Sunday

209 Almighty and everlasting God, who hast revealed thyself as Father, Son, and Holy Spirit, and dost ever live and reign in the perfect unity of love : Grant that we may always hold firmly and joyfully to this faith, and, living in praise of thy divine majesty, may finally be one in thee; who art three Persons in one God, world without end.

Second Sunday after Pentecost

1928Eng, Occasional Prayers

210 Remember, O Lord, what thou hast wrought in us, and not what we deserve; and as thou hast called us to thy service, make us worthy of our calling; through Jesus Christ our Lord.

Third Sunday after Pentecost

1662 : Trinity 9

Fourth Sunday after Pentecost

211   O God, who, calling Abraham to go forth to a country which thou wouldest show him, didst promise that in him all the families of the earth would be blessed : Fulfil thy promise in us, we pray thee, giving us such faith in thee as thou shalt count unto us for righteousness : that in us and through us thy purpose may be fulfilled; through Jesus Christ our Lord.

Fifth Sunday after Pentecost

1662 : Trinity 19

Sixth Sunday after Pentecost

1662 : Advent 2

Seventh Sunday after Pentecost

1662 : Saint Simon and Saint Jude

Eighth Sunday after Pentecost

212   O Lord Jesus Christ, who hast ordained the signs whereby we are assured of thy gracious work in us : Grant that, being born anew of water and the Spirit, we may by faith receive thy precious Body and Blood, and, in union with thee, offer ourselves a living sacrifice, holy and acceptable to the Father, who liveth and reigneth with thee and the Holy Spirit, ever one God, world without end.

Ninth Sunday after Pentecost

213   O God, the Creator and Father of all mankind, who
by thy Holy Spirit hast made a diversity of peoples one
in the confession of thy name : Lead them, we beseech
thee, by the same Spirit to display to the whole earth
one mind in belief and one passion for righteousness;
through Jesus Christ our Lord.

Tenth Sunday after Pentecost

214   O Lord, who hast called us to be thy witnesses to all
the nations : Have mercy upon us, who have known
thy will but have failed to do it. Cleanse us from unbelief and sloth, and fill us with hope and zeal, that we
may do thy work, and bear thy cross, and bide thy time,
and see thy glory; who with the Father and the Holy
Spirit art one God, world without end.

Eleventh Sunday after Pentecost

215   Almighty God, Giver of all good things, who by thy
one Spirit hast appointed a diversity of ministrations
in thy Church : Mercifully behold thy servants who are
called to the ministry, and so fill them with thy Holy
Spirit, that, both by word and good example, they may
faithfully and joyfully serve thee, to the glory of thy
name and the building up of thy Church; through Jesus
Christ our Lord.

Source : no 5

Twelfth Sunday after Pentecost

1662 : Trinity 6

Thirteenth Sunday after Pentecost

216   Look graciously upon us, O Holy Spirit, and give us for our hallowing thoughts that pass into prayer, prayers that pass into love, and love that passeth into life with thee for ever.

Fourteenth Sunday after Pentecost

217   O Lord, who hast promised that thy joy would be in us, so that our joy might be full : Grant that, living close to thee, we may learn to rejoice and give thanks in all things; for thy loving mercy's sake.

Fifteenth Sunday after Pentecost

218   Go before us, O Lord, in all our doings with thy most gracious favour, and further us with thy continual help; that in all our works, begun, continued, and ended, in thee, we may glorify thy holy name, and finally by thy mercy obtain everlasting life; through Jesus Christ our Lord.

Source : Greg (198); it is one of six collects in 1549, said after the offertory when there is no communion; it begins 'Prevent us, O Lord . . . '. In the same form it appears in 1662 ordination rites as the prayer immediately before the blessing.

Sixteenth Sunday after Pentecost

219   Almighty God, whose gracious will it is that thy Son should empty himself and become like us : Grant that we, with the example of his earthly life continually before us, and with the Holy Spirit working in our hearts, may be changed into his likeness; through Jesus Christ our Lord.

Seventeenth Sunday after Pentecost

220 Almighty God, who hast given a day of rest to thy people
and, through thy Spirit in the Church, hast consecrated
the first day of the week to be a perpetual memorial of
thy Son's resurrection : Grant that we may so use thy
gift that, refreshed and strengthened in soul and body,
we may serve thee faithfully all the days of our life;
through the same Jesus Christ our Lord.

Eighteenth Sunday after Pentecost

1662 : Quinquagesima

Nineteenth Sunday after Pentecost

221 Almighty God and heavenly Father, whose Son Jesus
Christ shared in Nazareth the life of an earthly home :
Send down thy blessing, we beseech thee, upon all
Christian families, that parents taught by the spirit of
understanding and wisdom, and children by the spirit
of obedience and reverence, may be bound each to each
by mutual love; through him who became a child, and
learned obedience to thy will, even Jesus Christ our
Lord.

Source : The preamble comes from a Prayer for the Home in
1928Eng Baptism service and also appears in ASB : Christmas
2, collect 1.

Twentieth Sunday after Pentecost

222 Almighty God, who hast manifested thy Son Jesus
Christ to be a light to mankind : Grant that we thy
people, being nourished by thy word and sacraments,
may be strengthened to show forth to all men the unsearchable riches of Christ, so that he may be known,
adored, and obeyed, to the ends of the earth; who liveth

and reigneth with thee and the Holy Spirit, one God, world without end.

Twenty-First Sunday after Pentecost

223   O God, who movest in love unceasing, and dost give to each man his appointed work : Help us steadfastly, and as in thy sight, to fulfil the duties of our calling; that when our Lord shall take account of us, we may be found faithful in that which is least, and enter into his eternal joy.

Twenty-Second Sunday after Pentecost

224   O God the Redeemer, who didst send thy servant Moses to lead thy people out of bondage and affliction : Give to us and to all nations' leaders obedient to thee, to teach us to know and to keep thy laws, and to bring us on our way to that country which thou hast prepared for us; through Jesus Christ our Lord.

Twenty-Third Sunday after Pentecost

225   Lord Jesus, who for our sake didst become poor, that by thy poverty we might become rich : Grant to thy people so to give of their substance as to acknowledge that they belong wholly to thee; for thine own sake.

Twenty-Fourth Sunday after Pentecost

1662 : Trinity 4

Twenty-Fifth Sunday after Pentecost

1662 : Trinity 13

Twenty-Sixth Sunday after Pentecost

1662 : Epiphany 6

Twenty-Seventh Sunday after Pentecost

226   O Christ our God who wilt come to judge the world
in the manhood which thou hast assumed : We pray
thee to sanctify us wholly, that in the day of thy coming we may be raised up to live and reign with thee for
ever.

Next Sunday before Advent

227   Make us, we beseech thee, O Lord our God, watchful
in awaiting the coming of thy Son, Christ our Lord;
that when he shall come and knock, he may find us not
sleeping in sin, but awake, and rejoicing in his praises;
through the same Jesus Christ our Lord.

A version of this appears as the Concluding Prayer for Monday in the First Week of Advent in the Roman Divine Office.

THE JOINT LITURGICAL GROUP AND *MODERN COLLECTS* [JLG IS GIVEN FIRST, FOLLOWED BY SAMC]

Ninth Sunday before Christmas

JLG uses an amended version of the CSI Collect for the Ninth
Sunday before Easter (not Easter 9 as it says in *The Daily Office,* 1968).

228   Almighty God, who hast created the heavens and the
earth, and hast made man in thine own image : Grant
us in all thy works to perceive thy hand, and ever to
praise thee for thy wisdom and love; through Jesus
Christ our Lord.

229   We praise you Almighty God for creating all things in
time and space and for making man in your own im-

age : Lead us to recognise your hand in all you have created and always to praise you for your wisdom and love; through Jesus Christ our Lord who with you and the Holy Spirit reigns supreme over all things, now and ever.

Eighth Sunday before Christmas

JLG uses an amended version of 1662 : Epiphany 6.

230   O God, whose blessed Son was manifested that he might destroy the works of the devil, and make us thy sons and heirs of eternal life : Grant that, having this hope, we may purify ourselves even as he is pure; that we may be made like unto him in his eternal and glorious kingdom : where with thee, O Father, he is alive and reigns in the unity of the Holy Spirit, one God, world without end.

231   Almighty God, whose blessed Son came to destroy evil, making us sons of God and heirs of eternal life : Grant that, uplifted by this hope, we may grow in grace until we are like him who reigns, and is to come again in glory, the same Jesus Christ our Lord.

Seventh Sunday before Christmas

JLG uses 1662 : Epiphany 2 without amendment (see collect 23). This is the South African modernised version.

232   Almighty God, by whom all things are created and ordered to serve your loving purposes : Grant us your peace all the days of our life; through Jesus Christ our Lord.

Sixth Sunday before Christmas

JLG's collect is a much shortened version of CSI : Pentecost 4.

233   O God, who didst promise to faithful Abraham that in

him all the families of the earth would be blessed : Grant us a firm faith, that in us thy promises may be fulfilled; through Jesus Christ our Lord.

The South African rewrite was the basis of one of the finest contemporary collects, the ASB collect for the Seventh Sunday before Christmas.

234   God, Almighty Father, whose chosen servant Abraham faithfully obeyed your call and rejoiced in your promise that all families on earth would be blessed in him : Grant us so firm a faith that your promises may be fulfilled in us; through Jesus Christ our Lord.

Fifth Sunday before Christmas

JLG amends CSI : Pentecost 22.

235   O God the Redeemer, who didst send thy servant Moses to lead thy people out of slavery and affliction : Rescue us from enslavement to sin and bring us to the country which thou hast prepared for us; through Jesus Christ our Lord.

236   Lord God, Redeemer of Israel, who sent your servant Moses to lead your people out of slavery and affliction : Free us from the tyranny of sin and death and bring us to the promised land of your glory where we may live in perfect union with you and the Holy Spirit; through Jesus Christ our Lord.

Fourth Sunday before Christmas : Advent 1

JLG uses 1662 : Advent 1 and simply changes the conclusion to 'alive and reigns' from 'liveth and reigneth'. *Modern Collects* performs a limited modernisation.

237   Almighty God, give us grace to cast away the works of darkness and to put on the armour of light now in the time of this earthly life in which your Son Jesus

Christ came to us in great humility : So that, in the
last day, when he shall come again in his glorious majesty to judge the living and the dead, we may rise again
in his kingdom of light; who lives and reigns with you
and the Holy Spirit, one God, now and for ever.

Third Sunday before Christmas : Advent 2

JLG uses 1662 : Advent 2 unamended. The South African
modernisation shows what damage can be done to the structure and meaning of a collect.

238   Blessed Lord, who caused all Holy Scriptures to be written for our learning : Help us to hear, read, and understand them that strengthened by your Holy Word
we may ever be upheld by the assurance of eternal life
in our Saviour Jesus Christ.

Second Sunday before Christmas : Advent 3

JLG uses 1662 : Advent 3 unamended. *Modern Collects* provides a prayer to correspond with lections about John the Baptist based on 1662 : Advent 3.

239   Almighty God, who sent John the Baptist to herald the
coming of your Son : Grant that the ministers and
stewards of your truth may prepare for his coming again
by turning our disobedient hearts to the holy wisdom
of your law; through Jesus Christ our Lord.

First Sunday before Christmas : Advent 4

JLG goes to a quite different source for its collect, Colquhoun
(no 556).

240   O God, who didst choose the blessed Virgin Mary to
become the mother of our Saviour : Grant that we, having in remembrance her exceeding faith and love, may
in all things seek to do thy will, and evermore rejoice

in thy salvation; through Jesus Christ thy Son, our only Mediator and Advocate.

South Africa follows the provision for the Second Sunday after Christmas in 1928Eng (see collect 19).

241   Almighty God, who wonderfully created us in your image and yet more wonderfully restored us through your Son, Jesus Christ : Grant us to share in his divine life as he shares our humanity; who now lives and reigns with you in the unity of the Holy Spirit one God, for ever and ever.

Christmas Day

JLG's first collect is newly translated from the *Roman Missal*.

242   O God, who hast made this most holy night to shine with the brightness of thy one true Light : Grant that we who have known the revelation of his light on earth may attain the fulness of his joy in heaven; through Jesus Christ our Lord.

243   Heavenly Father, who made this most holy night to shine with the brightness of your one true light : Grant that we who have known the revelation of his light on earth may also know the fulness of his joy hereafter; through Jesus Christ our Lord.

JLG's second collect is 1662 Christmas Day, with an amended conclusion. South Africa has an entirely new collect.

244   All praise to you, Almighty God, heavenly King, who sent your Son into the world when he took our nature upon him and was born in the stable at Bethlehem : Grant, that as we have been born again in him, so he may evermore live in us and reign on earth as in heaven with you and the Holy Spirit now and for ever.

First Sunday after Christmas

JLG amends CSI : Christmas 2.

245   O God, who by the shining of a star didst lead the wise
men to the worship of thy Son : Guide by thy light the
nations of the earth that the world may be filled with
thy glory; through Jesus Christ our Lord.

Modern Collects goes for something much bolder.

246   Almighty God, by whose Word and Wisdom the bril-
liant constellations declare your glory and who led the
wise men by the light of a star to your infant Son to
worship in him the glory of the Word made flesh : Guide
by your truth the nations of the earth that the whole
world may be filled with your glory; through Jesus
Christ our Lord.

Second Sunday after Christmas

JLG again uses the Colquhoun collection (no 321).

247   O God, whose blessed Son came into the world to do
thy will : Grant that we may ever have the pattern of
his holy life before our eyes and find it our delight to
do thy will and finish thy work; through the same Jesus
Christ.

Modern Collects makes only slight amendments.

248   Heavenly Father, whose blessed Son came into the world
to do your will : Grant that we may have the pattern
of his holy life always before our eyes and delight in
working for the fulfilment of your kingdom; through
Jesus Christ our Lord.

Third Sunday after Christmas

JLG uses the CSI collect for Christmas 4, amending the conclusion to 'for thy name's sake, who with the Father and the
Holy Spirit art one God for ever and ever'.

Modern Collects offers a much more extensive revision, which was further developed in the ASB collect for Epiphany 1.

249   Almighty God, who proclaimed Jesus to be your beloved Son when the Holy Spirit came down upon him
at his baptism in the Jordan : Grant that we who have
been baptised in his name may rejoice in being your
sons and the servants of all; through Jesus Christ our
Lord.

Fourth Sunday after Christmas

JLG uses the prayer from the 1928Eng Occasional Prayers which CSI has for Pentecost 2. *Modern Collects* has a version of this that draws on the original in the Leonine sacramentary; it is also used, with slight modification, in ASB, though the credit for it is given in Jasper-Bradshaw to the Church of England Liturgical Commission!

250   Almighty God, by whose grace alone we have been ac-
cepted and called to your service : Strengthen us by your
Spirit and make us worthy of our calling; through Jesus
Christ our Lord.

Fifth Sunday after Christmas

JLG describes this collect as 'CSI, Christmas 6 (amended)'; it is, in fact, a total rewrite that retains the key phrases 'the poverty . . . thy grace' and 'of our lives thy glory may be revealed'.

251   Almighty God, who in Christ makest all things new :
Transform the poverty of our nature into the riches of
thy grace, that by the renewal of our lives thy glory may
be revealed; through Jesus Christ our Lord.

Modern Collects modernises it by substituting 'makes' for 'makest' and 'your' for 'thy'; the key change is of 'by' for 'into', giving God's grace as the cause of the transformation.

Sixth Sunday after Christmas

JLG uses 1662 : Trinity 21 unchanged; this is the South African version.

252   Merciful Lord, Grant us your faithful people pardon and peace that we may be cleansed from our sins and serve you with a quiet mind; through Jesus Christ our Lord.

Extra Sundays after Christmas

The first JLG collect is that of 1662 : Trinity 9 (with 'pray' substituted for 'beseech'); the second is 1662 : Trinity 1. The 1968 Report calls them collects for the Seventh and Eighth Sundays after Christmas. *Modern Collects* follows JLG with modernised versions of the 1662 collects.

253   Grant us, Lord, the spirit to think and do always those things that are right : That we who cannot do anything good without you may be enabled to live according to your will.

254   Almighty God, because of the weakness of our nature we can do nothing good without you : Grant us your help that we may please you both in will and deed; through Jesus Christ our Lord.

Ninth Sunday before Easter

JLG uses 1662 : Epiphany 1 unamended. South Africa provided a new collect for the lectionary theme of Christ the Teacher.

255   Lord God of wisdom and truth known to men in your Son Jesus Christ, the revelation of your glory : Grant that we may know him and understand his teaching that in him we may share the fulness of eternal life; through Jesus Christ our Lord.

Eighth Sunday before Easter

JLG again uses a 1662 collect, this time for Trinity 20, and amends it by removing the preliminary 'O'. There is a new South African collect for the theme of Christ the Healer.

256   Almighty and everliving God, whose Son Jesus Christ came healing the sick and restoring your people to fulness of life : Look with mercy on the anguish of this world and, by your healing power, make whole both men and nations; through our Lord and Saviour Jesus Christ who lives and reigns with you and the Holy Spirit, one God, now and for ever.

Seventh Sunday before Easter

JLG uses 1662 : Epiphany 3 unamended. South Africa has a new collect on the theme of Christ, Worker of Miracles, a modified version of which appears in ASB for Epiphany 3.

257   All thanks to you Almighty God whose Son revealed in signs and miracles the wonder of your saving love : Look with mercy on our weaknesses and in all trouble and danger help and defend us by your mighty power; through Jesus Christ our Lord.

Ash Wednesday

JLG uses the 1662 collect unamended; *Modern Collects* tries for a new one.

258   Almighty and holy God, whose love reaches out even when you must condemn and whose mercy is shown to all who truly repent : Instil in us a new and contrite spirit that we may admit our guilt and receive from you forgiveness and peace; through Jesus Christ our Lord.

Sixth Sunday before Easter : Lent 1

JLG again takes, and amends, a collect from Colquhoun (no 1301), which first appeared in Bright (pp. 237–38).

259   Lord Jesus Christ, who wast in all points tempted as
       we are : Strengthen us, we pray thee, in our manifold
       temptations; and as thou knowest our weaknesses, so
       may we know thee mighty to save; who with the Fa-
       ther and the Holy Spirit art one God for ever and ever.

Modern Collects returns to Cranmer's collect of 1549 (no 33).

260   Holy Father, whose Son Jesus Christ fasted forty days
       in the desert : Give us grace to discipline ourselves in
       humble submission to your Spirit that we may lead up-
       right and holy lives to your honour and glory; through
       Jesus Christ our Lord.

Fifth Sunday before Easter : Lent 2

JLG uses 1662 : Trinity 18 unamended; SAMC tries something new.

261   God the source of all power whose Son Jesus Christ
       prayed for his disciples that, in the conflicts of the world
       you would keep them from the evil one : Strengthen
       us to resist every assault and temptation and to follow
       you, the only God; through Jesus Christ our Lord.

Fourth Sunday before Easter : Lent 3

JLG draws its collect from the provision for the Monday of
Holy Week in 1928Amer (no 45) and so puts it into the position it occupies in ASB. *Modern Collects* has another new collect.

262   Almighty God, whose Son entered into his kingdom
       when he was lifted up on the Cross : Train us to be
       faithful in the fellowship of his sufferings that we may
       follow him to his triumph; through Jesus Christ our
       Lord.

Third Sunday before Easter : Lent 4

The new collect for the Transfiguration introduced in 1928Eng provides the JLG collect for this Sunday. *Modern Collects* has a very poor attempt at modernisation.

263   Almighty Father, whose Son was revealed in glory before he suffered on the Cross : Grant that in seeing his divine majesty with the eye of faith we may be strengthened to follow him and through death may share his glory; through Jesus Christ our Lord.

Second Sunday before Easter : Lent 5 : Passion Sunday

JLG has abridged and strengthened a Passiontide collect from 1929Scot (no 39).

264   O God, who by the cross and passion of thy Son Jesus Christ didst save and deliver mankind : Grant that by steadfast faith in his sacrifice we may triumph in the power of his victory; through the same Jesus Christ our Lord.

Modern Collects begins the process of modernisation.

265   Holy God and Lord of Life, who by the suffering, death, and resurrection of your Son Jesus Christ delivered and saved mankind : Grant that by faith in his sacrifice on the Cross we may triumph in the power of his victory; through the same Jesus Christ our Lord.

First Sunday before Easter : Palm Sunday

JLG repeats 1662 : Palm Sunday unamended. This is the South African version.

266   Almighty and Everliving God, who, in your love for man sent your Son our saviour Jesus Christ to take our nature and to die on the Cross : Mercifully grant that following the example of his great humility we may share

with him in the glory of his resurrection; through the
same Jesus Christ our Lord.

Maundy Thursday

JLG and the 1968 Report make no separate provision for
Maundy Thursday; *Modern Collects* provides two prayers. The
first is a version of the Corpus Christi collect attributed to
Aquinas.

267   Almighty God, whose Son the Lord Jesus Christ gave
us a wonderful Sacrament of his Body and Blood to represent his death and to celebrate his resurrection :
Strengthen our devotion to him in these holy mysteries
and through him renew our unity with him and with
one another that we may grow in grace and in the
knowledge of our Salvation; through the same Jesus
Christ our Lord.

The second prayer functions as a collect for the Triduum and
was also used as the second collect for Good Friday and for
Easter Even.

268   Holy and Everliving God who revealed the glory of your
Son when he was exalted on the Cross : Accept our
praise and thanksgiving for the power of his victory and
grant us never to be afraid to suffer or to die with him;
our crucified King who lives and reigns in all eternity
with you and the Holy Spirit one God for ever and ever.

Good Friday

JLG uses 1662 with an amended conclusion. The first SA collect is a modernisation of 1662.

269   Almighty Father hear our prayer and look with favour
on this your family for which our Lord Jesus Christ was
ready to be betrayed into the hands of sinful men and

to suffer death upon the Cross; who lives and reigns
with you and the Holy Spirit one God, now and for ever.

Easter Even

JLG does not have a collect for Easter Even; the 1968 Report uses the 1662 collect. The first South African collect is
again a modernisation of 1662.

270   Grant Lord that as we are baptized into the death of
your Son our Saviour Jesus Christ : So by continually
putting to death our sinful nature we may be buried
with him and through the grave and gate of death may
pass to our joyful resurrection; through Jesus Christ our
Lord who died and was buried and rose again for us
and now reigns with you and the Holy Spirit, one God
for ever and ever.

Easter Day

JLG uses the additional collect from 1928Eng. *Modern Collects* provides a new one.

271   Lord of all life, we praise you that through Christ's
resurrection the old order of sin and death is overcome
and all things made new in him : Grant that being dead
to sin and alive to you in union with Christ Jesus we
may live and reign with him in glory; to whom with
you and the Holy Spirit be praise and honour, glory
and might now and in all eternity.

First Sunday after Easter

JLG finds its collect in Macnutt's *The Prayer Manual* (no 398).

272   Almighty God, who hast given unto us the true bread
that comes down from heaven, even thy Son Jesus
Christ : Grant that we may be fed by him who gives
life to the world, that we may abide in him and he in

us; who is alive and reigns with thee and the Holy Spirit, one God for ever and ever.

SA

273   Almighty Father, who gave your Son to die for our sins and to rise again for our justification : Grant that malice may not affect us nor evil corrupt us and that we may serve you continually in holiness and truth; through Jesus Christ our Lord.

Source: The first line is from 1662 : Easter 1 (as no 203); the general development also follows no 60.

Second Sunday after Easter

The JLG collect again comes from Colquhoun (no 324).

274   Be thou thyself, O Lord, we pray thee, the Shepherd of thy people : that we who are protected by thy care may be strengthened by thy risen presence; for thy Name's sake.

275   Almighty God of peace, whose Son Jesus Christ gave himself in sacrifice for sin on the holy Cross and by his resurrection from the dead was declared to be your Son the great shepherd of your sheep : By the Blood of his eternal covenant make us perfect in all goodness that we may do your will; through Jesus Christ our Lord.

See the discussion of 'Good Shepherd' collects in the Introduction.

Third Sunday after Easter

JLG draws its collect from the Church of England Series 2 Burial Service (amended).

276   Merciful God, who hast made thy Son Jesus Christ to be the resurrection and the life of all the faithful : Raise us, we pray thee, from the death of sin unto the life of righteousness, that we may seek those things which are

above; where he is alive and reigns with thee and the Holy Spirit, one God, for ever and ever.

This is a radical abbreviation of the collect from the 1662 Burial Service. The weak 'that we may seek those things that are above' replaces the stronger petition 'when we shall depart this life, we may rest in him'. The version in *Modern Collects* removes this part of the petition entirely.

277 Merciful God, who has made your Son Jesus Christ to be the resurrection and the life of all who believe in him : Raise us from the death of sin into the life of righteousness; through the same Jesus Christ our Lord who lives and reigns with you and the Holy Spirit now and for ever.

Fourth Sunday after Easter

JLG uses a slightly modified version of the 1662 collect for Saint Philip and Saint James's Day. It inserts 'so' after 'Grant us' and omits the names of the apostles.

278 Almighty God, whom truly to know is everlasting life : Grant us so perfectly to know thy Son Jesus Christ to be the way, the truth, and the life; that, following the steps of thy holy apostles, we may steadfastly walk in the way that leadeth to eternal life; through the same thy Son Jesus Christ our Lord.

Modern Collects returns to 1662.

279 Almighty God, who alone can order the unruly wills and passions of sinful men : Grant your people grace to love what you command and to desire what you promise that among all the attractions of the world our hearts may be firmly fixed where true joy is found; through Jesus Christ our Lord.

Fifth Sunday after Easter

JLG uses 1662 : Trinity 12 unamended.

280   Almighty Father, whose realm extends beyond the
bounds of space and time : Grant us so to live within
this world of transient things that we may hold fast to
what endures for ever; through Jesus Christ our Lord
who lives and reigns with you and the Holy Spirit now
and for ever.

Ascension Day

JLG uses the 1662 collect, amending only the conclusion. *Modern Collects* has a new and not very successful collect.

281   Sovereign Lord of the universe whose Son our Saviour
Jesus Christ ascended in triumph to rule in love and
glory over all creation : As in our flesh Christ reigns
supreme in heaven and earth so may the world and all
else you have made obey his will and all mankind acknowledge his authority that we may know the glorious fulfilment of your kingdom when you, our Lord and
God, shall be all in all.

Sixth Sunday after Easter

An amended version of the Ascensiontide post-communion
prayer, composed by Bishop Dowden, from 1929Scot is used
by JLG.

282   Almighty God, whose Son Jesus Christ ascended far
above all heavens that he might fill all things : Grant
that thy Church on earth may be filled with his presence and that he may remain with us always, even unto
the end of the world, through the same Jesus Christ our
Lord.

Pentecost

The 1662 Whitsunday collect is used by JLG with a modernised conclusion.

First Sunday after Pentecost : Trinity Sunday

JLG uses the collect from CSI : Pentecost 1.

Second Sunday after Pentecost

JLG uses the second Good Friday collect from 1662. *Modern Collects* modernises the same collect.

283   Almighty and Eternal God, by whose Spirit the whole body of your faithful people is being made one and directed in accordance with your will : Hear our prayer for all members of your holy Church that each in his vocation and ministry may serve you in sincerity and truth; through our Lord and Saviour Jesus Christ.

Third Sunday after Pentecost

JLG uses the 1662 collect for Easter Even. The 1968 Report does the same, even though it has used the collect already.

SA

284   Most Gracious God who through our Saviour Christ has assured mankind of eternal life and in Baptism has made us one with him : Grant that being made free from sin we may be raised up to new life in him; who reigns with you and the Holy Spirit, one God, now and for ever.

Fourth Sunday after Pentecost

JLG uses 1662 : Easter 2.

SA

285   Almighty God, who gave your only Son to be for us

a sacrifice for sin and also an example of godly life :
Give us grace always to receive him with thankfulness
as our Saviour and Lord and in the freedom of your
Spirit to follow the pattern of his most holy life; through
Jesus Christ our Lord.

Fifth Sunday after Pentecost

JLG uses 1662 : Easter 3.

SA

286   Almighty God who shows to those who have gone as-
      tray the light of your truth that they may return to the
      way of godliness : Grant that we who have been ad-
      mitted to the fellowship of Christ's religion may always
      discern and avoid what is false and faithfully bear wit-
      ness to the law of love; through Jesus Christ our Lord.

Sixth Sunday after Pentecost

JLG uses 1662 : Trinity 19.

SA

287   Most Holy Lord God, who created man in the begin-
      ning and in our dire need gave us a Saviour, the New
      Man, born of our flesh, that in him we might receive
      new birth : Keep us reconciled to one another as you
      have reconciled us to yourself that we may grow up into
      the maturity of the true man; your Son Jesus Christ
      our Lord.

Seventh Sunday after Pentecost

JLG uses the 1662 collect for Quinquagesima (the Next Sunday before Lent) with the single change—substituting 'Spirit'
for 'Ghost'—already made by CSI, which uses it as the collect for the Eighteenth Sunday after Pentecost. It is also used,
in modernised form, in *Modern Collects*.

288 Lord, who taught us that anything we do without love is worthless : Pour into our hearts that most excellent gift of love, the true bond of peace and source of all virtues without which whoever lives is counted dead before you : Grant this for the sake of your only Son Jesus Christ; who lives and reigns with you and the Holy Spirit, one God, now and for ever.

Eighth Sunday after Pentecost

The 1929Scot : Whitsunday post-communion collect is used by JLG.

SA

289 Almighty God, who sent your Holy Spirit to be the life and power of your Church : Mercifully grant that we may receive the gifts of his grace and yield the fruit of the Spirit in love and joy and peace; through Jesus Christ our Lord.

Ninth Sunday after Pentecost

JLG uses 1662 : Lent 2.

SA

290 Lord of all power and might, who has called us to fight by your side against the tyranny of evil : Arm us with the weapons of righteousness that we may be equipped to repulse all assaults of the enemy and to stand fast in the power of the Spirit; through Jesus Christ our Lord.

Tenth Sunday after Pentecost

JLG uses 1662 : Easter 5 with a slight amendment to the conclusion.

SA

291   God of all truth and peace whose mind is revealed in
       Christ : Grant that as he humbled himself assuming the
       status of a slave so may we yield ourselves to your ser-
       vice in union with him and may care for one another
       according to your will; through Jesus Christ our Lord.

Eleventh Sunday after Pentecost

JLG uses a prayer of Saint Augustine, which is further adapted
in *Modern Collects*.

292   O Lord, who hast taught us that whatever is done to
       the least of thy brethren is done to thee : Make us ever
       willing to minister to the needs of others; to thy praise
       and glory, who with the Father and the Holy Spirit art
       God over all, blessed for ever.

293   God Almighty, who has taught us that whatever is done
       to the least of men is done to Christ : Make us aware
       of the needs of others and always ready to relieve them
       according to your loving purposes; through Jesus Christ
       our Lord.

Twelfth Sunday after Pentecost

An amended collect from an apostle's feast day in 1662 is again
the source of the JLG provision; this is a version of the collect for Saint Bartholomew.

294   Almighty and everlasting God, who didst give to thine
       apostles grace truly to believe and to preach thy Word :
       Grant, we pray thee, to thy Church to love that Word
       which they believed, and both to preach and receive the
       same; through Jesus Christ our Lord.

SA

295   God our heavenly Father, who revealed your love by
       sending your only Son into the world that all might live
       through him : May we your messengers proclaim by

word and deed the presence of your kingdom and be strengthened in our resolution to work and witness for it; through Jesus Christ our Lord.

Thirteenth Sunday after Pentecost

JLG uses a modified version of 1928Amer provision for the Tuesday of Holy Week.

SA

296 God our loving Father who gave your only Son to suffer and to die for man : Grant that when we are found worthy to endure suffering for Christ's Name we may rejoice in our calling and be enabled to bear our part in completing his sufferings for the sake of your Church; through Jesus Christ our Lord.

Fourteenth Sunday after Pentecost

The JLG collect is taken from *A Book of Public Worship* (compiled by John Huxtable, John March, Romilly Micklem, and James Todd).

297 O God, who hast taught us to keep all thy commandments by loving thee and our neighbour : Grant us the spirit of grace and peace, that we may be devoted to thee with our whole heart and united to each other with a pure will; through Jesus Christ our Lord.

SA

298 Almighty God, who has taught us that unless we love one another we cannot fulfil your law : Of your goodness give us a true concern for our fellow men that in sharing one another's joys and burdens we may perform your will; through Jesus Christ our Lord.

Fifteenth Sunday after Pentecost

JLG uses 1662 : Trinity 15. The SA collect is apparently based, like the CSI collect for the Nineteenth Sunday after Pentecost (no 221), on the Prayer for the Home in the 1928Eng form for the baptism of infants.

299   God our Heavenly Father, whose Son knew the mutual trust and care of an earthly home : Watch over the homes of your people and grant that families may be enabled to hold together in love and godly discipline; through Jesus Christ our Lord.

Sixteenth Sunday after Pentecost

JLG uses 1662 : Trinity 5.

SA

300   Almighty God, the judge of all who wield your power : Guide by your wisdom those who bear responsibility for the affairs of this world that, through their obedience to your law they may set forward justice and maintain peace for all mankind; through Jesus Christ our Lord.

Seventeenth Sunday after Pentecost

JLG uses 1662 : Trinity 7.

SA

301   Almighty God, who in your wisdom has [Aus : have] so ordered our earthly life that we should [Aus : must] walk by faith and not by sight : Give us such trust in your fatherly care that in the face of all perplexities we may give proof of our faith by the courage of our lives; through Jesus Christ our Lord.

This collect, not used in ASB or in SAAPB, reappears in AusAC (Twenty-Seventh Ordinary Sunday) with the variations noted.

Eighteenth Sunday after Pentecost

The JLG collect in *The Daily Office* has no quoted source. It is included in the 1968 Report with a note to that effect. It is used as the (revised) collect for Pentecost 15 in ASB and described, in Jasper-Bradshaw, as a translation of the collect for Christ the King from the pre-Vatican II *Roman Missal*. The Liturgical Commission's Commentary to ASB gives the Scottish Prayer Book as the source. It was also used, in a different version, in AmerBCP (Proper 29) and CanBAS (Proper 34).

302 O God, who hast willed to restore all things in thy beloved Son, the king of all : Grant that the families of the nations, divided and rent asunder by the wounds of sin, may be subject to his most gracious rule; who is alive and reigns with thee in the unity of the Holy Spirit, one God, world without end.

SA

303 Almighty and Eternal God, who gave your only Son Jesus Christ that in him we might have eternal life : Keep us in mind of the greatness of your gift that we may give ourselves in thankful service for his sake; who with you and the Holy Spirit lives and reigns, one God, now and for ever.

A further version of this collect appears in SAAPB (Twenty-Seventh Sunday of the Year) (no 621).

Nineteenth Sunday after Pentecost

JLG uses 1662 : Easter 4.

SA

304 Almighty and eternal God : increase in us your gifts of faith and hope and love that loving all you command and trusting in your promises we may by faith attain

to the fulness of your eternal joy; through Jesus Christ our Lord.

Twentieth Sunday after Pentecost

JLG uses 1662 : Trinity 6. *Modern Collects* does the same. Unfortunately the last four collects in the series, all of them versions of those in 1662, are very clumsy attempts at modernisation. In this collect the graphic 'pour into our hearts' is replaced by the more prosaic 'inspire us', and the reason—that we should love God above all things and so obtain God's promises—is obscured by introducing the idea of loving God 'in all and above all', even though it involves a return, in part, to 1549.

305   Merciful God, who has prepared for those who love you such things as pass man's understanding : Inspire us with such love for you that loving you in all and above all we may obtain your promises which exceed all that we can desire; through Jesus Christ who lives and reigns with you and the Holy Spirit, one God, now and for ever.

Twenty-First Sunday after Pentecost

JLG uses 1662 : Trinity 4 with an amended conclusion. The *Modern Collects* version, probably the worst collect in the collection, follows the 1662 collect initially but then goes its own unfortunate way. The original collect was a petition for the increase and multiplication of God's mercy, but that reference is entirely missing here.

306   God the Protector of the faithful without whom nothing is strong, nothing is holy : Grant that by endurance in temptation and adversity we may be proved and made ready for the life of the world to come; through Jesus Christ our Lord.

In 1989 SAAPB there is another version, much closer to the original, used on the Thirty-Fourth Sunday of the Year.

Extra Sundays after Pentecost

Both JLG collects are from 1662 : the first is Trinity 22, the second Trinity 25, next before Advent. The 1968 Report calls them the collects of the Twenty-Second and Twenty-Third Sundays after Pentecost. *Modern Collects* uses the same two prayers. The attempt to modernise them again reveals the difficulties and pitfalls of the whole process. 1662's 'adversities' here become 'hindrances' and 'singleness of mind' replaces being 'devoutly given' to serving in good works.

307 Lord God, we pray you to keep your household the Church in continual godliness that through your protection it may be free from all hindrances and may serve you in singleness of mind to the glory of your Name; through Jesus Christ our Lord.

The force of the final collect is entirely lost by changing the opening words from 'stir up'. The ASB version, for Pentecost 22, restores the opening and the indication that the reward will come from God.

308 Almighty God, stir up the wills of your faithful people that plentifully bearing the fruit of good works they may be plentifully rewarded; through Jesus Christ our Lord.

Chapter Four

CONTEMPORARY COLLECTS
1973–1989

Advent to the Beginning of Lent

309   Almighty God, give us grace to cast away the works of darkness, and put on the armour of light, now in the time of this mortal life in which your Son Jesus Christ came to visit [Can : omits 'visit'] us in great humility; that in the last day, when he shall come again in his glorious majesty to judge both [SA : omits 'both'] the living and the dead, we may rise to the life immortal; through him who lives and reigns with you and the Holy Spirit, one God, now and forever.

Source : 1549/1662 : Advent 1 (no 1)
Use : AmerBCP, ASB, CanBAS, IrAPB, SAAPB [second collect], WalesBCP : Advent 1 [first collect]

---

310   Almighty Father your Son came to us in humility as our saviour and at the last day he will come again in glory as our judge : give us grace to turn away from darkness to the light of Christ that we may be ready to welcome him and to enter into his kingdom; where he lives and reigns with you and the Holy Spirit one God, for ever and ever.

Source : as no 309
Use : SAAPB : Advent 1 [first collect]

311 Come, Lord, in might and deliver us from the sins which threaten to enslave us, that under thy protection we may stand fast in the freedom of thy gospel; who lives and reigns . . . .

Source : based on the *Excita* collect for Advent 1 in SM (no i)
Use : WalesBCP : Advent 1 [second collect]

312 Blessed Lord [Can : Eternal God], who caused all holy Scriptures to be written for our learning : help us [Amer : Grant us so] [Ir : Help us so] [SA : Teach us so] to hear them, to read, mark, learn, and inwardly digest them that, through patience, and the comfort of your holy word, [Amer : omits ', through patience, . . . holy word',] we may embrace and for [Amer : omits 'for'] ever hold fast the [Ir : inserts 'blessed'] hope of everlasting life, which you have given us in our Saviour Jesus Christ.

Source : 1549/1662 : Advent 2 (no 2)
Use : ASB, IrAPB, SAAPB : Advent 2; AmerBCP : Proper 28; CanBAS : Proper 32

313 Blessed Lord you gave us the Scriptures to point the way to salvation : teach us to hear them, read them and study them with love and prayer and strengthen us by their inspiration to hold firm the hope of eternal life; through Jesus Christ our Lord

Source : as no 312
Use : SAAPB : Advent 2 [first collect]

314 Merciful God, who sent your messengers the prophets to preach repentance and prepare the way of salvation :

Give us grace to heed their warnings and forsake our sins, that we may greet with joy the coming of Jesus Christ our Redeemer*; who lives and reigns with you and the Holy Sprit, one God, now and for ever.

*AusAC follows AmerAuthS and reads : 'the coming of our Redeemer, Jesus Christ our Lord, who lives . . . '.

Source : based on CSI : Advent 3 (no 189)
Use : AmerBCP, AusAC : Advent 2

---

315   Awaken our hearts, Lord, we beseech thee, to prepare the way for the advent of thine only-begotten Son; that with minds purified by the grace of his coming, we may serve thee faithfully all our days; through the same Jesus Christ our Lord, who lives . . . .

Source : SM : Advent 2 (no ii)
Use : WalesBCP : Advent 2

---

316   Almighty God, who sent your servant John the Baptist to prepare your people for the coming of your Son [Can : to welcome the Messiah] : inspire [Can : inserts 'us,'] the ministers and stewards of your truth [Can : inserts a comma here] to turn our disobedient hearts to the law of love [Can : to you]; that when he comes again in glory, we may stand with confidence before him as our judge; who is alive and reigns with you and the Holy Spirit, one God, now and for ever.

CanBAS concludes : 'that when the Christ shall come again to be our judge, we may stand with confidence before his glory; who is alive . . .'.

Source : 1662 : Advent 3 (no 40); changed to refer specifically to John the Baptist and not just to 'thy messenger'
Use : ASB, IrAPB, SAAPB : Advent 3; CanBAS : Advent 2

---

317   Almighty God, you sent John the Baptist to prepare the
      way for the coming of your Son : Guide the ministers
      and stewards of your truth to make our disobedient
      hearts obey the law of love; that when Christ comes
      again in glory to judge the world we may stand with
      confidence before him, who lives . . . .

Source : as no 316
Use : IrAPB : Advent 3

---

318   Merciful Father you sent John the Baptist to announce
      the coming of your Son : inspire all who minister in
      your Church to prepare for his coming again by turn-
      ing us from disobedience to your loving service; through
      Jesus Christ our Lord.

Source : a much simplified and shortened version of no 316
Use : SAAPB : Advent 3 [first collect]

---

319   Stir up your power, O Lord, and with great might come
      among us; and, because we are sorely hindered by our
      sins, let your bountiful grace and mercy speedily help
      and deliver us; through Jesus Christ our Lord, to whom
      with you and the Holy Spirit, be honor and glory, now
      and for ever.

Source : derived from Gel (1211) and SM : Advent 4 (no iv);
this is the same source as the 1549/1662 collects (nos 6 and
7). It had a different transitional form in AmerAuthS.

Use : AmerBCP : Advent 3

320   Raise up your mighty power, O Lord, and come among
      us; and, because we are hindered and bound by our
      sins, let your plentiful grace and mercy speedily help
      and deliver us; through Jesus Christ our Lord . . . .

---

321   God of power and mercy, you call us once again to celebrate the coming of your Son. Remove those things
which hinder love of you, that when he comes, he may
find us waiting in awe and wonder for him who lives
and reigns with you and the Holy Spirit, one God, now
and for ever.

Source : new
Use : CanBAS : Advent 3

---

322   Give ear, Lord, to our prayers, and by thy gracious
visitation lighten the darkness of our minds; through
Jesus Christ, who lives . . . .

Source : 1549 : Advent 3 (no 3)
Use : WalesBCP : Advent 3

323   Heavenly Father, who [IR and SA : you] chose the Virgin Mary, full of grace, to be the mother of our Lord
and Saviour : fill us with your grace, that in all things
we may [SA : inserts ', like her,'] accept your holy will
and with her rejoice in your salvation; through Jesus
Christ our Lord.

CanBAS has the same first line, but then continues 'now fill
us with your grace, that we in all things may embrace your
will and with her rejoice in your salvation . . . '.

Source : Colquhoun (no 556); adapted by JLG (no 241) for
Advent 4
Use : ASB, AusAC, CanBAS, IrAPB, SAAPB : Advent 4 [first
collect]

---

324   Purify our conscience, Almighty God, by your daily visitation, that your Son Jesus Christ, at his coming, may
find in us a mansion prepared for himself; who lives
and reigns with you, in the unity of the Holy Spirit,
one God, now and for ever.

Source : One of a number of versions of a Gelasian collect (Gel [1127], Greg [809], Gallic. vetus [40]) translated by Bright (16).

Use : AmerBCP : Advent 4

Another version was printed in AmerAuthS.

325 Mighty Lord, cleanse our consciences, we pray, and bring light to the darkness of our hearts by the visitation of our Savior Jesus Christ; that when he comes, he may find in us a mansion prepared for himself, who now lives and reigns . . . .

Use : AmerAuthS : Advent 4; 'darkness of our heart' occurs in 1549 : Advent 3 (no 3).

A simplified version is given in SAAPB.

326 Almighty and eternal God, purify our hearts and minds that when your Son Jesus Christ comes again in glory, he may find in us a home prepared for himself; who is alive and reigns with you in the unity of the Holy Spirit, now and for ever.

Use : SAAPB : Advent 4 [second collect]

A fourth version, closer to the original, is given in AusAC.

327 Cleanse our consciences, O Lord, and enlighten our hearts, through the daily presence of your Son Jesus Christ : that when he comes again in glory to be our judge we may be found acceptable in his sight; who lives and reigns . . . .

Use : AusAC : Advent 1

Christmas Eve and Christmas Day

328 O God, you make us glad by the yearly festival of the birth of your only Son Jesus Christ : Grant that we, who joyfully receive him as our Redeemer, may with sure confidence behold him when he comes to be our

Judge; who lives and reigns with you and the Holy Spirit, one God, now and for ever.

Source : This collect, used in 1549 (no 9), returned to use in 1928Eng (Christmas Eve) and 1928Amer and 1929Scot (Christmas Day). There are at least four slightly different versions of it currently in use (nos 329–32).

Use : AmerBCP : Christmas Day [first collect]. AmerAuthS had a different address : 'O God, in our joyful remembrance of the birth . . . '. Christ was then received faithfully rather than joyfully.

---

329   Almighty God, you make us glad with the yearly remembrance of the birth of your Son Jesus Christ. Grant that, as we joyfully receive him for our redeemer, we may with sure confidence behold him when he shall come to be our judge; who is alive and reigns with you and the Holy Spirit, one God, now and for ever.

Source : as no 328
Use : ASB and IrAPB : Christmas Eve. The Welsh version, used on Christmas Day, begins 'Heavenly Father, who makes us glad . . . ' and inserts 'so' after 'our redeemer'. It concludes 'through the same Jesus Christ our Lord, who lives . . . .'.

---

330   O God, you make us glad with the yearly remembrance of the birth of your only Son, Jesus Christ : grant that we may joyfully receive him as our redeemer and with sure confidence stand before him when he comes to be our judge; who lives and reigns with you and the Holy Spirit, one God, world without end.

Source : as no 328
Use : SAAPB : Christmas Eve [second collect]

---

331   God our Father, we rejoice to remember the birth of your Son : help us by faith to receive him as our

redeemer that we may face him with confidence when he comes to be our judge; who is alive and reigns . . . .

Source : as no 328 but much simplified
Use : SAAPB : Christmas Eve [first collect]

---

332   Almighty God, you make us glad with the yearly expectation of the birthday of your Son Jesus Christ : grant that, as we joyfully receive him for our redeemer, so we may with sure confidence behold him when he shall come to be our judge; who lives and reigns with you and the Holy Spirit, one God, now and for ever.

Source : as no 328
Use : AusAC : Advent 3

---

333   O God [SA : Eternal God], you have caused this holy night to shine with the brightness of the true Light [SA : the Light of life] : Grant that we, who have known the mystery [SA : revelation] of that Light on earth, may also enjoy him perfectly in heaven; where with you and the Holy Spirit he lives and reigns, one God, in glory everlasting.

Source : Gel (5), Greg (36), SM : Mass at Cockcrow (no vi)
Use : AmerBCP : Christmas Day [second collect]; SAAPB [second collect provided for midnight]
The SA version is a cross between that of AmerBCP and that of ASB, with an addition of its own. AmerAuths had a quite different collect which is the basis of AmerBCP Christmas 1.

---

334   Eternal God, who made this most holy night to shine with the brightness of your one true light : bring us, who have known the revelation of that light on earth, to see the radiance of your heavenly glory; through Jesus Christ our Lord.

Source : as no 333

Use : ASB, AusAC, IrAPB : for use at midnight or in the early morning

---

335   Eternal God, this holy night is radiant with the brilliance of your one true light. As we have known the revelation of that light on earth, bring us to see the splendour of your heavenly glory; through Jesus Christ our Lord, who is alive . . . .

Source : as no 333
Use : CanBAS : Midnight

---

336   Heavenly Father, you made this holy night radiant with the brightness of your Son Jesus Christ : help us to welcome him as the world's true Light and bring us to eternal joy in his kingdom; where he lives and reigns . . . .

Source : as no 333
Use : SAAPB : Midnight [first collect]

CanBAS is alone in providing a collect for midnight, one for during the day, and this collect for the early morning.

337   O God our Father, whose Word has come among us in the Holy Child of Bethlehem, may the light of faith illumine our hearts and shine in our words and deeds; through him who is Christ our Lord, who lives and reigns . . .

Source : new
Use : CanBAS : Christmas Morning

---

338   Almighty God, you have given [SA : given us] your only-begotten Son to take our nature upon him, and to be born [this day] of a pure virgin : Grant that we, who have been born again and made your children by adoption and grace, may daily be renewed by your Holy Spirit; through our Lord Jesus Christ, to whom with

you and the same Spirit be honor and glory, now and for ever.

Source : 1549/1662 (no 8)
Use : AmerBCP : Christmas Day [third collect]; SAAPB : Christmas Day and Christmas 1 [second collect]

---

339   Almighty God, who hast given thy only-begotten Son to take our nature upon him, and as at this time to be born of a pure Virgin : grant that we, rejoicing in the coming of thy living and eternal Word, may daily be renewed by thy Holy Spirit; through the same . . . .

Source : as no 338
Use : WalesBCP : Christmas Day

ASB/IrAPB and AusAC give this collect a very different form, akin to the post-*Sanctus* of the Eucharistic prayer; it follows the SAMC version.

340   All praise to you, Almighty God and heavenly king, who sent your Son into the world to take our nature upon him and to be born of a pure virgin. Grant that, as we are born again in him, so he may continually dwell in us and reign on earth as he reigns in heaven with you and the Holy Spirit, now and for ever.

Source : as no 338 but follows the SAMC version (no 245)
Use : ASB, AusAC, IrAPB : Christmas Day

---

341   Almighty God, in the birth of your Son you have poured on us the new light of your incarnate Word, and shown us the fulness of your love : Help us to walk in his light and dwell in his love that we may know the fulness of his joy; who lives and reigns . . . .

Source : derived from AmerBCP : Christmas 1 (no 342)
Use : IrAPB : Christmas Day

First Sunday after Christmas

342   Almighty God, you have poured upon us the new light
of your incarnate Word : Grant that this light, enkindled
in our hearts, may shine forth in our lives; through Jesus
Christ our Lord, who lives and reigns with you, in the
unity of the Holy Spirit, one God, now and for ever.

Source : SM : Christmas Day Stational Mass at Saint Anasta-
sia; Greg (42); 1928Amer : Christmas 2 (no 18). In 1973
AmerAuthS it was the second collect for Christmas Day (no
343 below).

Use : AmerBCP : First Sunday after Christmas Day. This
replaces the provision in AmerAuthS (no 400).

343   Almighty Father, by whom the world has been filled
with the new light of your incarnate Word : Grant, we
pray, that as he kindles the flame of faith and love in
our hearts, so his light may shine forth in our lives, who
now lives . . . .

It has been re-used in AusAC : Christmas During the Day
(second service).

---

344   Almighty God, you have shed upon us the new light
of your incarnate Word. May this light, enkindled in
our hearts, shine forth in our lives; through Jesus Christ
our Lord, who lives . . . .

Source : 1928Amer : Christmas 2 (no 18); as no 341
Use : CanBAS : Christmas 1

ASB has two collects for Christmas 1, for use in different years.
The first derives from the Leonine Sacramentary and was used
for the 1928Eng provision from the Circumcision to the
Epiphany (collect 19; see also collect 20). In most other
provinces, it is used for the Second Sunday after Christmas.
It has five versions.

345   Almighty God, who wonderfully created us in your own image and yet more wonderfully restored us through your Son Jesus Christ : grant that, as he came to share in our humanity, so we may share the life of his divinity; who is alive and reigns with you and the Holy Spirit one God, now and for ever.

Source : 1928Eng (no 19)
Use : ASB and IrAPB : Christmas 1 (Year 1)

---

346   O God, who wonderfully created, and yet more wonderfully restored, the dignity of human nature : Grant that we may share the divine life of him who humbled himself to share our humanity, your Son Jesus Christ; who lives and reigns with you, in the unity of the Holy Spirit, one God, for ever and ever.

Source : as no 345
Use : AmerBCP : Second Sunday after Christmas

---

347   Almighty Father, you wonderfully created us in your own image and yet more wonderfully restored us : grant that as your Son our Lord Jesus Christ shared our humanity, so we may be partakers of his divine nature; through the same your Son Jesus Christ, who is alive and reigns with you and the Holy Spirit, now and for ever.

Source : as no 345
Use : SAAPB : Second Sunday after Christmas [second collect]

---

348   Almighty God, you wonderfully created and yet more wonderfully restored our human nature. May we share the divine life of your Son Jesus Christ, who humbled himself to share our humanity, and now lives and reigns

. . . .

Source : as no 345
Use : CanBAS : Christmas During the Day

---

349   God our Father you wonderfully created us in your image and yet more wonderfully restored us through your
Son Jesus Christ : grant that we may share his divine
life as he shares our humanity; who is alive and reigns
with you in the unity of the Holy Spirit one God, for
ever and ever.

Source : as no 345
Use : SA : Second Sunday after Christmas [first collect]

The second collect in ASB, also used in IrAPB, reveals some
of the limitations of the ASB lectionary. Whereas in Year 1,
the Gospel is John 1:14-18, in Year 2 it is a premature reading of Luke 2:22-40, and the collect is that which is also
provided for February 2.

350   Almighty Father, whose Son Jesus Christ was presented
in the Temple and acclaimed the glory of Israel and the
light of the nations : grant that in him we may be
presented to you and in the world may reflect his glory;
through Jesus Christ our Lord.

Source : 1549/1662 for the Purification (no 106)
Use : ASB, IrAPB : Christmas 2

---

351   Heavenly Father you sent your Son into the world to
do your will : keep the pattern of his life always before
our eyes and inspire us to work for the coming of his
kingdom; who is alive and reigns . . . .

Source : nos 247, 248
Use : SAAPB : Christmas 1 [first collect]

The first day of January, the Circumcision of Christ in 1549/1662, now carries a variety of names, some referring only to the naming of Jesus, some to the Holy Name and others also to the Circumcision. The collects reflect this diversity.

352   Eternal Father, you gave your incarnate Son the holy name of Jesus to be the sign of our salvation : Plant in every heart, we pray, the love of him who is the Savior of the world, our Lord Jesus Christ; who lives and reigns with you and the Holy Spirit, one God, in glory everlasting.

Source : The Cambridge Bede Book
Use : AmerBCP : The Holy Name, January 1

---

353   Eternal Father, we give thanks for your incarnate Son, whose name is our salvation. Plant in every heart, we pray, the love of him who is the Saviour of the world, our Lord Jesus Christ; who lives and reigns with you and the Holy Spirit, one God, in glory everlasting.

Source : from AmerBCP (no 352)
Use : CanBAS : The Naming of Jesus

---

354   Almighty God, whose blessed Son was circumcised in obedience to the law for man's sake and given the Name that is above every name : give us grace faithfully to bear his Name, to worship him in the freedom of the Spirit, and to proclaim him as the Saviour of mankind, who is alive and reigns with you and the Holy Spirit, one God, now and for ever.

Source : composite from 1549/1662 and the Church of England Liturgical Commission, based on Acts 4:10 and 12
Use : ASB : The Naming of Jesus, or the Circumcision of Christ. AusAC has a modified version of this, omitting 'for man's sake' and changing the second sentence to 'grant that we, obedient to his commands, and faithfully bearing his

Name, may worship him in the freedom of the Spirit and proclaim him as Saviour of the world, who lives . . . '.

---

355   Almighty God, whose only Son was made a member
       of the old Israel by circumcision in obedience to the Law
       and was named Jesus : Grant that we who have been
       called into the New Israel by baptism and given a new
       name may constantly obey your holy will; for the sake
       of Jesus Christ our Lord.

Source : 1662 : The Circumcision (no 16)
Use : SAMC

---

356   Almighty God, who has given thy Son Jesus Christ the
       Name which is above every name, and has taught us
       that there is none other whereby we may be saved : grant
       that rejoicing in his Name we may ever strive to pro-
       claim it to all people; through the same Jesus Christ
       our Lord.

Source : 1929Scot (no 135)
Use : WalesBCP : The Naming of Jesus

---

357   Merciful Father you have taught us that there is salva-
       tion in no other name than in the name of Jesus : teach
       us to glorify his name and make your salvation known
       to all the world; through Jesus Christ our Lord.

Source : 1928Eng (no 134)
Use : SAAPB : The Holy Name of Jesus : The Circumcision
of Christ

---

358   Father Almighty, you named your Son Jesus because
       he came to bring salvation to the world : Fulfil the prom-
       ise of his holy Name, and in your mercy save us from
       our sins; through him who lives and reigns with you
       and the Holy Spirit, one God, for ever.

Source : new
Use : IrAPB : The Naming of Jesus

---

359   God our Father, you gave to your incarnate Son the
name of Jesus to be a sign of our salvation. May every
tongue confess that Jesus Christ is Lord to your eternal glory; for he now lives and reigns with you and the
Holy Spirit, one God, for ever and ever.

Source : new, but related to other provisions
Use : AusAPB : The Naming and Circumcision of our Lord
Jesus Christ

---

360   God of power and life, the glory of all who believe in
you, fill the world with your splendour and show the
nations the light of your truth; through Jesus Christ your
Son our Lord, who is alive . . . .

Source : Roman Missal : Christmas 2
Use : CanBAS : Christmas 2

The same limitations found with Christmas 1 are found with
Christmas 2 in ASB/IrAPB. Year 1 has a 'holy family' collect; Year 2 is an Epiphany collect.

361   Heavenly Father, whose blessed Son shared at Nazareth
the life of an earthly home : help us to live as the holy
family, united in love and obedience, and bring us at
last to our home in heaven; through Jesus Christ our
Lord.

Source : Jasper-Bradshaw describes this as 'a new collect by
the Revision Committee of the General Synod' with a preamble borrowed from a collect in the 1928Eng baptism of infants. That prayer has a different address to God but has
'whose blessed Son . . . earthly home'. The remainder of
the collect is not new but a slightly amended version of the
reformed *Roman Missal* collect for the feast of the Holy Fam-

ily (Sunday within the Octave of Christmas) (cp no 299).
Use : ASB, IrAPB : Christmas 2

Epiphany

362 O God, by the leading of a star you manifested your
     only Son to the peoples of the earth : Lead us, who know
     you now by faith, to your presence, where we may see
     your glory face to face; through Jesus Christ our Lord,
     who lives and reigns with you and the Holy Spirit, one
     God, now and for ever.

Source : 1928Amer (no 21)
Use : AmerBCP : Epiphany, January 6

---

363 Almighty Father, by the leading of a star you revealed
     your only-begotten Son to the peoples of the earth : in
     your mercy grant that we who know you now by faith,
     may after this life come to the vision of your glorious
     Godhead; through Jesus Christ our Lord.

Source : 1928Amer/Eng (no 21)
Use : SAAPB : Epiphany [second collect]

---

364 God, who didst give thy only-begotten Son to be a light
     to all nations : mercifully grant that we, who know thee
     now by faith, may after this life enjoy the vision of thy
     glorious Godhead; through Jesus Christ our Lord.

Source : as no 363, with an altered first line
Use : WalesBCP : Epiphany

---

365 Eternal God, who by the shining of a star led the wise
     men to the worship of your Son : guide by his light the
     nations of the earth, that the whole world may behold
     your glory; through Jesus Christ our Lord.

Source : CSI : Christmas 2 (no 191)

Use : ASB, AusAC : Epiphany; ASB and IrAPB : Christmas 2 (Year 2)

---

366 Eternal God, who by a star led wise men to the worship of your Son: Guide by your light the nations of the earth, that the whole world may know your glory; through Jesus Christ our Lord, who lives and reigns . . . .

Source : as no 365
Use : CanBAS : Epiphany

---

367 O God, the giver of light, you led the wise men to worship your Son : Bring all men to the light of your truth, that the world may be filled with your glory; through Jesus Christ our Lord, who lives and reigns . . . .

Source : as no 365
Use : IrAPB : Epiphany

---

368 Sovereign Lord by a star you led the wise men to an Infant who is the Light of the world : let his light shine on every nation and fill the whole world with your glory; through Jesus Christ our Lord.

Source : New; it lacks the power and creativeness of the SAMC collect used for Christmas 1 and Epiphany (no 246).
Use : SAAPB : Epiphany

Epiphany 1 : Baptism of Jesus

369 Father in heaven, who at the baptism of Jesus in the River Jordan proclaimed him your beloved Son and anointed him with the Holy Spirit : Grant that all who have been baptized into his Name may keep the covenant they have made, and boldly confess him as Lord and Savior; who with you and the Holy Spirit lives and reigns, one God, in glory everlasting.

Source : new, but see 8, 179, 181
Use : AmerBCP : First Sunday of Epiphany : Baptism of Our Lord. The AmerAuthS version predates the development of the baptismal covenant in the 1979 Prayer Book. The 1973 version spoke of the baptized being 'found worthy of their calling to be your adopted sons and heirs with him of everlasting life'.

The WalesBCP uses the 1549/1662 collect for Epiphany 5 on Epiphany 1 and observes the baptism of the Lord on Epiphany 2 with this collect, which appears to be derived from AmerBCP but with the loss of the reference to the baptismal covenant.

370   Almighty God, our heavenly Father, who at the baptism of Christ our Lord in Jordan didst declare him to be thy beloved Son : grant that we who have been baptised into him may always confess him as Lord and Saviour, who now lives and reigns . . . .

Source : no 369
Use : WalesBCP : Epiphany 2 : Baptism of the Lord

---

371   Almighty God, who anointed Jesus at his baptism with the Holy Spirit and revealed him as your beloved Son : inspire us, your children, who are born of water and the Spirit, to surrender our lives to your service, that we may rejoice to be called the sons of God; through Jesus Christ our Lord.

Source : A revision of CSI : Christmas 4 (no 193); 'your children born of water and the Spirit' comes from the Roman collect.
Use : ASB/IrAPB : Epiphany 1; AusAC : First Ordinary Sunday

---

372   Eternal Father, who at the baptism of Jesus revealed him to be your Son, anointing him with the Holy Spirit,

keep your children, born of water and the Spirit, faithful to their calling; through Jesus Christ our Lord, who lives and reigns . . . .

Source : no 371
Use : CanBAS : Baptism of the Lord : Proper 1

---

373   Heavenly Father you revealed Jesus as your beloved Son when the Holy Spirit came upon him at his baptism in the Jordan : grant that we, who have been baptized in him may rejoice to be your children and the servants of all; through Jesus Christ our Lord.

Source : It follows closely the collect for Christmas 3 in SAMC (no 249) but substitutes 'revealed' for 'proclaimed'. It draws 'rejoice to be . . . and the servants of all' from CSI collect for Christmas 4 (no 193).
Use : SAAPB : First Sunday of the Year [first collect]

After Epiphany 1, the various calendars and lectionaries change course and no common themes are pursued. The collects until the end of Epiphany are not, therefore, given in comparative order.

374   Almighty God, whose Son our Savior Jesus Christ is the light of the world : Grant that your people, illumined by your Word and Sacraments, may shine with the radiance of Christ's glory, that he may be known, worshiped, and obeyed to the ends of the earth; through Jesus Christ our Lord, who with you and the Holy Spirit lives and reigns, one God, now and for ever.

Source : new; based on CSI : Pentecost 20 (no 222)
Use : AmerBCP : Second Sunday of the Epiphany

There are two further versions of this : the first in AusAC, the second in CanBAS.

375   Almighty God, who gave your Son our Saviour Jesus
       Christ to be the light of the world : bring us by your
       Word and sacraments to shine with the radiance of his
       glory; that he may be known, worshipped and obeyed,
       even to the ends of the earth; who lives . . . .

Source : no 374
Use : AusAC: Christmas 2

---

376   Almighty God, your Son Jesus Christ is the light of the
       world. May your people, illumined by your word and
       sacraments, shine with the radiance of his glory, that
       he may be known, worshipped, and obeyed to the ends
       of the earth; who lives and reigns . . . .

Source : no 374
Use : CanBAS : Epiphany 2

---

377   Give us grace, O Lord, to answer readily the call of our
       Saviour Jesus Christ and proclaim to all people the Good
       News of his salvation, that we and the whole world may
       perceive the glory of his marvelous works; who lives and
       reigns with you and the Holy Spirit, one God for ever
       and ever.

Source : new; written by Massey Shepherd
Use : AmerBCP : Third Sunday of Epiphany

---

378   Almighty and everlasting God, you govern all things
       both in heaven and on earth : Mercifully hear the sup-
       plications of your people, and in our time grant us peace;
       through Jesus Christ our Lord, who lives and reigns
       with you and the Holy Spirit, one God, for ever and
       ever.

Source : 1662 : Epiphany 2 (no 23)
Use : AmerBCP : Fourth Sunday of Epiphany

---

379   Set us free, O God from the bondage of our sins, and
      give us [AusAC : inserts 'we pray'] the liberty of abun-
      dant life which you have made known to us in your Son
      our Savior Jesus Christ; who lives and reigns with you,
      in the unity of the Holy Spirit, one God, now and for
      ever.

Source : new; written by Massey Shepherd
Use : AmerBCP : Fifth Sunday of Epiphany; AusAC: Third
Ordinary Sunday

---

380   O God, the strength of all who put their trust in you :
      Mercifully accept our prayers; and because in our weak-
      ness we can do nothing good without you, give us the
      help of your grace, that in keeping your commandments
      we may please you both in will and deed; through Jesus
      Christ our Lord, who lives and reigns with you and the
      Holy Spirit, one God, for ever and ever.

Source : 1662 : Trinity 1 (no 72)
Use : AmerBCP : Sixth Sunday of Epiphany

---

381   O Lord, you have taught us that [Can : Almighty God,
      we are taught by your word that] without love what-
      ever we do is worth nothing [ASB and Can : all our
      doings without love are nothing worth;] : Send your
      Holy Spirit and pour into our hearts your greatest [ASB
      and Can : that most excellent] gift, which is love [ASB
      and Can : gift of love], the true bond of peace and of
      all virtue [ASB : virtues], without which whoever lives
      is accounted [ASB : counted] dead before you. Grant
      this for the sake of your only Son Jesus Christ, who lives
      and reigns with you and the Holy Spirit, one God, now
      and for ever.

The CanBAS version ends at 'all virtue'.

Source : 1549/1662 : Quinquagesima (no 31)

Use : AmerBCP : Seventh Sunday after Epiphany; ASB : Pentecost 7; CanBAS : Proper 21; see also no 609.

---

382   Most loving Father, whose will it is for us to give thanks for all things, to fear nothing but loss of you, and to cast all our care on you who care for us : Preserve us from faithless fears and worldly anxieties, that no clouds of this mortal life may hide from us the light of that love which is immortal, and which you have manifested to us in your Son Jesus Christ our Lord; who lives and reigns with you, in the unity of the Holy Spirit, one God, now and for ever.

Source : An original collect by Bright (234–35), it was used in 1928Amer among the Family Prayers (596). The provision in AmerAuthS (no 383) was different, though based on Bright's prayer; it did not pass in AmerBCP but was used in AusAC. No 382 is closer to Bright's original.
Use : AmerBCP : Eighth Sunday after Epiphany

---

383   Most loving Father, whose will it is for us to cast all our care on you, who care for us : Preserve us from faithless fears and worldly anxieties, that no clouds of this mortal life may hide from us the light of that love which you have made known to us in your Son, Jesus Christ our Lord, who lives . . . .

Source : See no 382.
Use : AmerAuthS; modified version in AusAC : Sixth Ordinary Sunday : omits 'who care for us' and has 'no cloud may hide us', omitting 'of this mortal life'; it also omits 'your Son' from the conclusion.

---

384   O God, who before the passion of your only-begotten Son revealed his glory upon the holy mountain : grant to us that we, beholding by faith the light of his countenance, may be strengthened to bear our cross, and

be changed into his likeness from glory to glory; through Jesus Christ our Lord; who lives and reigns with you and the Holy Spirit, one God, for ever and ever.

Source : 1928Eng (See nos 128, 411-15.)
Use : AmerBCP : Last Sunday of Epiphany (See no 128.)

---

385   Almighty God, by whose [Ir : your] grace alone we are [Ir : have been] accepted and called to your service : strengthen [Ir : and inspire] us by your Holy Spirit and make us worthy of our calling; through Jesus Christ our Lord.

Source : A version of 'Remember, O Lord', CSI (no 211); the immediate source is SAMC (no 250).
Use : ASB : Epiphany 2; AusAC : Second Ordinary Sunday; also SAAPB [first collect] and IrAPB with slight modifications

---

Both SA and CanBAS have a version of this prayer :

386   Heavenly Father by your grace alone you accepted us and called us to your service : strengthen us by your Spirit and make us worthy of our calling; through Jesus Christ our Lord.

Source : See no 385.
Use : SA : Second Sunday of the Year/Epiphany 2

---

387   Almighty God, by grace alone you call us and accept us in your service. Strengthen us by your Spirit, and make us worthy of your call; through Jesus Christ our Lord, who lives and reigns . . . .

Source : See no 385.
Use : CanBAS : Epiphany 3/Proper 3

---

388   Almighty God, whose [Can and SA : your] Son revealed in signs and miracles the wonder of your saving love;

renew [Ir : Enrich] your people [SA : us] with [AusAC
and SA : by] your heavenly grace, and in all [SA : omits
'all'] our weakness sustain us by your mighty power;
through Jesus Christ our Lord.

Source : SAMC : Seventh Sunday before Easter (no 257)
Use : ASB and IrAPB : Epiphany 3; AusAC : Fourteenth Or-
dinary Sunday; CanBAS : Seventh Sunday after Epiphany/
Proper 7; SAAPB : Fourteenth Sunday of the Year

---

389 Almighty [Can : Living] God, in Christ you make all
things new. Transform the poverty of our nature by the
riches of your grace, and in the renewal of our lives make
known your heavenly [Can : omits 'heavenly'] glory;
through Jesus Christ our Lord.

Source : CSI : Christmas 6 (no 195); JLG/SAMC : Christmas
5 (no 252)
Use : ASB, IrAPB, CanBAS : Epiphany 4; AusAC : Lent 4

---

390 God our Father in Christ you make all things new :
transform the poverty of our nature by the riches of your
grace and reveal your glory in the renewal of our lives;
through Jesus Christ our Lord.

Source : See no 389.
Use : SAAPB : Third Sunday of the Year/Epiphany 3

---

391 Merciful Lord you are the only giver of pardon and
peace : cleanse us your faithful people from our sins
that we may serve you with a quiet mind; through Jesus
Christ our Lord.

Source : 1662 : Trinity 21 (no 96) by way of SAMC (no 253)
Use : SAAPB : Fourth Sunday of the Year/Epiphany 4 [first
collect]

---

392   Merciful Lord, grant to your faithful people pardon and peace, that we may be cleansed from all our sins and serve you with a quiet mind; through Jesus Christ our Lord . . . .

Source : See no 391.
Use : CanBAS : Fifth Sunday after Epiphany/Proper 5; SAAPB : Fourth Sunday of the Year/Epiphany 4 [second collect]; ASB and Ir : Seventh Sunday before Easter

---

393   Give us, Lord, we pray, the spirit to think and to [Ir : omits 'to'] do always those things that are right : that we who can do no good thing without you may have power to live according to your [Ir : inserts 'holy'] will; through Jesus Christ our Lord.

Source : 1662 : Trinity 9 (no 81); cp AmerBCP : Proper 14 (no 559)
Use : ASB and IrAPB : Epiphany 5

---

394   Heavenly Father, whose blessed Son was revealed that he might destroy the works of the devil and make us the sons of God and heirs of eternal life : grant that we, having this hope, may purify ourselves even as he is pure; that when he shall appear in power and great glory we may be made like him in his eternal and glorious kingdom; where he is alive and reigns with you and the Holy Spirit, one God, now and for ever.

Source : 1662 : Epiphany 6 (no 28)
Use : ASB : Epiphany 6; IrAPB : Eighth Sunday before Christmas

---

395   O God, whose blessed Son came into the world that he might destroy the works of the devil and make us children of God and heirs of eternal life : Grant that, having this hope we may purify ourselves as he is pure;

that, when he comes again with power and great glory, we may be made like him in his eternal and glorious kingdom; where he lives and reigns with you and the Holy Spirit, one God, for ever and ever.

Source : as no 394
Use : AmerBCP : Proper 27

---

396 Heavenly Father, your Son taught us in parables : Enable your Church to speak to the minds of people of every generation by constantly renewing us through the Holy Spirit that we may fully proclaim the everlasting Gospel; through Jesus Christ our Lord.

Source : new
Use : IrAPB : Epiphany 6

WalesBCP uses 'Remember, Lord, what thou hast wrought in us' for Epiphany 3 and 1549/1662 : Epiphany 1 for Epiphany 5. The following two collects appear to be new.

397 Almighty and everliving God, whose power and glory are revealed in thy Son Jesus Christ : renew and strengthen us with thy grace, that we who worship thee in thy Church may joyfully witness to thy glory in the world; through the same our Saviour Jesus Christ.

Source : new
Use : WalesBCP : Epiphany 4

---

398 Almighty Lord and everlasting God, we beseech thee to direct, sanctify, and govern both our hearts and bodies, in the ways of thy laws, and in the works of thy commandments; that through thy most mighty protection, both here and ever, we may be preserved in body and soul; through our Lord and Saviour Jesus Christ.

Source : new

Use : WalesBCP : Epiphany 6

---

399   Almighty and everliving [Ir : everlasting] God [SA : Merciful Father], whose [SA : your] Son Jesus Christ healed the sick and restored them to wholeness [SA : fulness] of life : look with compassion on the anguish of the world, and [SA : heal the affliction of your people,] by your healing [Can : omits 'healing'] power make whole both men [Can : omits 'both men'; inserts 'all peoples'] and nations [AusAC : make whole every person and nation] [Ir : omits everything after 'world' and substitutes 'and heal the afflictions of your people]; through our Lord and Saviour Jesus Christ . . . .

Source : SAMC (no 257)
Use : ASB and IrAPB : Eighth Sunday before Easter; CanBAS : Sixth Sunday after Epiphany/Proper 6; AusAC : Twenty-Third Ordinary Sunday; SAAPB : Twenty-Third Sunday.

The AmerAuthS collect for Christmas 1 was among those discarded in 1979.

400   Almighty God, who in the incarnation of your eternal Word have revealed the source and perfection of all true religion : Grant that we may entrust our lives to him, on whom is built the whole salvation of mankind, our Savior Jesus Christ, who now lives . . . .

Source : Leo (1248); translated by Bright (22)
Use : AmerAuthS : Christmas 1

It was re-used in an expanded version in AusAC.

401   Almighty God, who in the incarnation of your eternal Word revealed the source and perfection of all true religion : grant us so fully to manifest Christ in our lives that people of all races and creeds may be drawn to him

who is their whole salvation, our Saviour Jesus Christ,
who lives . . . .

Source : See no 400.
Use : AusAC : Twentieth Ordinary Sunday

Ash Wednesday to Pentecost

402   Almighty and everlasting God, you hate [Can : de-
spise] nothing you have made and forgive the sins of
all [ASB : inserts 'those'] who are penitent : create and
make [SA : omits 'and make'] in us new and contrite
hearts,

US : that we, worthily lamenting our sins and acknowledging our wretchedness [Can : brokenness], may obtain of you,

ASB : that, lamenting our sins and acknowledging our
wretchedness, we may receive from you,

Ir : that we may be truly sorry for our sins, and obtain
from you,

SA : that lamenting our sins and acknowledging our
weakness, we may obtain from you,

the God of all mercy, perfect remission and forgiveness
[ASB : perfect forgiveness and peace]; through Jesus
Christ our Lord, who lives and reigns with you and the
Holy Spirit, one God, for ever and ever.

Source : new in 1549; 1662 : Ash Wednesday (no 32)
Use : AmerBCP, ASB, IrAPB, CanBAS, SAAPB : Ash Wednesday [second collect]

---

403   Almighty and holy God your Son, in obedience to the
Spirit fasted forty days in the desert : give us grace to
discipline ourselves that we may press on towards Easter
with eager faith and love; through Jesus Christ our
Lord.

Source : SAMC (no 260)
Use : SAAPB : Ash Wednesday [first collect]

---

404 Almighty God, whose blessed Son was led by the Spirit
to be tempted by Satan : come quickly to help us who
are assaulted by many temptations; and, as you know
the weaknesses of each of us, let each find you mighty
to save; through Jesus Christ your Son our Lord, who
lives and reigns with you and the Holy Spirit, one God,
now and for ever.

Source : an original prayer by Bright (237–38), 'For the
Tempted', which was addressed to Christ
Use : AmerBCP : First Sunday in Lent

---

405 Almighty God, whose Son Jesus Christ [Can : omits
'Jesus Christ'] fasted forty days in the wilderness, and
was tempted as we are, yet without sin [Ir : yet did not
sin] [Can : but did not sin] : give us grace to discipline
ourselves in obedience [Can : submission] to your Spirit;
and [Can : that], as you know our weakness, so may
we [Can : we may] know your power to save [Ir : saving power]; through Jesus Christ our Lord.

Source : a compound of JLG (no 260) and SAMC (no 261)
collects for Lent 1. The central section is drawn from 261.
The final section 'as you know . . . power to save' is from
the Bright collect used in no 404, but by way of no 260 which
itself gives Colquhoun (no 1301) as the source. The 1549 collect (no 33) is a remote ancestor and partial inspiration. The
account of the collect in Jasper-Bradshaw (273–74) is about
as misleading as it is possible to be. A detailed analysis would
look like this.

> Almighty God (new)
> whose Son Jesus Christ fasted forty days in the (no 261)
>   wilderness (replaces 'desert' in no 261)

Give us grace to (no 33)
  discipline ourselves in (no 261)
  obedience (replaces 'humble submission' in no 261)
  to your spirit (no 261)
and that as your know our weakness (nos 260, 404 :
    changed from plural)
  so we may know (no 260)
  your power (new)
  to save (no 260)

Use: ASB : Lent 1

---

406   Merciful Father your Son was tempted as we are yet
      without sin : be with us in our weakness that we may
      know your power to save; through Jesus Christ our
      Lord.

Source : nos 260/261
Use : SAAPB : Lent 1 [first collect]

---

407   Almighty God, your Son fasted forty days and forty
      nights in the desert : give us grace to use such discipline,
      that our flesh being subdued to the Spirit, we may al-
      ways obey your will in righteousness and holiness, to
      your honour and glory; through Jesus Christ our Lord.

Source : 1549/1662 : Lent 1 (no 33)
Use : SAAPB : Lent 1 [second collect]

---

408   O God, whose glory it is always to have mercy : Be gra-
      cious to all who have gone astray from your ways, and
      bring them again with penitent hearts and steadfast faith
      to embrace and hold fast the unchangeable truth of your
      Word, Jesus Christ your Son; who with you and the
      Holy Spirit lives and reigns, one God, for ever and ever.

Source : Good Friday Solemn collects; Missale Gallic. vetus
(107), Gel (413), Greg (351)

Use : AmerBCP : Second Sunday in Lent

---

409   Lord God Almighty, grant your people grace to with-
      stand the temptations of the world, the flesh, and the
      devil, and with pure hearts and minds to follow you,
      the only God; through Jesus Christ our Lord.

Source : 1662 : Trinity 18 (nos 91/92)
Use : ASB : Lent 2

---

410   Loving Lord, grant your people grace to resist the temp-
      tations of the world, the flesh and the devil, and with
      pure hearts to follow you the only God; through Jesus
      Christ our Lord.

Source : as no 409
Use : SAAPB : Lent 3 [second collect]

The Transfiguration lections are now widely used in the Tem-
porale, though their position varies across the Communion.
In ASB and IrAPB they are used in both years on Lent 4.
The collect is a slightly adapted version that provided for the
Feast of the Transfiguration in 1928Eng and 1929Scot. In
SAAPB the lections are used on Lent 2, but the collect has
no reference to the Transfiguration. CanBAS also has it on
Lent 2 and uses the ASB collect. In NZPB the Transfiguration lections are used on Epiphany 4 with two collects referring to the event, the first derived from that in ASB, the other
original. In AmerBCP the Last Sunday after Epiphany
celebrates the Transfiguration and uses the 1928Eng collect
for the feast on that occasion (no 382); the collect used for
the feast is one by William Reed Huntington.

411   Almighty Father the disciples saw your Son in glory be-
      fore he suffered on the cross : grant that by faith in his
      death and resurrection we may triumph in the power
      of his victory; through Jesus Christ our Lord.

Source : 'grant that . . . victory' from no 265; 'power of his victory' appears first in no 39
Use : SAAPB : Lent 2 [first collect]

412   Almighty Father, your Son was revealed in majesty before he suffered death upon the cross : give us faith to perceive his glory and strengthen us to bear the cross; through the same Jesus Christ our Lord.

Use : SAAPB : Lent 2 [second collect]

413   Almighty Father [Can : God], whose Son was revealed in majesty before he suffered death upon the cross : give us faith to perceive his glory, that we may be strengthened to suffer with him and be changed into his likeness [Can : being strengthened by his grace we may be changed into his likeness], from glory to glory; who is alive and reigns with you and the Holy Spirit, one God, now and for ever.

Use : ASB and IrAPB : Lent 4/Third Sunday before Easter; CanBAS : Lent 2

414   Almighty Father your Son was revealed in glory before he suffered on the cross : grant that by faith in his death and resurrection we may triumph in the power of his victory; through Jesus Christ our Lord.

Source : as no 411
Use : SAAPB : The Transfiguration

415   God, who before the Passion of thy only-begotten Son revealed his majesty on the holy mount : grant that we thy servants may see his glory and be strengthened to bear the cross; through the same Jesus Christ our Lord.

Use : WalesBCP : Passion Sunday/Lent 5

416   God of life and glory, your Son was revealed in splendour before he suffered death upon the cross; grant that we, beholding his majesty, may be strengthened to follow him and be changed into his likeness from glory

to glory; for he lives and reigns with you and the Holy Spirit, one God now and for ever.

Use : NZ : Epiphany 4 and used for the Transfiguration

---

417   Lord God Almighty, your Son prayed for his disciples, that in all the conflicts of the world you would deliver them from the power of the devil : Strengthen us to resist every assault and temptation, and to follow you, the only God; through Jesus Christ our Lord.

Source : SAMC (no 261)
Use : IrAPB : Lent 2

---

418   Almighty God, you know [ASB : see] that we have no power in ourselves to help ourselves : Keep us both outwardly in our bodies and inwardly in our souls, that we may be defended from all adversities which may happen to the body, and from all evil thoughts which may assault and hurt the soul; through Jesus Christ our Lord, who lives and reigns with you and the Holy Spirit, one God, for ever and ever.

Source : 1662 : Lent 2 (no 34)
Use : AmerBCP : Third Sunday in Lent; ASB : Pentecost 9

---

419   Gracious Father your Son is the source of living water : grant that the gift of his Spirit may be to us a spring of water welling up to eternal life; through Jesus Christ our Lord.

Source : new
Use : SAAPB [first collect]

CanBAS has a different collect for Year A from that provided for Years B and C:

420   Almighty God, whose Son Jesus Christ gives the water of eternal life, may we always thirst for you, the spring

and source of goodness; through him who lives and reigns with you and the Holy Spirit, one God, now and for ever.

Source : new
Use : CanBAS : Lent 3 (Year A)

---

421   Father of mercy, alone we have no power in ourselves to help ourselves. When we are discouraged by our weakness, strengthen us to follow Christ, our pattern and our hope; who lives . . . .

Source : first line from no 418
Use : CanBAS : Lent 3 (Years B and C)

---

422   Lord God, your Son Jesus Christ suffered before he entered his glory : Make us willing to deny ourselves, take up the cross, and follow in his footsteps, that we may share in his eternal joy; who lives and reigns . . . .

Source : a version of AmerBCP : Monday in Holy Week (no 445); 'follow in his footsteps' appears in no 148
Use : IrAPB : Lent 3

---

423   Gracious Father, whose blessed Son Jesus Christ came down from heaven to be the true bread which gives life to the world : Evermore give us this bread, that he may live in us, and we in him; who lives and reigns with you and the Holy Spirit, one God, now and for ever.

Source : This is a collect by F. B. Macnutt (*The Prayer Manual,* London 1952, no 488 [JLG : no 398] used by JLG and CECal for Easter 1 [no 272]). In fact both nos 488 and 398 are 'bread' collects!

Use : AmerBCP : Fourth Sunday in Lent; CanBAS—Years B and C

---

424   Eternal Father your Son is the Light of the world : dispel the darkness of our sins with your celestial brightness; through Jesus Christ our Lord.

Source : new, but put together from various pieces
Use : SAAPB : Lent 4 [first collect]

---

425   Almighty God, through the waters of baptism your Son has made us children of light. May we ever walk in his light and show forth your glory in the world; through Jesus Christ our Lord, who is alive . . . .

Source : nos 150, 342
Use : CanBAS : Lent 4 (Year A)

---

426   Almighty God, you alone can bring into order the unruly wills and affections of sinners : Grant your people grace to love what you command and desire what you promise; that, among the swift and varied changes of the world, our hearts may surely there be fixed where true joys are to be found; through Jesus Christ our Lord, who lives and reigns with you and the Holy Spirit, one God, now and for ever.

Source : 1662 : Easter 4 (no 63)
Use : AmerBCP : Fifth Sunday in Lent

---

427   Almighty God, you only can control our disordered wills and passions : grant that we may love what you command and desire what you promise, that among the many and varied changes of the world, our hearts may be firmly fixed where true joys may be found; through Jesus Christ our Lord.

Source : as no 426
Use : SAAPB : Fourth Sunday after Easter [second collect]

428   Almighty God, who alone can bring order to the unruly wills and passions of sinful men : give us grace,
to love what you command and to desire what you
promise, that in all the changes and chances of this
world, our hearts may surely there be fixed where lasting joys are to be found; through Jesus Christ our Lord,

Source : as no 426
Use : ASB : Easter 4

---

429   Almighty God, you alone can order the unruly wills and
passions of sinful men : grant to your people that they
may love what you command and desire what you
promise, that so, among the many and varied changes
of the world, our hearts may surely there be fixed where
true joys are to be found; through Jesus Christ our Lord.

Source : as no 426
Use : AusPB : Third Sunday after Easter

---

430   Almighty God, you alone can order the unruly wills and
affections of sinful men : Grant that your people may
love what you command, and desire what you promise; that in the various changes of the world our hearts
may ever there be fixed where true joys are to be found;
through Jesus Christ our Lord.

Source : as no 426
Use : IrAPB : Pentecost 19

---

431   Most merciful God, who by the death and resurrection
of your Son Jesus Christ delivered and saved mankind :
grant that by faith in him who suffered on the cross,
we may triumph in the power of his victory; through
Jesus Christ our Lord.

Source : a Latin collect translated in 1929Scot (no 39)
Use : ASB : Lent 5; AusAC : Tuesday before Easter

---

432   Holy God and Lord of life by the death and resurrection of your Son Jesus Christ you delivered and saved the world : grant that by faith in him who suffered on the cross we may triumph in the power of his victory; through Jesus Christ our Lord.

Source : SAMC (no 266)
Use : SAAPB : Lent 5 [first collect]

---

433   Loving Father, you delivered and saved us all by the cross and passion of your Son Jesus Christ : grant that by steadfast faith in the merits of his sacrifice we may find help and salvation, and may triumph in the power of his victory; through Jesus Christ our Lord.

Source : SAMC (no 264)
Use : SAAPB : Lent 5 [second collect]

---

434   Grant, O merciful Father, that, as you saved mankind by the cross and passion of your Son Jesus Christ; so, trusting in the power of his sacrifice, we may share in the glory of his victory; through Jesus Christ our Lord.

Source : as no 431
Use : IrAPB : Lent 5

---

435   Almighty God, your Son came into the world to free us all from sin and death. Breathe upon us with the power of your Spirit, that we may be raised to new life in Christ, and serve you in holiness and righteousness all our days; through the same Jesus Christ, our Lord.

Source : as no 431
Use : CanBAS : Lent 5 (Year A)

---

436   Most merciful God, by the death and resurrection of your Son Jesus Christ, you created humanity anew. May the power of his victorious cross transform those

who turn in faith to him who lives and reigns with you
and the Holy Spirit, one God, now and for ever.

Source : as no 431
Use : CanBAS : Lent 5 (Years B and C)

---

437   Almighty and everliving God, in your tender love for
the human race you sent your Son our Savior Jesus
Christ to take upon him our nature, and to suffer death
upon the cross, giving us the example of his great humility : Mercifully grant that we may walk in the way
of his suffering, and also share in his resurrection;
through Jesus Christ our Lord, who lives and reigns
with you and the Holy Spirit, one God, for ever and
ever.

Source : 1549/1662 : Palm Sunday (no 44)
Use : AmerBCP : Sunday of the Passion : Palm Sunday

---

438   Almighty and everlasting God [SA : Father], who [SA :
omits 'who'] in your tender love towards mankind [SA :
inserts 'you'] sent your Son our Saviour Jesus Christ
to take upon him our flesh [SA : nature] and to suffer
death upon the cross : grant that we may follow the example of his patience and humility [SA : omits 'and humility'], and also be made partakers of his resurrection;
through Jesus Christ our Lord.

Source : as 437
Use : ASB and SA : Palm Sunday [second collect]. See also
the Canadian version (no. 642).

---

439   Almighty and everlasting God, in your tender love towards mankind you sent your Son our Saviour Jesus
Christ to take our human nature and to suffer death
upon the cross; Grant that following the example of his

patience and humility we may be made partakers of his resurrection; through Jesus Christ our Lord.

Source : as no 437
Use : IrAPB : Palm Sunday

---

440   Almighty and everliving God, in your tender love towards us you sent your Son to take our nature upon him, and to suffer death upon the cross; grant that we may follow the example of his great humility and share in his glorious resurrection; through him who lives and reigns with you and the Holy Spirit, one God now and for ever.

Source : as no 437
Use : NZ : Lent 6 : Palm Sunday [second collect]

---

441   Eternal Father your Son our Saviour Jesus Christ fulfilled your will by taking our nature and giving his life for us : help us to follow the example of his humility by walking in the way of the cross; through Jesus Christ our Lord.

Source : as no 437
Use : SAAPB : Palm Sunday [first collect]

---

442   Father of mankind [Aus and SA : Father of all], who [SA : you] gave your only-begotten Son [SA : only Son Jesus Christ] to take upon himself the form of a servant and to be obedient even to death on a cross : give us the same mind that was in Christ Jesus that, sharing in his humility, we may come to be with him in his glory; who is alive . . . .

Source : as no 437
Use : ASB : Pentecost 10; AusAC and SAAPB : Thirtieth Sunday

---

443   Lord Jesus Christ, you humbled yourself in taking the form of a servant, and in obedience died on the cross for our salvation : Give us the mind to follow you and proclaim you as Lord and King, to the glory of God the Father.

Source : as no 437
Use : IrAPB : Pentecost 10

444   Almighty God, whose Son was crucified yet entered into glory, may we, walking in the way of the cross, find it is for us the way of life; through Jesus Christ our Lord, who is alive . . . .

Source : no 445
Use : CanBAS : Palm Sunday [for the Procession] and Monday in Holy Week

445   Almighty God, whose most dear Son went not up to joy but first [Aus : omits 'but first'; inserts 'before'] he suffered pain, and entered not into glory before he was crucified : Mercifully grant that we, walking in the way of the [Ir : his] cross, may find it none other than the way of life and peace; through Jesus Christ your Son our Lord, who lives and reigns with you and the Holy Spirit, one God, for ever and ever.

Source : no 45
Use : AmerBCP and IrAPB : Monday in Holy Week; ASB : Lent 3; AusAC : Palm Sunday

446   O God, [Ir : inserts 'who'] by [SA : Merciful Father, through] the passion of your blessed [SA : omits 'blessed'] Son you [Ir : omits 'you'] made an instrument of shameful death to be for us the means [SA : way] of life : Grant us so to [SA : grant that we may] glory in the cross of Christ, that we may gladly suffer

shame and loss for the sake of your Son our Savior Jesus Christ [SA : and gladly suffer for his sake]; who lives and reigns with you and the Holy Spirit, one God, for ever and ever.

Source : 1928Eng : Holy Cross Day (no 139)
Use : AmerBCP and IrAPB : Tuesday in Holy Week; SAAPB : Thirteenth Sunday

---

447 O God, by the passion of your blessed Son, you made an instrument of shameful death to be for us the means of life. May our lives be so transformed by his passion that we may witness to his grace; who lives . . . .

Source : no 446
Use : CanBAS : Tuesday in Holy Week

---

448 Almighty God who in the passion of your blessed Son made an instrument of shameful death to be for us the means of life and peace : grant us so to glory in the cross of Christ that we may gladly suffer for his sake; who lives . . . .

Source : no 446
Use : AusAC : Wednesday before Easter

---

449 Lord God, whose blessed Son our Savior gave his body to be whipped and his face to be spit upon : Give us grace to accept joyfully the sufferings of the present time, confident of the glory that shall be revealed; through Jesus Christ your Son our Lord, who lives and reigns with you and the Holy Spirit, one God, for ever and ever.

Source : no 46
Use : AmerBCP : Wednesday in Holy Week

---

450   Lord God, your Son our Saviour gave his body to be
whipped and turned his face for men to spit upon. Give
your servants grace to accept suffering for his sake, confident of the glory that will be revealed, through Jesus
Christ our Lord who is alive . . . .

Source : no 449
Use : CanBAS : Wednesday in Holy Week

---

451   Lord God, whose blessed Son our Saviour gave his back
to the smiters and did not hide his face from shame :
give us grace to endure [Aus : accept] the sufferings of
this present time with sure confidence in the glory that
shall be revealed; through Jesus Christ [Ir : your Son]
our Lord.

Source : no 449
Use : ASB and IrAPB : Pentecost 13; IrAPB : Wednesday
in Holy Week; AusAC : Good Friday

---

452   Heavenly Father, you anointed your Son Jesus Christ
with the Holy Spirit and with power to bring to man
the blessings of your kingdom. Anoint your Church with
the same Holy Spirit, that we who share in his suffering and his victory may bear witness to the gospel of
salvation; through Jesus Christ our Lord.

Source : new
Use : ASB : Blessing of the Oils

---

453   Heavenly Father you anointed your Son Jesus Christ
with the Holy Spirit and with power to bring us the
blessings of your kingdom : grant that we, who share
in his sufferings and victory may receive the benefits
of his anointing; who lives and reigns with you and the
Holy Spirit, one God, for ever and ever.

Source : no 452

Use : SAAPB : Maundy Thursday : Chrism Eucharist (when there is no Renewal of Vows)

---

454 Almighty Father, whose dear Son, on the night before he suffered, instituted the Sacrament of his Body and Blood : Mercifully grant that we may receive it thankfully in remembrance of Jesus Christ our Lord, who in these holy mysteries gives us a pledge of eternal life; and who lives and reigns with you and the Holy Spirit, one God, for ever and ever.

Source : 1928Amer (no 48)
Use : AmerBCP : Maundy Thursday

---

455 Almighty and heavenly Father, we thank you that in this wonderful sacrament you have given us the memorial of the passion of your Son Jesus Christ. Grant us so to reverence the sacred mysteries of his body and blood, that we may know within ourselves and show forth in our lives the fruits of his redemption; who is alive and reigns with you and the Holy Spirit, one God, now and for ever.

Source : See Introduction.
Use : ASB and IrAPB : Maundy Thursday [first collect]

---

456 God our Father, whose Son our Lord Jesus Christ in a wonderful Sacrament has left us a memorial of his passion : Grant us so to venerate the sacred mysteries of his Body and Blood, that we may ever perceive within ourselves the fruit of his redemption; who lives and reigns with you and the Holy Spirit, one God, for ever and ever.

Source : See Introduction.
Use : AmerBCP : Of the Holy Eucharist

---

457   Father, your Son our Lord Jesus Christ, in a wonderful sacrament gave us a memorial of his passion : grant that we may venerate the sacred mysteries of his body and blood, and perceive within ourselves the fruit of his redemption; who lives and reigns with you, in the unity of the Holy Spirit, one God, world without end.

Source : See Introduction.
Use : SAAPB : Maundy Thursday : Evening Eucharist [third collect]

---

458   Almighty God your Son our Lord Jesus Christ gave us the wonderful sacrament of his body and blood to represent his death and to celebrate his resurrection : strengthen our devotion to him in these holy mysteries and through them renew our unity with him and with one another that we may grow in grace and in the knowledge of our salvation; through Jesus Christ our Lord.

Source : SAMC (no 267)
Use : SAAPB : Maundy Thursday : Evening Eucharist [second collect] and Corpus Christi [first collect]

---

459   Gracious and merciful God, in a wonderful sacrament you have given us a memorial of the passion of your Son Jesus Christ; grant that we who receive these sacred mysteries may grow up into him in all things until we come to your eternal joy; through our Saviour Jesus Christ.

Use : NZ : Maundy Thursday [third collect]

---

460   O God, your Son Jesus Christ has left to us this meal of bread and wine in which we share his body and his blood. May we who celebrate this sign of his great love

show in our lives the fruits of his redemption; through Jesus Christ our Lord, who lives . . . .

Source : new
Use : CanBAS : Maundy Thursday

---

461   Grant Lord, that we who receive the body and blood of our Lord Jesus Christ may be the means by which the work of his incarnation shall go forward; take, consecrate, break and distribute us, to be for others a means of your grace, and vehicles of your eternal love; through Jesus Christ our Lord.

Source : new; derived from St. Augustine
Use : AusAC : Maundy Thursday (1) and Twenty-Second Sunday

---

462   Almighty [SA : Heavenly] Father [Can : God], whose [Can and SA : your] Son Jesus Christ [SA : omits 'Jesus Christ'] has taught us that what [SA : anything] we do for the least of our brethren [Can : your children] [SA : our neighbours] we do also [SA : omits 'also'] for him : give us the will to be the servant of others [Can : serve others] as he was the servant of all, who gave up his life and died for us, yet [Can : but] is alive and reigns with you and the Holy Spirit, one God, now and for ever.

SAAPB continues 'for him : open our eyes to the needs of others and give us the will to serve you in them; through Jesus Christ our Lord'.

Source : JLG (no 292) for line 1 (it is addressed to Christ as Lord)
Use : ASB and AusAC : Maundy Thursday [second collect]; ASB : Pentecost 11; CanBAS : Proper 14; AusAC and SAAPB : Twenty-Fifth Sunday

---

463   Almighty God, your Son Jesus Christ washed the disciples' feet : Give us the will to be the servant of others as he was the servant of all; who gave up his life and died for us, yet is alive and reigns with you and the Holy Spirit, one God, now and for ever.

Source : no 462
Use : IrAPB : Maundy Thursday [second collect]

---

464   Everlasting God, your Son Jesus Christ girded himself with a towel and washed his disciples' feet; grant us the will to be the servant of others as he was servant of all, who gave up his life and died for us, yet lives and reigns with you and the Holy Spirit, one God now and for ever.

Source : no 462 in part
Use : NZ : Maundy Thursday [fourth collect]

---

465   Almighty God, we pray you graciously to behold [Can : look graciously, we pray on] this your family, for whom our Lord Jesus Christ was willing to be betrayed, and given into the hands of sinners, and to suffer death upon the cross; who now lives and reigns with you and the Holy Spirit, one God, for ever and ever.

Source : no 50
Use : AmerBCP and CanBAS : Good Friday

---

466   Almighty Father, hear our prayer and look with mercy on this your family for which our Lord Jesus Christ was ready to be betrayed into the hands of sinners and to suffer death on the cross; who is alive . . . .

Source : SAMC : nos 27, 50
Use : SAAPB : Good Friday

---

467   Almighty Father, look with mercy on this your family for which our Lord Jesus Christ was content to be

betrayed and given up into the hands of wicked men and to suffer death upon the cross; who is alive and glorified . . . .

Source : no 50
Use : ASB [first collect]; IrAPB : Good Friday

---

468 Almighty and everlasting God, by whose Spirit the whole body of the Church is governed and sanctified : hear our prayer which we offer for all your faithful people; that each in his vocation and ministry may serve you in holiness and truth to the glory of your Name; through our Lord and Saviour Jesus Christ.

Source : no 51
Use : ASB : Good Friday [second collect] and Pentecost 2

---

469 Merciful God, who made all men and hate nothing that you have made : you desire not the death of a sinner but rather that he should be converted and live. Have mercy upon your ancient people the Jews, and upon all who have not known you, or who deny the faith of Christ crucified; take from them all ignorance, hardness of heart, and contempt for your word, and so fetch them home to your fold that they may be one flock under one shepherd; through Jesus Christ our Lord.

Source : nos 52/53
Use : ASB : Good Friday [third collect]

---

470 O God, Creator of heaven and earth : Grant that, as the crucified body of your dear Son was laid in the tomb and rested on this holy Sabbath, so we may await with him the coming of the third day, and rise with him to newness of life; who now lives and reigns with you and the Holy Spirit, one God, for ever and ever.

Source : new; by Bishop Otis Charles

Use : AmerBCP and CanBAS : Holy Saturday; CanBAS :
omits 'Grant that' and changes 'so we may' to 'so may we'.

---

471   Lord God our Father, maker of heaven and earth : grant
that, as the crucified body of your dear Son was laid
in the tomb to await the glory that should be revealed,
so we may endure the darkness of this present time in
sure confidence that we shall rise with him; who lives
 . . . .

Source : no 470
Use : AusAC : Easter Eve

---

472   Grant, Lord, that we who are baptized into the death
of your Son our Saviour Jesus Christ may continually
put to death our evil desires and be buried with him;
that through the grave and gate of death we may pass
to our joyful resurrection; through his merits, who died
and was buried and rose again for us, your Son Jesus
Christ our Lord.

Source : 1662 : Easter Even (no 55); cp SAMC (no 270)
Use : ASB : Easter Eve

---

473   Grant, Lord, that we who are baptized into the death
of your Son Jesus Christ, may die to sin, and be buried with him; and that through the grave and gate of
death, we may come to our joyful resurrection; through
him who died and rose again for us, our Lord and
Saviour Jesus Christ.

Source : as no 472
Use : IrAPB : Easter Eve

---

474   O God,* who for our redemption gave your only-
begotten Son to the death of the cross, and by his glorious resurrection delivered us from the power of our

enemy : Grant us so to die daily to sin, that we may evermore live with him in the joy of his resurrection; through Jesus Christ your Son our Lord, who lives and reigns with you and the Holy Spirit, one God, now and for ever.

*In AmerBCP on p. 295 [the Easter Vigil], this collect has the opening words 'Almighty God'.

Source : 1928Amer (no 57)
Use : AmerBCP : Easter Day; AusAC : Tenth Ordinary Sunday

---

475 Lord of all life and power, who through the mighty resurrection of your Son overcame the old order of sin and death to make all things new in him : grant that we, being dead to sin and alive to you in Jesus Christ may reign with him in glory; to whom with you and the Holy Spirit be praise and honour, glory and might, now and in all eternity.

Source : as no 474 but by way of SAMC (no 271)
Use : ASB : Easter Day [first collect]; AusAC : Day

---

476 Lord of life and power, through the mighty resurrection of your Son, you have [SA : omits 'have'] overcome the old order of sin and death and have [SA : omits 'have'] made all things new in him. May we [SA : grant that we], being dead to sin and alive to you in Jesus Christ, [SA : inserts 'may'] reign with him in glory, who with you and the Holy Spirit is alive, one God, now and for ever [SA : to whom with you and the Holy Spirit be praise and honour, glory and might now and in all eternity].

Source : as no 474
Use : CanBAS : During the Day; SAAPB : Day [first collect]

---

477   Almighty God, who through your only-begotten Son Jesus Christ overcame death and opened to us the gate of everlasting life; Grant that we, who celebrate with joy the day of the Lord's resurrection, may be raised from the death of sin by your life-giving Spirit; through Jesus Christ our Lord, who lives and reigns with you and the Holy Spirit, one God, now and for ever.

Source : 1549/1662 (no 56)
Use : AmerBCP : Easter Day; IrAPB [second collect]

---

478   Almighty God, you have conquered death through your dearly beloved Son Jesus Christ and opened to us the gate of everlasting life : grant us by your grace to set our mind on things above, so that by your continual help our whole life may be transformed; through Jesus Christ our Lord, who is alive . . . .

Source : as no 480
Use : AusPB : Easter Midnight/Early Morning/Day [first collect]

---

479   Almighty God, who through your only-begotten Son Jesus Christ overcame death and opened to us the gate of everlasting life : we humbly beseech you that as by your special grace going before us you put into our minds good desires, so by your continued help we may bring them to good effect; through Jesus Christ our Lord, who is alive . . . .

Source : as no 477
Use : ASB : Easter Day [second collect]

---

480   Almighty Father, through your only begotten Son Jesus Christ you overcame death and opened to us the gate of everlasting life : we humbly pray that as by your grace

you put into our minds good desires, so by your continual help we may bring them to fulfilment; through
Jesus Christ our Lord, who lives . . . .

Source : as no 486
Use : SAAPB : Day [second collect]

---

481   All praise to you, our God and Father, you raised your
Son in triumph from the grave conquering sin and
death, and opening for all mankind the way to eternal
life : Grant us so to die daily to sin that we may rise
and live with him in the joy of his resurrection; who
lives and reigns with you and the Holy Spirit, one God,
now and for ever.

Source : as no 474
Use : IrAPB : Easter Day [first collect]

---

482   God our Father, by raising Christ your Son you conquered the power of death and opened for us the way
to eternal life. In our celebration today raise us up and
renew our lives by the Spirit that is within us. Grant
this through our Lord Jesus Christ, your Son, who lives
and reigns . . . .

Source : Roman Sacramentary, ICEL translation : Easter Day
[first collect]; it has 'Let our celebration' rather than 'In our
celebration'
Use : AusPB : Day [second collect]

---

483   O God, who made this most holy night to shine with
the glory of the Lord's resurrection : Stir up in your
Church that Spirit of adoption which is given to us in
Baptism, that we being renewed both in body and mind,
may worship you in sincerity and truth; through Jesus
Christ our Lord, who lives and reigns with you, in the
unity of the Holy Spirit, one God, for ever and ever.

Source : SM : Vigil Mass; Gel (454), Greg (377), Bobbio (258)
Use : AmerBCP : Easter Day

---

484   Lord God, you have brightened this night with the radiance of the risen Christ. Quicken the spirit of sonship in your Church; renew us in mind and body to give you whole-hearted service. Grant this through our Lord Jesus Christ, your Son, who lives and reigns . . . .

Source : as no 483
Use : AusPB : Easter at Night

---

485   Lord God you have brightened this night with the radiance of the risen Christ : May this light so shine within the Church that we may be renewed in mind and body and serve you with all our being; through Jesus Christ our Lord.

Source : as no 483
Use : SAAPB : Easter Vigil

---

486   Almighty God, who by the resurrection of your Son brought into our darkness the brightness of your one true light : so kindle our hearts at this Paschal feast that we may burn with heavenly desires and with pure hearts attain to the feast of everlasting light; through Jesus Christ our Lord, who lives . . . .

Source : derived from the blessing on the Paschal Candle in AmerBCP (p. 285)
Use : AusAC : Night/Early Morning

---

487   Eternal Giver of life and light, this holy night shines with the radiance of the risen Christ. Renew your Church with the Spirit given to us in baptism, that we may worship you in sincerity and truth, and shine as

a light in the world; through Jesus Christ our Lord, who is alive . . . .

Source : as no 483
Use : CanBAS : Easter Vigil

---

488   Grant, we pray, Almighty God, that we who celebrate with awe the Paschal feast may be found worthy to attain to everlasting joys; through Jesus Christ our Lord, who lives and reigns with you and the Holy Spirit, one God, now and for ever.

Source : 1928Amer : Tuesday in Easter Week (no 59)
Use : AmerBCP : Monday in Easter Week

---

489   O God, who by the glorious resurrection of your Son Jesus Christ destroyed death and brought life and immortality to light : Grant that we, who have been raised with him, may abide in his presence and rejoice in the hope of eternal glory; through Jesus Christ our Lord, to whom, with you and the Holy Spirit, be dominion and praise for ever and ever.

Source : Colquhoun (no 302)
Use : AmerBCP : Tuesday in Easter Week

---

490   O God, whose blessed Son made himself known to his disciples in the breaking of bread : Open the eyes of our faith, that we may behold him in all his redeeming work; who lives and reigns with you, in the unity of the Holy Spirit, one God, now and for ever.

Source : 1928Amer : Monday in Easter Week (no 58)
Use : AmerBCP : Wednesday in Easter Week and Third Sunday of Easter

---

491   Almighty God, your Son Jesus Christ after his resur-
       rection appeared to his disciples on the Emmaus Road
       and made himself known in the breaking of bread :
       Open our eyes that we may know him in all his redeem-
       ing work; who lives . . . .

Source : as no 490
Use : IrAPB : Monday in Easter Week and Easter 2 (Year 1)

---

492   O God, your Son made himself known to his disciples
       in the breaking of bread. Open the eyes of our faith,
       that we may see him in his redeeming work, who is alive
       . . . .

Source : as no 490
Use : CanBAS : Third Sunday of Easter

---

493   Almighty and everlasting God, who in the Paschal mys-
       tery established the new covenant of reconciliation :
       Grant that all who have been reborn into the fellow-
       ship of Christ's Body may show forth in their lives what
       they profess by their faith; through Jesus Christ our
       Lord, who lives and reigns with you and the Holy Spirit,
       one God, for ever and ever.

Source : SM : Friday of Easter Week (cp 1549/1662 : Easter
3); Bright (pp. 56–57); Greg (423)
Use : AmerBCP : Thursday in Easter Week and Second Sunday of Easter

---

494   Almighty and everliving God, who by the suffering and
       death of your Son Jesus Christ established a new cove-
       nant of reconciliation : grant that we who have been
       reborn into the fellowship of Christ's Body may show
       forth in our lives what we profess by our faith; through
       Jesus Christ our Lord.

Source : as no 493
Use : AusAC : Eighth Ordinary Sunday

---

495 Almighty Father, who gave your only Son to die for our sins and to rise for our justification : Give us grace so to put away the leaven of malice and wickedness, that we may always serve you in pureness of living and truth; through Jesus Christ your Son our Lord, who lives and reigns with you and the Holy Spirit, one God, now and for ever.

Source : 1549 : Second Celebration on Easter Day, Tuesday in Easter Week, and Easter 1; 1662 : Easter 1 (no 60)
Use : AmerBCP : Friday in Easter Week

---

496 We thank you, heavenly Father, that you have delivered us from the dominion of sin and death and brought us into the kingdom of your Son; and we pray that, as by his death he has recalled us to life, so by his love he may raise us to eternal joy; who lives and reigns with you, in the unity of the Holy Spirit, one God, now and for ever.

Source : revision of Bright (58); a Mozarabic prayer
Use : AmerBCP : Saturday in Easter Week

---

497 We thank you, heavenly Father, for delivering [Aus : that you have delivered] us from the power of darkness, and bringing us into the kingdom of your Son; and we pray that, as by his death he has recalled us to life, so by his presence abiding in us he may raise us to joys eternal; through Jesus Christ your Son . . . .

Source : as no 496
Use : AmerAuthS : Saturday in Easter Week; AusAC : Lent 5

498   Almighty Father, who in your great mercy made glad
the disciples with the sight of the risen Lord : give us
such knowledge of his presence with us, that we may
be strengthened and sustained by his risen life and serve
you continually in righteousness and truth; through
Jesus Christ our Lord.

Source : new; by the Church of England Liturgical Commission
Use : ASB : Easter 1

---

499   Almighty and eternal God, the strength of those who
believe and the hope of those who doubt, may we, who
have not seen, have faith and receive the fullness of
Christ's blessing, who is alive . . . .

Source : new
Use : CanBAS : Second Sunday of Easter

---

500   Merciful Father, you gave Jesus Christ to be for us the
bread of life, that those who come to him should never
hunger. Draw us to our Lord in faith and love, that
we may eat and drink with him, at his table in his kingdom, where he lives . . . .

Source : new
Use : IrAPB : Easter 1

---

501   God of peace,
    by the blood of the eternal covenant
    you brought again from the dead our Lord Jesus
    the great shepherd of the sheep;
    make us perfect in every good work,
    and work in us that which is pleasing and good;
    through Jesus Christ to whom be glory for ever and ever.

Source : See the discussion of Good Shepherd collects in the Introduction.

Use : NZ : Second Sunday after Easter

---

502   [Can : O] God of peace, who [SA : you] brought again from the dead our Lord Jesus Christ, that [SA and Can : the] great shepherd of the sheep, by the blood of the eternal covenant : make us perfect in every good work to do your will, and work in us that which is well-pleasing in your sight [SA : in all goodness that we may do your will and make us what you would have us be]; through Jesus Christ our Lord.

Source : See the discussion of Good Shepherd collects in the Introduction.

Use : ASB : Easter 2; SAAPB and AusAC : Easter 3; Can-BAS : Fourth Sunday of Easter

---

503   Merciful Father, you gave your Son Jesus Christ to be the good shepherd, and in his love for us to give his life and rise again : Keep us always under his protection, and give us grace to follow in his steps; through Jesus Christ our Lord

Source : See the discussion of Good Shepherd collects in the Introduction.

Use : IrAPB : Easter 2 (Year 2)

---

504   O God, whose Son Jesus is the good shepherd of your people : Grant that when we hear his voice we may know him who calls us each by name, and follow where he leads; who, with you and the Holy Spirit, lives and reigns, one God, for ever and ever.

Source : New; by Massey Shepherd; see the discussion of Good Shepherd collects in the Introduction.

Use : AmerBCP : Fourth Sunday of Easter

---

505   Almighty God, whose Son Jesus Christ is the resurrection and the life of all who put their trust in him : raise
us, we pray, from the death of sin to the life of righteousness; that we may [Aus : inserts 'ever'] seek the
things which are above, where he reigns with you and
the Holy Spirit, one God, now and forever.

Source : 1549 : Funeral Mass; 1662 : Burial Service (See no
276.)
Use : ASB : Easter 3; AusAC : Easter 1

---

506   Almighty God, you raised your Son from death to be
the resurrection and the life for all believers : Raise us
to true life in him that we may seek the things which
are above, where Christ reigns with you and the Holy
Spirit, for ever.

Source : as no 505
Use : IrAPB : Easter 3

---

507   Almighty God, whom truly to know is everlasting life :
Grant us so perfectly to know your Son Jesus Christ
to be the way, the truth, and the life, that we may steadfastly follow his steps in the way that leads to eternal
life; through Jesus Christ your Son our Lord, who lives
and reigns with you and the Holy Spirit, one God, for
ever and ever.

Source : The original of this collect was that provided in 1549
(no 110) for the feast of Saint Philip and Saint James (May
1), which had John 14 as the gospel. There is a JLG version
(no. 278).
Use : AmerBCP : Fifth Sunday of Easter

508   Almighty Father, whom truly to know is eternal life :
       teach us to know your Son Jesus Christ as the way, the
       truth, and the life; that, following in the steps of your
       apostles Philip and James, we may walk in the way that
       leads to eternal life; through our Saviour Jesus Christ.

Use : NZ : Saint Philip and Saint James, Apostles

ASB changes the petition.

> . . . that we may follow the steps of your holy apostles
> Philip and James, and walk steadfastly in the way that
> leads to your glory; through Jesus Christ our Lord.

Source : 1662
Use : ASB : Saint Philip and Saint James, Apostles

---

509   Eternal God, whose [SA : your] Son Jesus Christ is for
       all mankind [SA : omits 'for all mankind'] the way, the
       truth, and the life : grant us to [SA : grant that we may]
       walk in his way, to [SA : omits 'to'] rejoice in his truth,
       and to [SA : omits 'to'] share his risen life; who is alive
       . . . .

Source : new; prepared by the Church of England Liturgical
Commission
Use : ASB and IrAPB : Ninth Sunday before Easter; SAAPB :
Eighteenth Sunday

---

510   Living Father, who has given thine only Son to be the
       Way, the Truth, and the Life : grant that in him we
       may faithfully seek thee, joyfully find thee and for ever
       possess thee, God blessed for ever.

Source : no 509
Use : WalesBCP : Third Sunday after Easter

---

511   Almighty God, you have given us your Son Jesus Christ
      to be the way, the truth and the life : Help us in faith
      to follow him as your apostles did, and bring us to eter-
      nal life; through Jesus Christ our Lord.

Source : no 509
Use : IrAPB : Easter 4

---

512   Almighty God, your Son Jesus Christ is the way, the
      truth, and the life. Give us grace to love one another
      and walk in the way of his commandments, who lives
      and reigns with you and the Holy Spirit, one God, now
      and for ever.

Source : no 509
Use : CanBAS : Fifth Sunday of Easter

---

513   Eternal God, your [AusAC : whose] Son Jesus Christ
      is the way, the truth and the life for all creation; grant
      us grace to walk in his way, to rejoice in his truth, and
      to share his risen life; who lives and reigns with you
      and the Holy Spirit, one God now and for ever.

Source : no 509
Use : NZ : Fourth Sunday after Easter; AusAC : Sunday after
the Ascension

---

514   Sovereign Lord and Father through the death and resur-
      rection of your Son all creation is renewed and by faith
      we are born again : make us grow up into him and bring
      us to the fulness of Christ; who is alive and reigns . . . .

Source : new
Use : SAAPB : Fourth Sunday after Easter

---

515   O [Can : Merciful] God, you have prepared for those
      who love you such good things as surpass [ASB : pass]

our understanding [Can : riches beyond imagination] :
Pour into our hearts such love towards you, that we,
loving you in all things and [ASB and Can : omit 'in
all things and'] above all things, may obtain your
promises, which exceed all that we can desire; through
Jesus Christ our Lord, who lives and reigns with you
and the Holy Spirit, one God, for ever and ever.

Source : 1662 : Trinity 6 (no 78)
Use : AmerBCP and CanBAS : Sixth Sunday of Easter; ASB
and IrAPB : Last Sunday after Pentecost

---

516   Eternal Father your kingdom extends beyond space and
time : grant that in this world of changing things we
may hold fast to what endures for ever; through Jesus
Christ our Lord.

Source : SAMC (no 280)
Use : SAAPB : Fifth Sunday after Easter [first collect]

---

517   Loving Father, all that is good comes from you : give
us your humble servants your inspiration, that we may
be holy in thought and deed; through Jesus Christ our
Lord.

Source : new
Use : SAAPB : Fifth Sunday after Easter [second collect]

---

518   Lord Jesus Christ, you returned to the glory of your
Father, and sent the Holy Spirit to be with us for ever.
May we, knowing his presence and power, be led into
the way of truth and come to the glory of your kingdom; where you live and reign . . . .

Source : new
Use : IrAPB : Easter 5

---

519   Eternal Father your Son ascended far above the heavens
and holds all authority in this world and the next : grant
us the faith to know that he lives in his Church on earth
and at the end of time the whole world will see his glory;
who lives and reigns . . . .

Source : JLG (no 282); see no 520.
Use : SAAPB : Ascension Eve

---

520   Almighty God, whose blessed Son our Savior Jesus
Christ ascended far above all heavens that he might fill
all things : Mercifully give us faith to perceive that, according to his promises, he abides with his Church on
earth, even to the end of the ages; through Jesus Christ
our Lord, who lives and reigns with you and the Holy
Spirit, one God, in glory everlasting.

Source : 1929Scot : Ascensiontide post-communion
Use : AmerBCP : Ascension Day (cp ASB : Pentecost 21 [no
524])

---

521   Grant, we pray, Almighty God, that as we believe your
only-begotten Son our Lord Jesus Christ [Aus : omits
'our Lord Jesus Christ'] to have ascended into heaven,
so we may also in heart and mind there ascend, and
with him continually dwell; who lives and reigns with
you and the Holy Spirit, one God, for ever and ever.

Source : 1662 (no 65)
Use : AmerBCP : Ascension Day; SA : Ascension Day [second
collect]; AusAC [first collect]

---

522   Almighty God, as we believe your only-begotten Son
our Lord Jesus Christ to have ascended into the heavens,
so may we also [Ir : heavens : Grant that we] in heart
and mind thither [Ir : also] ascend and with him continually dwell; who is alive . . . .

Source : as no 521
Use : ASB and IrAPB : Ascension Day

---

523   Almighty God, your Son Jesus Christ ascended to the
      throne of heaven that he might rule over all things as
      Lord. Keep the Church in the unity of the Spirit and
      in the bond of his peace, and bring the whole of crea-
      tion to worship at his feet, who is alive and reigns . . . .

Source : See no 524.
Use : CanBAS : Ascension Day

---

524   Eternal Father [Aus : Eternal God], whose Son Jesus
      Christ ascended to the throne of heaven that he might
      rule over all things as Lord : keep the Church in the
      unity of the Spirit and in the bond of [Aus : inserts 'his']
      peace, and bring the whole created order to worship at
      his feet; who is alive . . . .

Source : SAMC : Ascension Day (no 281); JLG : Easter 6 (no
282)
Use : ASB and IrAPB : Pentecost 21; AusAC : Ascension Day

---

525   Sovereign Lord your Son ascended in triumph to rule
      in love and glory over the whole universe : grant that
      all peoples may acknowledge the authority of his king-
      dom; through . . . .

Source : as no 524
Use : SAAPB : Ascension Day [first collect]

---

526   God our Father, make us joyful in the ascension of your
      Son Jesus Christ. May we follow him into the new cre-
      ation, for his ascension is our glory and our hope. We
      ask this through our Lord Jesus Christ . . . .

Source : Roman Sacramentary, ICEL translation
Use : AusPB : Ascension Day [second collect]

---

527   O God [ASB and Ir : Eternal God], the King of glory,
you have exalted your only Son Jesus Christ [ASB and
Ir : omit 'Jesus Christ'] with [Ir : in] great triumph to
your kingdom in heaven : Do not leave us [ASB and
Ir : Leave us not] comfortless [SA : desolate], but send
us [ASB and Ir : omit 'us'] your Holy Spirit to
strengthen us, and exalt us to that place where our Savior Christ has gone before [ASB and Ir : to the place
where Christ is gone before, and where with you and
the Holy Spirit he is worshipped and glorified now and
for ever]; who lives and reigns with you and the Holy
Spirit, one God in glory everlasting.

Source : The original, to which AmerBCP adheres very closely,
is 1662 (no 66).
Use : AmerBCP : Seventh Sunday after Easter : Sunday after
Ascension Day; ASB : Sunday after Ascension Day; SA :
Easter 6 [second collect]

---

528   Eternal God, the king of glory, you have exalted your
only Son with great triumph to be Lord of all; leave
us not comfortless but send your Holy Spirit to
strengthen us that we may labour for the coming of your
kingdom; through Jesus Christ our Lord, who lives and
reigns with you and the Spirit, one God now and for
ever.

Source : as no 527
Use : NZ : Sunday after Ascension Day [first collect]

---

529   Almighty God, you have exalted your only Son Jesus
Christ with great triumph to your kingdom in heaven.
Mercifully give us faith to know that, as he promised,

he abides with us on earth to the end of time; who is
alive . . . .

Source : See no 520.
Use : CanBAS : Seventh Sunday of Easter

530 Eternal Father through Jesus Christ our ascended Lord
you sent your Holy Spirit to be the bond of fellowship
in the Church : unify the whole created order in Christ
who reigns supreme over all things with you . . . .

Source : no 281
Use : SAAPB : Sixth Sunday after Easter [first collect]

531 God our Father when your Son ascended into heaven
he promised to send us the Holy Spirit : grant that we,
who have not been left as orphans may abide always
in that Spirit and be loving and obedient disciples of
your Son; who lives . . . .

Source : new
Use : SAAPB : Pentecost Eve

532 Almighty God, on this day you opened the way of eternal life to every race and nation by the promised gift
of your Holy Spirit : Shed abroad this gift throughout
the world by the preaching of the Gospel, that it may
reach to the ends of the earth; through Jesus Christ our
Lord, who lives and reigns with you, in the unity of
the Holy Spirit, one God, for ever and ever.

Source : new
Use : AmerBCP : Day of Pentecost : Whitsunday

533 O God, who on this day [ASB : as at this time] taught
the hearts of your faithful people by sending to them
the light of your Holy Spirit : Grant us by the same

Spirit to have a right judgment in all things, and evermore to rejoice in his holy comfort; through Jesus Christ
your Son our Lord, who lives and reigns with you, in
the unity of the Holy Spirit, one God, for ever and ever
[ASB : through the merits of Christ Jesus our Saviour
(SA : Jesus Christ our Saviour), who is alive and reigns
with you in the unity of the Spirit, one God, now and
for ever].

Source : 1662 (no 67)
Use : AmerBCP and ASB : Day of Pentecost : Whitsunday
(Whit Sunday); SAAPB : Day of Pentecost [second collect]

---

534   Almighty God, at this time you taught the hearts of your
faithful people by sending to them the light of your Holy
Spirit : Guide us by the same Spirit to have a right judgment in all things, and evermore to rejoice in his holy
comfort; through Jesus Christ our Saviour, who lives
and reigns . . . .

Source : as no 533
Use : IrAPB : Pentecost [first collect]

---

535   Almighty God, you kindled this day the light of your
Spirit in the hearts of your faithful people; may we by
the same Spirit have a right judgment in all things, and
evermore rejoice in your love and power; through Jesus
Christ our Saviour, who lives and reigns with you and
the Holy Spirit, one God now and for ever.

Source : new
Use : NZ : Day of Pentecost : Whitsunday [second collect]

---

536   Almighty God, who on the day of Pentecost sent the
Holy Spirit to the disciples, filling them with joy and
with boldness to preach the Gospel : Send us out in the
power of the same Spirit to witness to your truth, and

to draw all men to the fire of your love; through Jesus Christ our Lord.

Source : New; see no 538.
Use : IrAPB : Day of Pentecost [second collect]

---

537 Almighty God, on the day of Pentecost you sent your Holy Spirit to the disciples with the wind from heaven and in tongues of flame : inspire our hearts and set them on fire with his joy and power and send us out as witnesses to the wonder of your love; through Jesus Christ our Lord who lives . . . .

Source : new
Use : SAAPB : Pentecost [first collect]

---

538 Almighty God, who on the day of Pentecost sent your Holy Spirit to the disciples with the wind from heaven and in [Aus : with] tongues of flame, filling them with joy and boldness to preach the Gospel : send us out in the power of the same Spirit to witness to your truth and to draw all men [Aus : mankind] to the fire of your love; through Jesus Christ our Lord.

Source : new; composed by the Church of England Liturgical Commission
Use : ASB : Pentecost [second collect]; AusAC : Pentecost

---

539 Almighty and everliving God, who fulfilled the promises of Easter by sending us your Holy Spirit and opening to every race and nation the way of life eternal, keep us in the unity of your Spirit, that every tongue may tell of your glory; through Jesus Christ our Lord, who lives . . . .

Source : new; based on no 532
Use : CanBAS : Pentecost

Trinity Sunday

540   Almighty and everlasting God, you have given to us
your servants grace, by the confession of a true faith,
to acknowledge the glory of the eternal Trinity, and in
the power of your [ASB : the] divine Majesty to worship the Unity : Keep us steadfast in this faith and worship, and bring us at last to see you in your one and
eternal glory, O Father; who with the Son and the Holy
Spirit live and reign, one God, for ever and ever.

ASB concludes 'in this faith, that we may evermore be
defended from all adversities; through Jesus Christ our Lord,
who is alive and reigns with you and the Holy Spirit, one God,
now and for ever'.

Source : a revised version of 1549/1662 (no 71)
Use : AmerBCP and ASB : First Sunday after Pentecost :
Trinity Sunday; SAAPB : Trinity Sunday (second collect)

---

541   Almighty and eternal God, you have revealed yourself
as Father, Son, and Holy Spirit, and live and reign in
the perfect unity of love. Hold us firm in this faith, that
we may know you in all your ways and evermore rejoice in your eternal glory, who are three Persons in
one God, now and for ever.

Source : CSI (no 209)
Use : ASB : Trinity Sunday [second collect]; AusAC, IrAPB :
Trinity Sunday

---

542   Father, we praise you : through your Word and Holy
Spirit you created all things. You reveal your salvation
in all the world by sending to us Jesus Christ, the Word
made flesh. Through your Holy Spirit you give us a
share in your life and love. Fill us with the vision of
your glory, that we may always serve and praise you,
Father, Son, and Holy Spirit, one God, for ever and
ever.

Source : There are similarities with the Roman Sacramentary, ICEL translation, alternative collect for Most Holy Trinity.
Use : CanBAS : Trinity Sunday

---

543   Remember, O Lord, what you have wrought in us and not what we deserve; and, as you have called us to your service, make us worthy of our calling; through Jesus Christ our Lord, who lives and reigns with you and the Holy Spirit, one God, now and for ever.

Source : Translated by Armitage Robinson from the Leonine Sacramentary (no 976); this prayer was included among the Occasional Prayers in 1928Eng (no 210).
Use : AmerBCP : Proper 1; AusAC : Ash Wednesday

---

544   Almighty and merciful God, in your goodness keep us, we pray, from all things that may hurt us, that we, being ready both in mind and body, may accomplish with free hearts those things which belong to your purpose; through Jesus Christ your Son our Lord, who lives and reigns with you and the Holy Spirit, one God, for ever and ever.

Source : 1662 : Trinity 20 (nos 94/95)
Use : AmerBCP : Proper 2

---

545   Grant, O Lord, that the course of this world may be peaceably governed by your providence; and that your Church may joyfully serve you in confidence and serenity; through Jesus Christ our Lord, who lives and reigns with you and the Holy Spirit, one God, for ever and ever.

Source : 1662 : Trinity 5 (no 77)
Use : AmerBCP : Proper 3

---

546   O God, your never-failing providence sets in order all
       things both in heaven and earth : Put away from us,
       we entreat you, all hurtful things, and give us those
       things which are profitable for us; through Jesus Christ
       our Lord, who lives and reigns with you and the Holy
       Spirit, one God, for ever and ever.

Source : 1662 : Trinity 8 (no 80)
Use : AmerBCP : Proper 4

547   O God, from whom all good proceeds : Grant that by
       your inspiration we may think those things that are
       right, and by your merciful guiding may do them;
       through Jesus Christ our Lord, who lives and reigns
       with you and the Holy Spirit, one God, for ever and
       ever.

Source : 1662 : Easter 5 (no 64)
Use : AmerBCP : Proper 5

548   Keep, O Lord, your household the Church in your
       steadfast faith and love, that through your grace we may
       proclaim your truth with boldness, and minister your
       justice with compassion; for the sake of our Savior Jesus
       Christ, who lives and reigns with you and the Holy
       Spirit, one God, now and for ever.

Source : new, but see nos 27, 73/74, 97.
Use : AmerBCP : Proper 6

549   O Lord, make us have perpetual love and reverence
       for your holy Name, for you never fail to help and gov-
       ern those whom you have set upon the sure foundation
       of your loving kindness; through Jesus Christ our Lord,
       who lives and reigns with you and the Holy Spirit, one
       God, for ever and ever.

Source : 1549/1662 : Trinity 2 (nos 73/74)
Use : AmerBCP : Proper 7

---

550   Almighty God, you have built your Church upon the foundation of the apostles and prophets, Jesus Christ himself being the chief cornerstone : Grant us so to be joined together [Can : Join us together] in unity of spirit by their teaching, that we may be made [Can : become] a holy temple acceptable to you; through Jesus Christ our Lord, who lives and reigns with you and the Holy Spirit, one God, for ever and ever.

Source : 1549/1662 : Simon and Jude (no 122)
Use : AmerBCP : Proper 8; CanBAS : Proper 27. Proper 8 is for use on the Sunday closest to 29 June, the feast of Saints Peter and Paul, and so it picks up from the feast the theme of the apostles.

---

551   O God, you have taught us to keep all your commandments by loving you and our neighbor : Grant us the grace of your Holy Spirit, that we may be devoted to you with our whole heart, and united to one another with pure affection; through Jesus Christ our Lord, who lives and reigns with you and the Holy Spirit, one God, for ever and ever.

Use : AmerBCP : Proper 9

552   Heavenly Father, you have taught us that in loving you and our fellow men we keep your commandments : Give us the spirit of grace and peace that we, united to one another in brotherly love, may serve you with our whole heart; through Jesus Christ our Lord.

Use : IrAPB : Pentecost 16

553   Almighty God [SA : Merciful Lord], you have taught us through your Son that love is the fulfilling of the law.

Grant that we may love you with our whole heart and our neighbours as ourselves; through Jesus Christ our Lord.

Use : ASB : Pentecost 16; AusAC and SAAPB : Seventh Sunday

554　Almighty God, you have taught us through your Son that love fulfils the law. May we love you with all our heart, all our soul, all our mind, and all our strength, and may we love our neighbour as ourselves; through Jesus Christ our Lord . . . .

Source : The common source for nos 551–54 is a prayer for one of the September Masses in the Leonine Sacramentary (971). It was translated by Bright (*Ancient Collects* 77) and by Frank Colquhoun (*Parish Prayers,* no 1555). Another version was provided by Huxtable, et al., in *A Book of Public Worship* and this appears in JLG and CECal (Fourteenth Sunday after Pentecost [no 297]). SAMC provided another version of it (no 298). The various versions provide an interesting illustration of the possibilities for developing a collect. At one AmerBCP follows Bright's version fairly closely and is loyal to the Leonine text; at the other, CanBAS keeps the basic theme whilst following and paraphrasing the Lord's summary of the law rather than the Leonine collect.
Use : CanBAS : Proper 13

555　O Lord, mercifully receive the prayers of your people who call upon you, and grant that they may know and understand what things they ought to do, and also may have grace and power faithfully to accomplish them; through Jesus Christ our Lord, who lives and reigns with you and the Holy Spirit, one God, now and for ever.

Source : 1549/1662 : First Sunday after Epiphany (no 22)
Use : AmerBCP : Proper 10

---

556 Almighty God, the fountain of all wisdom, you know our necessities before we ask and our ignorance in asking : Have compassion on our weakness, and mercifully give us those things which for our unworthiness we dare not, and for our blindness we cannot ask; through the worthiness of your Son Jesus Christ our Lord, who lives and reigns with you and the Holy Spirit, one God, now and for ever.

Source : new in 1549; 1549/1662 : Prayers 'when there is no communion'
Use : AmerBCP : Proper 11

---

557 O God [ASB : Lord God], the protector of all who trust in you, without whom nothing is strong, nothing is holy : Increase and multiply upon us your mercy; that, with you as [ASB : you being] our ruler and guide, we may so pass through things temporal, that we [ASB : inserts 'finally'] lose not the things eternal; through Jesus Christ our Lord, who lives and reigns with you and the Holy Spirit, one God, for ever and ever.

Source : 1662 : Trinity 4 (no 76)
Use : AmerBCP : Proper 12; Can : Proper 17; ASB : Pentecost 14

---

558 Let your continual mercy, O Lord, cleanse and defend your Church; and, because it cannot continue in safety without your help, protect and govern it always by your goodness; through Jesus Christ our Lord, who lives and reigns with you and the Holy Spirit, one God, for ever and ever.

Source : 1662 : Trinity 16 (no 89)
Use : AmerBCP : Proper 13

---

559   Grant to us, Lord, we pray, the spirit to think and do always those things that are right, that we, who cannot exist without you, may by you be enabled to live according to your will; through Jesus Christ our Lord, who lives and reigns with you and the Holy Spirit, one God, for ever and ever.

Source : 1662 : Trinity 9 (no 81)
Use : AmerBCP : Proper 14; see also no 393.

The Canadian book has another version of this which is closer to that of 1662, and there is a South African one as well.

560   Almighty God, grant us [SA : Grant to us, Lord] the Spirit [SA : spirit] to think and do always those things that are [SA : what is] right, [SA : inserts 'so'] that we who can do nothing [SA : cannot do anything] good without you, may [SA : inserts 'be enabled to'] live according to your holy [SA : omits 'holy'] will; through Jesus Christ our Lord . . . .

Use : CanBAS : Proper 8; SAAPB : Fifth Sunday

---

561   Almighty God, you have given your only Son to be for us a sacrifice for sin, and also an example of godly life : Give us grace to receive thankfully the fruits of his redeeming work, and to follow daily in the blessed steps of his most holy life; through Jesus Christ our Lord, who lives and reigns with you and the Holy Spirit, one God, for ever and ever.

Source : 1549/1662 : Easter 2 (no 61)
Use : AmerBCP : Proper 15

---

562   Almighty Father, you have given your only Son to be for us a sacrifice for sin and an example of godly life : give us grace that we may always thankfully receive the immeasurable benefit of his sacrifice, and also daily en-

deavour to follow his holy life; through Jesus Christ our Lord.

Source : as no 561, by way of no 285
Use : SAAPB : Easter 3 [second collect]

---

563   Grant, O merciful God, that your Church, being gathered together in unity by your Holy Spirit, may show forth your power among all peoples, to the glory of your Name; through Jesus Christ our Lord, who lives and reigns with you and the Holy Spirit, one God, for ever and ever.

Source : 1928Amer : Tuesday in Whitsunday Week (no 70)
Use : AmerBCP : Proper 16; CanBAS : Proper 26

---

564   Lord of all power and might, the [Can : omits everything before 'Author'] author and giver of all good things : Graft in our hearts the love of your Name; increase in us true religion; nourish us with [Can : in] all goodness; and bring forth in us the fruit of good works [ASB and Can, following 1662 : and of your great mercy keep us in the same]; through Jesus Christ our Lord, who lives and reigns with you and the Holy Spirit, one God, for ever and ever.

Source : 1662 : Trinity 7 (no 79)
Use : AmerBCP : Proper 17; ASB and IrAPB : Pentecost 17;
CanBAS : Proper 22

---

565   Grant us, O Lord, to trust in you with all our hearts; for, as you always resist the proud who confide in their own strength, so you never forsake those who make their boast of your mercy; through Jesus Christ our Lord, who lives and reigns with you and the Holy Spirit, one God, now and for ever.

Source : Leo (540); translated by Bright 74
Use : AmerBCP : Proper 18

---

566   O God, because without you we are not able to please
you [ASB and Can : Almighty God, without you we
are not able to please you. Mercifully . . .], mercifully grant that your Holy Spirit may in all things direct
and rule our hearts; through Jesus Christ our Lord, who
lives and reigns with you and the Holy Spirit, one God,
now and for ever.

Source : 1662 : Trinity 19 (no 93)
Use : AmerBCP : Proper 19; ASB and IrAPB : Pentecost 6;
CanBAS : Proper 11

---

567   Grant us, Lord, not to be anxious about earthly things,
but to love things heavenly; and even now, while we
are placed among things that are passing away, to hold
fast to those that shall endure; through Jesus Christ our
Lord, who lives and reigns with you and the Holy Spirit,
one God, for ever and ever.

Source : Leo (173); translated by Bright 79
Use : AmerBCP : Proper 20; AusAC : Twelfth Sunday

---

568   O God, you declare your almighty power chiefly in
showing mercy and pity : Grant us the fullness of your
grace, that we, running to obtain your promises, may
become partakers of your heavenly treasure; through
Jesus Christ our Lord, who lives and reigns with you
and the Holy Spirit, one God, for ever and ever.

Source : 1549/1662 : Trinity 11 (nos 83/84)
Use : AmerBCP : Proper 21

---

569   Almighty and everlasting God, you are always more
ready to hear than we to pray, and to give more than

we either desire or deserve : Pour upon us the abundance of your mercy, forgiving us those things of which our conscience is afraid, and giving us those good things for [ASB : omits 'for'] which we are not worthy to ask, except [ASB : save] through the merits and mediation of Jesus Christ our Savior; who lives and reigns with you and the Holy Spirit, one God, for ever and ever.

Source : 1662 : Trinity 12 (no 85)
Use : AmerBCP : Proper 22; ASB : Easter 5

---

570   Lord, we pray that your grace may always precede and follow us, that we may continually be given to good works; through Jesus Christ our Lord, who lives and reigns with you and the Holy Spirit, one God, for ever and ever.

Source : 1662 : Trinity 17 (no 90)
Use : AmerBCP : Proper 23

---

571   Almighty and everlasting God, in Christ you have revealed your glory among the nations : Preserve the works of your mercy, that your Church throughout the world may persevere with steadfast faith in the confession of your Name; through Jesus Christ our Lord, who lives and reigns with you and the Holy Spirit, one God, for ever and ever.

Source : Gel (401), Mis. Gallican. vetus (95), Greg (339), SM : Good Friday solemn collects; translated in Bright (98)
Use : AmerBCP : Proper 24

---

572   Almighty and everlasting God, increase in us the gifts of faith, hope, and charity; and, that we may obtain what you promise, make us love what you command; through Jesus Christ our Lord, who lives and reigns with you and the Holy Spirit, one God, for ever and ever.

Source : 1662 : Trinity 14 (no 87)
Use : AmerBCP : Proper 25

---

573   Almighty and merciful God, it is only by your gift that your faithful people offer you true and laudable service : Grant that we may run without stumbling to obtain your heavenly promises; through Jesus Christ our Lord, who lives and reigns with you and the Holy Spirit, one God, now and for ever.

Source : 1662 : Trinity 13 (no 86)
Use : AmerBCP : Proper 26

---

574   Almighty and everlasting God, whose will it is to restore all things in your well-beloved Son, the King of kings and Lord of lords [Can : our Lord and King] : Mercifully [Can : omits 'Mercifully'] grant that the peoples of the earth, [Can : inserts 'now'] divided and enslaved by sin, may be freed and brought together under his most gracious [Can : omits 'most gracious'; inserts 'gentle and loving'] rule; who lives and reigns with you and the Holy Spirit, one God, now and for ever.

Source : translation by Howard Galley from the pre-Vatican II Roman Missal collect for the feast of Christ the King, introduced by Pius XI in 1925; see no 302.
Use : AmerBCP : Proper 29; CanBAS : Proper 34

---

575   Almighty God, whose will is to restore all things in your beloved Son, the king of all : govern the hearts and minds of those in authority, and bring the families of the nations, divided and torn apart by the ravages of sin, to be subject to his just and gentle rule ; who is alive and reigns with you and the Holy Spirit, one God, now and for ever.

Source : as no 574
Use : ASB : Pentecost 15; AusAC : Thirty-Fourth Sunday

---

576 Lord God our Father, through our Saviour Jesus Christ
you have assured mankind of eternal life and in baptism have made us one with him. Deliver us from the
death of sin and raise us to new life in your love, in
the fellowship of the Holy Spirit, by the grace of our
Lord Jesus Christ.

Source : New; see SAMC : Pentecost 3 (no 284) and collects
for Easter Eve and Baptism/Confirmation.
Use : ASB and IrAPB : Pentecost 3

---

577 Almighty God [SA : Father], you have broken the
tyranny of sin and have [SA : omits 'have'] sent the Spirit
of your Son into our hearts whereby we call you Father. Give us grace to dedicate our freedom to your service, that all mankind may be brought to the glorious
liberty of the sons of God; through Jesus Christ our
Lord.

SA omits 'whereby we call you Father' after 'hearts' and continues 'take and receive our freedom and bring us into the
glorious liberty of the children of God'.

Source : a new collect by the Church of England Liturgical
Commission. An inclusive version appears in the Canadian
liturgy (no 578 below).
Use : ASB : Pentecost 4; AusAC and SAAPB : Fifteenth
Sunday

578 Almighty God, you have broken the tyranny of sin and
sent into our hearts the Spirit of your Son. Give us grace
to dedicate our freedom to your service, that all people
may know the glorious liberty of the children of God;
through Jesus Christ our Lord . . . .

Source : new
Use : CanBAS : Proper 20

---

579   Almighty God, you show to those who are in error the
light of your truth, that they may return to the way of
righteousness. May we and all who have been admitted to the fellowship of Christ's religion reject those
things which are contrary to our profession and follow
all such things as are agreeable to the same; through
Jesus Christ our Lord.

Source : 1662 : Easter 3 (no 62)
Use : ASB : Pentecost 5

---

580   Almighty God, who [Aus and Can : you] sent [Aus :
send] your Holy Spirit to be the life and light of your
Church [Aus : all your people] : open our hearts to the
riches of his grace, that we may bring forth the fruit
of the Spirit in love and joy and peace [Can : in love,
joy, and peace]; through Jesus Christ our Lord.

Source : new; Jasper-Bradshaw sees Gal 5:16-22 and the Whitsunday Post-Communion of 1929Scot as sources; see no 289
Use : ASB : Pentecost 8; CanBAS : Proper 19; AusAC : Easter
5

---

581   Almighty God [SA : Father of justice and love], who
called [Can and SA : you call] your Church to witness
that you were [SA : are] in Christ reconciling men [SA :
the world] to yourself [Can : that in Christ we are reconciled to you] : help us so [SA : omits 'so'] to proclaim
[SA : inserts 'boldly'] the good news of your love, that
all who hear it may be reconciled [Can : turn] to you
[SA : inserts 'and work together for peace and justice'];
through him who died for us and rose again and reigns
with you and the Holy Spirit, one God, now and for
ever.

Source : new
Use : ASB : Pentecost 12; CanBAS : Proper 24; SAAPB : Eleventh Sunday

---

582   Almighty God, you have made us for yourself and our hearts are restless till they find their rest in you. Teach us to offer ourselves to your service, that here we may have your peace, and in the world to come may see you face to face; through Jesus Christ our Lord.

Source : new; (1) Augustine's *Confessions;* (2) Matt 5:8; (3) 1 Cor 13:12
Use : ASB : Pentecost 18; AusAC : Seventeenth Sunday

---

583   Almighty God, you have made us for yourself, and our hearts are restless until they find their rest in you. May we find peace in your service, and in the world to come, see you face to face; through Jesus Christ our Lord . . . .

Source : no 583
Use : CanBAS : Proper 15

---

584   Almighty and everlasting [Aus and Can : everliving] God, increase in us your gift of faith; that, forsaking what lies behind and reaching out to that which [Can : omits 'that which'; inserts 'what'] is before, we may run the way of your commandments and win the crown of everlasting joy; through Jesus Christ our Lord.

Source : new; (1) Phil 3:13, Heb 12:1, 1 Cor 9:24-25; (2) 1549/1662 : Trinity 11 (nos 83/84)
Use : ASB and IrAPB : Pentecost 19; AusAC : Ninth Ordinary Sunday; CanBAS : Proper 29

---

585   Almighty God, your Son has opened for us a new and living way into your presence. Give us pure hearts and

constant [ASB : steadfast] wills to worship you in spirit and in truth; through Jesus Christ our Lord . . . .

Source : new; (1) Heb 10:19-23; (2) John 4:24
Use : ASB : Pentecost 20; AusAC : Twenty-Eighth Ordinary Sunday; CanBAS : Proper 16

---

586   Lord God of the nations, you have revealed your will to all people and promised us your saving help. May we hear and do what you command, that the darkness may be overcome by the power of your light; through your Son Jesus Christ our Lord . . . .

Source : new
Use : CanBAS : Ninth Sunday after Epiphany : Proper 9

---

587   O God, you have assured the human family of eternal life through Jesus Christ our Saviour. Deliver us from the death of sin and raise us to new life in him, who lives and reigns . . . .

Source : nos 284, 576
Use : CanBAS : Proper 10

---

588   O God our defender, storms rage about us and cause us to be afraid. Rescue your people from despair, deliver your sons and daughters from fear, and preserve us all from unbelief; through your Son, Jesus Christ our Lord . . . .

Source : new
Use : CanBAS : Proper 12

---

589   Almighty God, your Son Jesus Christ fed the hungry with the bread of his life and the word of his kingdom. Renew your people with your heavenly grace, and in all our weakness sustain us by your true and living bread, who lives and reigns . . . .

Source : new; second line from no 388
Use : CanBAS : Proper 18

590 Almighty God, in our baptism you adopted us for your
own. Quicken, we pray, your Spirit within us, that we,
being renewed in body and mind, may worship you in
sincerity and truth; through Jesus Christ our Lord
. . . .

Source : nos 483/484
Use : CanBAS : Proper 28

591 Almighty God, you sent your Son Jesus Christ to be
the light of the world. Free us from all that darkens and
ensnares us, and bring us to eternal light and joy;
through the power of him who is alive . . . .

Source : new, from fragments; cp no 424
Use : CanBAS : Proper 33

592 Almighty God, you have [Ir : omits 'have'] [Aus : who]
created the heavens and the earth and made man [Can :
omits 'made man'; inserts 'ourselves'] [Aus : inserts
'and woman'] in your own [Can : omits 'own'] image.
Teach us to discern your hand in all your works, and
to serve you with reverence and thanksgiving; through
Jesus Christ our Lord, who with you and the Holy Spirit
reigns supreme over all things, now and for ever.

Source : new; preamble from CSI : Ninth Sunday before Easter
(no 196); see also SAMC (no 228)
Use : ASB and IrAPB : Ninth Sunday before Christmas;
CanBAS : Proper 25; SAAPB : Nineteenth Sunday (1);
AusAC : Twenty-Ninth Sunday

593 Almighty God, whose [Ir : your] chosen servant Abraham faithfully [Can : omits 'faithfully'] obeyed your

call and rejoiced [Can : omits 'and rejoiced'; inserts 'rejoicing'] in your promise that, in him, all the families
of the earth should be blessed [Can : that in him the
family of the earth is blessed] [Ir : to bless all the families of the earth in him] : give us a faith like his, that,
in us, your promises may be fulfilled [Ir : Strengthen
our faith, that in us your promise may be fulfilled];
through Jesus Christ our Lord.

Source : new; based on CSI : Pentecost 4 (no 211)
Use : ASB and IrAPB : Seventh Sunday before Christmas;
CanBAS : Proper 31 [standard ending]

---

594   Lord God our redeemer, who heard the cry of your
people and sent your servant Moses to lead them out
of slavery; free us from the tyranny of sin and death
and, by the leading of your Spirit, bring us to our
promised land; through Jesus Christ our Lord.

Source : new; based on CSI : Pentecost 22 (no 224); JLG/
SAMC (nos 235/236)
Use : ASB : Sixth Sunday before Christmas; CanBAS : Proper
30; AusAC : Lent 3

---

595   Lord God, Redeemer of Israel, you sent your servant
Moses to lead your people out of slavery and affliction :
Deliver us from the tyranny of sin and death and bring
us to the promised land, where we may live in perfect
union with you and the Holy Spirit; through Jesus
Christ our Lord.

Source : See no 593
Use : IrAPB : Sixth Sunday before Christmas

---

596   Almighty God, who spoke to the prophets that they
might make your will and purpose known : inspire the
guardians of your truth, that through the faithful wit-

ness of the few the children of earth may be made one with the saints in glory; by the power of Jesus Christ our Lord, who alone redeemed mankind and reigns with you and the Holy Spirit, one God, now and for ever.

Source : adapted from CSI : Advent 2 (no 188)
Use : ASB : Fifth Sunday before Christmas : AusAC : Sixteenth Sunday

---

597   Stir up, O Lord, the wills of your faithful people : that richly bearing the fruit of good works, they [Can : we] may by you be richly rewarded; through Jesus Christ our Lord.

Source : 1662 : Trinity 25 (no 100)
Use : ASB and IrAPB : Fifth Sunday before Christmas [second collect]; also ASB : Pentecost 22; CanBAS : Proper 23

---

598   Almighty God, you have called your people to bear witness to you : Give us grace to obey your commands and keep us truly faithful, that all nations may hear your voice, return to you, and glorify your name; through Jesus Christ our Lord.

Source : new
Use : IrAPB : Fifth Sunday before Christmas [first collect]

---

599   Almighty and eternal God, you have called us to be your people : Bring us to closer unity and fellowship with you and one another so that every member of your Church may serve you in holiness and truth; through our Lord and Saviour Jesus Christ.

Source : final clause from no 468
Use : IrAPB : Pentecost 2

---

600   Father, you have sent the Spirit of your Son into our hearts, and called us to the glorious liberty of your children : Give us grace to use our freedom in your service, and in our lives to follow in the footsteps of our Lord and Master, Jesus Christ, who lives . . . .

Source : See nos 577/578.
Use : IrAPB : Pentecost 4

601   Father, your love reaches out to all mankind, and you have commanded us to follow your Son our Saviour : Give us grace to do your will, and to share in your Church's mission to proclaim the gospel of your love to all the world; through Jesus Christ our Lord.

Source : new
Use : IrAPB : Pentecost 5

602   Almighty God, you call us to your service : Give us strength to put on the armour you provide that we may resist the assaults of the devil, and ever trust in the salvation which you have promised us in Jesus Christ our Lord.

Source : new
Use : IrAPB : Pentecost 9

603   Eternal Father, you gave your apostles grace to believe and to proclaim your word : Grant that your Church may love and preach the word which they believed, and give to all men grace to come to you, the only God; through Jesus Christ our Lord.

Source : 1549/1662 : Saint Bartholomew (nos 115/116)
Use : IrAPB : Pentecost 12

604   Lord God, you are the source of all power and might :
Govern the hearts and minds of those in authority, that
peace and justice may flourish on earth, and your
Church may ever serve you in godliness and joy;
through Jesus Christ our Lord.

Source : as no 574
Use : IrAPB : Pentecost 15

---

605   Almighty God, you gave your Son Jesus Christ to break
the power of evil : Free us from all darkness and temptation, and bring us to eternal light and joy; through
the power of him who lives and reigns . . . .

Source : cp no 591
Use : IrAPB : Pentecost 22

---

606   Merciful Lord, your Son is the resurrection and the life
of all who believe in him : raise us from the death of
sin into the life of righteousness; through Jesus Christ
our Lord.

Source : cp no 587
Use : SAAPB : Easter 2 (1)

---

607   Eternal and infinite God, you have inspired us to acknowledge the glory of the Trinity and in your divine
power to worship the Unity : keep us steadfast in this
faith and unite us in your boundless love; that we may
always praise you Father, Son and Holy Spirit, one
God, now and for ever.

Source : no 71
Use : SAAPB : Trinity Sunday

---

608   Lord God, we can do nothing good without you but
in your strength we can do all things : grant us the spirit

to think and do always whatever is right; through Jesus Christ our Lord.

Source : nos 81, 253; cp no 559
Use : SAAPB : Fifth Sunday of the Year

---

609   Gracious Father, you have taught us that love is the true bond of all virtues and without it anything we do is worthless : send your Holy Spirit and pour this great gift into our hearts; through Jesus Christ our Lord.

Source : nos 31, 288
Use : SAAPB : Eighth Sunday of the Year

---

610   Lord of all wisdom, you have so ordered our life that we walk by faith and not by sight : grant that in the darkness of this world we may witness to our faith by the courage of our lives; through Jesus Christ our Lord.

Source : no 301
Use : SAAPB : Ninth Sunday of the Year

---

611   Heavenly Father, your Son has taught us that in losing life we save it : put to death in us all that keeps us from the life you alone can give; through Jesus Christ our Lord.

Source : new
Use : SAAPB : Tenth Sunday of the Year

---

612   Merciful Lord, you have called us to offer ourselves as a living sacrifice to you : transform us by the renewal of our minds that we may know and do your perfect will; through Jesus Christ our Lord.

Source : new
Use : SAAPB : Twelfth Sunday of the Year

613   Eternal Lord, you spoke to the prophets to make your
      will and purpose known : inspire the guardians of your
      truth that through their witness all people may be made
      one with your saints; through Jesus Christ our Lord.

Source : no 596
Use : SAAPB : Sixteenth Sunday of the Year

---

614   Lord of heaven and earth, you sent your Holy Spirit
      to be the life and power of your Church : sow in our
      hearts the seeds of his grace that we may bring forth
      the fruit of the Spirit in love and joy and peace; through
      Jesus Christ our Lord.

Source : no 289; cp no 580
Use : SAAPB : Seventeenth Sunday of the Year

---

615   God our Saviour, your Son has promised that when two
      or three come together in his name he is there with
      them : open our eyes that we may see him and our hearts
      that we may love him; through Jesus Christ our Lord.

Source : new; based on the Prayer of Chrysostom
Use : SAAPB : Twentieth Sunday of the Year

---

616   Lord God, for the sake of the joy that lay ahead of him
      your Son endured the cross and accepted the shame :
      give us grace to bear our sufferings and bring us to the
      glory that shall be revealed; through Jesus Christ our
      Lord.

Source : no 46
Use : SAAPB : Twenty-First Sunday of the Year

---

617   Gracious Father, your Son Jesus Christ offered him-
      self in humble obedience to free us from our sins : grant
      us grace to receive him with thankfulness as our Saviour
      and Lord and in the freedom of your Spirit to follow

the pattern of his holy life; through Jesus Christ our Lord.

Source : no 285
Use : SAAPB : Twenty-Second Sunday of the Year

---

618   Gracious Father, Christ our Saviour in baptism made us one with him and assured us of eternal life : free us from sin and raise us to new life in him; who lives and reigns . . . .

Source : no 284; another version of no 576
Use : SAAPB : Twenty-Fourth Sunday of the Year

---

619   Heavenly Father, your Son has taught us that anything we do for the least of our neighbours we do for him : open our eyes to the needs of others and give us the will to serve you in them; through Jesus Christ our Lord.

Source : nos 292/293
Use : SAAPB : Twenty-Fifth Sunday of the Year

---

620   God, mighty to save, you have given us the shield of faith and the sword of the Spirit : strengthen us to resist all attacks of the enemy and to fight at your side against the tyranny of evil; through Jesus Christ our Lord.

Source : no 290
Use : SAAPB : Twenty-Sixth Sunday of the Year

---

621   Eternal Father, you gave your only Son Jesus Christ that in him we might have eternal life : reveal in us the greatness of your gift and inspire us to give ourselves to you in thankful service for his sake; who with you . . . .

Source : no 303
Use : SAAPB : Twenty-Seventh Sunday of the Year

---

622   God, the source of all power, your Son prayed that you
would keep his disciples from the evil one : strengthen
us to resist temptation and to follow you the only God;
through Jesus Christ our Lord.

Source : no 261; cp no 417
Use : SAAPB : Twenty-Eighth Sunday of the Year

---

623   Eternal God, in your loving mercy you have planted
within us the seed of faith : grant that it may grow until
we trust you with all our heart; through Jesus Christ
our Lord.

Source : new
Use : SAAPB : Twenty-Ninth Sunday of the Year

---

624   God our Father, your Son came in love to deliver us
and to equip us for eternal life : free us from all that
hinders us from running the race you have set before
us; through Jesus Christ our Lord.

Source : no 7
Use : SAAPB : Thirty-Second Sunday of the Year

---

625   Gracious Lord, your Son came to bring us good news
and power to transform our lives : grant that when he
comes again as judge we may be ready to meet him with
joy; through Jesus Christ our Lord.

Source : new
Use : SAAPB : Thirty-Third Sunday of the Year

---

626   Sovereign Lord, you are restoring all things in your Son
the King of the universe : free the people of the earth

from sin and bring them together under his gracious
rule; who lives . . . .

Source : no 302
Use : SAAPB : Thirty-Fourth Sunday of the Year : Christ
the King

---

627   Grant, Lord, that in all our dealings with one another
we may be subject to you, the Father of all, and follow
the pattern of your Son Jesus Christ, who, in obedience
to your will, gave up his life for us, yet lives and reigns
with you and the Holy Spirit, one God, now and for
ever.

Source : new
Use : AusAC : Sunday after Christmas

---

628   In all our doubts, dangers and perplexities, O Lord,
teach us what we ought to say; that we who can do no
good thing without you may have the power to speak
the truth; through Jesus Christ our Lord.

Source : new
Use : AusAC : Fourth Ordinary Sunday

---

629   O God of the nations of the earth, remember the mul-
titudes created in your image, who do not know the
redeeming work of our Saviour Jesus Christ; and grant
that by the prayers and labours of your holy Church,
they may be delivered from unbelief and brought to worship you; through him who is the resurrection and the
life of all mankind, your Son, Jesus Christ our Lord.

Source : AmerAuthS : For the Mission of the Church (no 14)
(640); it is based on the first of the Occasional Prayers 9, for
Mission, in 1928Eng. Another version of it appears in
AmerBCP : For the Mission of the Church [second collect]
(257). Hatchett describes it as 'a revised form of an occasional

prayer, "For the Spread of the Gospel", of the Indian Prayer
Book supplement' (Hatchett p. 213).
Use : AusAC : Fifth Ordinary Sunday

---

630   Lord God of wisdom and truth, you made yourself
known to the world in your Son Jesus Christ : grant
that we may know him and love him and through him
may share the fulness of eternal life; who now lives and
reigns with you and the Holy Spirit, one God, for ever
and ever.

Source : SAMC : Ninth Sunday before Easter (no 255)
Use : SAAPB : Sixth Sunday of the Year

---

631   Heavenly Father, you have delivered us from the power
of sin and brought us into the kingdom of your Son :
grant that he whose death has recalled us to life may
by his presence among us raise us to eternal joys;
through Jesus Christ our Lord.

Source : nos 496/497
Use : SAAPB : First Sunday after Easter

---

632   God our Father, your Son Jesus Christ lived in a family at Nazareth; Grant that in our families on earth we
may so learn to love and live together that we may rejoice as one family in your heavenly home; through
Jesus Christ our Lord.

Source : as no 361
Use : IrAPB : Pentecost 14

---

633   Grant, Lord, that we who have been redeemed from
our unworthiness and made fit by Christ's sacrifice to
share in his kingdom, may remember what we were and
what we are, and may forgive as we have been forgiven;
through Jesus Christ our Lord.

Source : new
Use : AusAC : Eleventh Ordinary Sunday

---

634   Almighty God, whose beloved Son for our sake willingly endured the agony and shame of the cross : give us courage and patience to take up our cross and follow him; who lives and reigns with you and the Holy Spirit, one God, now and for ever.

Source : AusAC gives AmerAuth S : Holy Cross, as the source. A slightly modified version appears in AmerBCP : Holy Cross (p. 252, no 6), and Hatchett correctly gives Milner-White and Briggs, *Daily Prayer,* 41, as the source (Hatchett p. 209).
Use : AusAC : Thirteenth Ordinary Sunday

---

635   Grant, Lord, that we may see in you the fulfilment of our need and may turn from all false satisfactions to feed on that true and living bread which you have given us in your Son Jesus Christ; who lives and reigns with you and the Holy Spirit, one God, now and for ever.

Source : new
Use : AusAC : Eighteenth Ordinary Sunday

---

636   Merciful Father, whose Son laid down his life that we might die to self and live in him; grant us so perfect a communion with him that in all the doubts and dangers that assail us our faith may not be found wanting; through Jesus Christ our Lord.

Source : new; based on AmerAuthS : Fifth Sunday after Pentecost; possible sources are nos 103 and 203.
Use : AusAC : Nineteenth Ordinary Sunday

---

637   Gracious Father, by whose mercy we are redeemed and made worthy : grant us ever to remember that our righteousness consists not in ourselves but in the merits of

your Son Jesus Christ; who lives and reigns with you and the Holy Spirit, one God, now and for ever.

Source : new
Use : AusAC : Twenty-Fourth Ordinary Sunday

---

638   Almighty Father, whose hand is open to fill all things living with plenteousness : make us ever thankful for your goodness; and grant that we, remembering the account we must one day give, may be faithful stewards of your bounty; through Jesus Christ our Lord.

Source : AmerAuthS : Stewardship of Creation. A version appears in AmerBCP (p. 259), and Hatchett gives the source as a collect in 1928Amer : For Faithfulness in the Use of this World's Goods; the original was apparently a 'Prayer for the Rich' in the Book of Offices proposed to the General Convention in 1889 (Hatchett p. 214).
Use : AusAC : Twenty-Sixth Ordinary Sunday

---

639   Almighty God, who gave your Son Jesus Christ to break the power of evil : free us from all that darkens and ensnares us and bring us to eternal light and joy; through the power of him who lives and reigns with you and the Holy Spirit, one God, now and for ever.

Source : 'Extensive reworking of an unpublished collect from a sub-committee of the Joint Liturgical Group, with line 3 from a collect for Trinity 23 in *Collects with the New Lectionary*, p. 30. As in *Collects, Series 3*, p. 28, Trinity 22' (AusAC p. 51). See nos 591 and 605.
Use : AusAC : Thirty-First Ordinary Sunday

---

640   Father of righteousness, Judge of all, in whose sight no one living can be justified but through the merits of your Son Jesus Christ : give us such confidence in his love toward us that we may lay hold on his gift of salvation,

and be delivered from the burden of our sins; through the same Jesus Christ our Saviour, who lives and reigns with you and the Holy Spirit, one God, now and for ever.

Source : new
Use : AusAC : Thirty-Second Ordinary Sunday

---

641   Almighty God, whose sovereign purpose none can make void : give us faith to be steadfast amid the tumults of this world, knowing that your kingdom shall come and your will be done, to your eternal glory; through Jesus Christ our Lord, who lives and reigns with you and the Holy Spirit, one God, now and for ever.

Source : AmerAuthS : Twenty-Sixth Sunday after Pentecost; the original source is Milner-White and Briggs, *Daily Prayer,* p. 20.
Use : AusAC : Thirty-Third Ordinary Sunday

---

642   Almighty and everliving God, in your tender love for all our human race you sent your Son our Saviour Jesus Christ to take our flesh and suffer death upon a cruel cross. May we follow the example of his great humility, and share in the glory of his resurrection; through Jesus Christ our Lord, who is alive and reigns with you and the Holy Spirit, one God, now and for ever.

Source : 1549/1662 : Palm Sunday (no 44); for modern versions see nos 437–442
Use : CanBAS : Sunday of the Passion (Palm Sunday) at the Eucharist

---

INDEX OF FIRST LINES

INDEX OF KEY WORDS

may be filled with his presence 282; Grant . . .
to thy C. 294; grant . . . unto thy C. 115, 116;
he abides in his C. on earth 520; he lives in his
C. on earth 519; in thy holy C. 51; into thy holy
C. 180; keep the C. in the unity of the Spirit 523,
524; Keep . . . thy C. 88; keep thy C. and household 27; labours of your holy C. 629; life and light
of your C. 580; life and power of your C. 289,
614; manifest in thy C. the like power and love
121; may this light so shine within the C. 485;
members of your holy C. 283; minister in your
C. 318; multiply thy C. 166; pour thy Spirit upon
thy C. 168; quicken the spirit of sonship in your
C. 484; renew your C. 487; sacred ministry of thy
C. 156; share in your C.'s mission 601; stir up in
your C. that Spirit 483; sufferings for the sake of
your C. 296; that your C. may joyfully serve you
545; that your C. may love and preach the word
603; that your C. throughout the world may persevere 571; thy C. being always preserved 107; thy
C. may joyfully serve thee 77; thy holy C. 109;
thy Spirit in the C. 220; thy whole C. in paradise
141; thy/your C. being gathered together 70, 563;
thy/your household the C. 97, 307; unity of thy
C. 173; universal C. 156; whole body of the C.
51, 468; your C. may ever serve you 604; your
household the C. 548; who called your C. to witness 581; worship thee in thy C. 397; zeal for thy
C. 131

circumcised	blessed Son was c. 354; Son to be c. 16
circumcision	by c. in obedience to the Law 355; true c. 16
citizens	c. of Jerusalem 172
city	holy c. 201
clean	pure and c. hearts 106
cleanse	c. and defend thy/your Church 89, 558; c. our consciences 325, 377; c. us from unbelief 214; c. us your faithful people 391
cleansed	c. from all our sins 392; c. from all their sins 96; c. from our sins 252
clouds	no c. of this mortal life 382, 383

comfort   c. all thy servants 200; c. and peace 135; c. of thy
                   grace 36; c. of thy/your holy Word 2; c. us in all
                   our afflictions 69; enlighten, visit and c. 200;
                   heavenly c. 141, 142; Holy Spirit to c. us 66; in
                   his holy c. 67, 533, 534; joy and c. 132

comforted   defended and c. 75

comforter   the C., even the Spirit of Truth 175

comfortless   do not leave us c. 527; leave us not c. 66, 528

coming   at his c. 324; c. again 239, 318; c. of his kingdom
                   351; c. of Jesus Christ 314; c. of the day when all
                   things shall be subject to him 188; c. of the third
                   day 470; c. of thy/your Son 227, 239, 316, 317,
                   318, 321; day of thy c. 226; final c. 189; first c.
                   4, 189; grace of his c. 315; second c. 4

command   fulfil his c. to make disciples 168; hear and do what
                   you c. 586; love that which thou dost c. 87; love
                   what you c. 279, 426, 427, 428, 429, 430, 572;
                   loving all you c. 304

commanded   you have c. us to follow your Son 601

commandest   c. him . . . to feed thy flock 113; love the thing
                   which thou c. 63

commandments   follow thy holy c. 114; fulfil thy holy c. 102; keep
                   all thy/your c. 297, 551; keep your c. 552; keep-
                   ing of thy c. 72; keeping your c. 380; run the way
                   of your c. 584; running the way of thy c. 84; walk
                   in the way of his c. 512; works of thy c. 398

commands   grace to obey your c. 598

commemorate   c. her example 131; c. the Blessed Mary Magda-
                   lene 125; c. the Conception of the Mother of our
                   Lord 144; c. the Nativity of the Mother of the
                   Lord 137; c. the saints of our nation 143

commemoration   c. of that sacrifice 169

communion   live in c. with thee 206; one c. and fellowship 123;
                   so perfect a c. with him 636

compassion   c. on our weakness 556; justice with c. 548; look
                   with c. on the anguish of the world 399

completing   c. his sufferings 296

conception   C. of the Mother of our Lord 144

concern   true c. for our fellow men 298

condemn   even when you must c. 258

crucified	before he was c. 45, 445; c. body 470, 471; c. King 268; faith of Christ c. 185, 469; Son was c. 444
crucify	c. him afresh 42
cry	c. of your people 594
cup	accept the c. 171; c. of blessing 171
custom	receipt of c. 117
daily	d. be renewed 8, 181, 338, 339; d. endeavour ourselves 61; d. endeavour to follow his holy life 562; d. presence 327; d. increase in thy Holy Spirit 187; d. visitation 324; die d. from/unto sin 57, 186, 474, 481; follow d. in the blessed steps 561; take up our cross d. 41, 201
danger	in all trouble and d. 257
dangers	doubts and d. that assail us 636; doubts, d. and perplexities 628; in all d. 75; in all our d. and necessities 24; so many and great d. 25, 26; support us in all our d. 26
darkens	all that d. and ensnares us 591, 639
darkness	called us out of d. 154; cast away the works of d. 1, 237, 309; d. may be overcome 586; d. of our heart 3; d. of our hearts 325; d. of our minds 322; d. of this present time 471; d. of this world 610; delivering us from the power of d. 497; dispel the d. of our sins 424; free us from all d. and temptation 605; from d. to light 197; into our d. 486; lighten the d. 322; to turn away from d. 310
daughters	deliver your sons and d. 588
day	as on this d. 174; coming of the third d. 470; d. of his appearing 140; d. of Pentecost 536, 537, 538; d. of rest 220; d. of the Lord's resurrection 477; d. of thy coming 226; especially this d. 153; last d. 1, 237, 309, 310; on this d. 532; one d. 638; the d. when all things shall be subject to him 188; the first d. of the week 220; this d. 14, 106, 533, 535
days	all our d. 315; all the d. of our life 17, 23, 177, 220, 232; forty d. 33, 260, 403, 405, 407
dead	brought again from the d. 501, 502; counted d. before you 288; d. before thee/you 31, 381; d. to

defence	our d. against all our enemies 35
defend	cleanse and d. thy/your Church 89, 558; d. us from all adversities 71; d. us from all error 69; help and d. us 24, 257; succour and d. us on earth 118
defended	d. against all adversity 30; d. and comforted 75; d. by thy mighty power 27; d. from all adversities 34, 418
delay	without d. 102, 114
delight	d. in working for the fulfilment of your kingdom 248; our d. to do thy will 247
deliver	d. the nations of the world 180; d. them from the power of the devil 417; d. us and equip us for eternal life 624; d. us from the death of sin 576, 587; d. us from the sins 311; d. us from the snares of the enemy 40; d. us from the tyranny of sin and death 595; d. your sons and daughters from fear 588; save and d. mankind 39, 264
delivered	being d. from the disquietude of this world 127; d. and saved mankind 265, 431; d. and saved the world 432; d. and saved us all 433; d. by thy goodness 29; d. from the burden of our sins 640; d. from unbelief 629; d. us from the dominion of sin and death 496; d. us from the power of our enemy 474; d. us from the power of sin 631; speedily d. us 6; speedily help and d. us 7, 319
deny	d. the faith of Christ crucified 469; willing to d. ourselves 422
depart	d. without hurt 133
departed	faithful d. 140, 142
departure	spake . . . of his d. 199
descend	d. in the likeness of fiery tongues 174
desert	fasted forty days in the d. 260, 403; forty nights in the d. 407
deserve	d. to be punished 36; either we desire or d. 85; not what we d. 210, 543; we either desire or d. 569
desire	d. not the death of a sinner 469; d. that which thou dost promise 63; d. what you promise 279, 426, 427, 428, 429, 430; either we d. or deserve 85; exceed all that we can d. 78, 305, 515; hearty d. to pray 75; we either d. or deserve 569

desires	evil d. 472; forsake all covetous d. 117; good d. 56, 479, 480; hearty d. 35; heavenly d. 486
despair	d. with Judas 170; rescue your people from d. 588
destitute	d. of thy manifold gifts 111
destroy	d. evil 231; d. the works of the devil 28, 230, 394, 395
devil	assaults of the d. 602; infections of the d. 91; power of the d. 417; the world, the flesh, and the d. 92, 409, 410; works of the d. 28, 230, 394, 395
devoted	d. to thee/you with our whole heart 297, 551
devotion	outward d. 166; strengthen our d. to him in these holy mysteries 267, 458
devout	d. prayers of the Church 98
devoutly	d. given to serve thee 97
die	d. daily from/to/unto sin 57, 186, 474, 481; d. for our sins 60, 203, 273, 495; d. on the Cross 266; d. to self and live in him 636; d. to sin 473; to suffer and to d. for man 296; to suffer or to d. with him 268
died	d. for our sake 38; d. for us 462, 463; d. on the cross 443
digest	inwardly d. 2, 312
dignity	d. of human nature 346
dimness	d. of this life 172
dire	in our d. need 287
direct	d. and rule our hearts 93, 566; d. and unite us 69; d., sanctify and govern 398
discern	d. and avoid 286; teach us to d. your hand in all your works 592
disciples	appeared to his d. on the Emmaus road 491; d.' feet 463, 464; faithful d. 194; fulfil his command to make d. 168; keep his d. from the evil one 622; known to his d. in the breaking of bread 490, 492; loving and obedient d. of your Son 531; made glad the d. 498; manifest himself to his d. 58; prayed for his d. 261, 417; sent the Holy Spirit to his/the d. 536, 537, 538; the coming of the Holy Spirit upon thy d. 187; the d. saw your Son in glory 411; to lead the d. 164
discipline	give us such grace to d. ourselves 260, 403, 405;

give us grace to use such d. 407; godly d. 299; the spirit of d. and love 150

discouraged d. by our weakness 421

diseases all our d. 125; d. of our souls 119, 120

disobedience turning us from d. 318

disobedient d. hearts 239, 316, 317; hearts of the d. 4

disordered d. wills and passions 427

dispel d. the darkness 424

disquietude d. of this world 127

dissension confessing thy faith without d. 176

distribute consecrate, break, and d. us 461

distrust d. thee, who art the Truth 205

divers d. gifts and graces of thy saints 153

diversity d. of ministrations 215; d. of peoples 213

divided d. and enslaved 574; d. and torn apart 575

divine d. life 241, 346, 348, 349; d. majesty 71, 124, 170, 209, 263, 540; d. nature 19, 20, 347; d. pity 38; d. power 607; d. providence 5

divinity life of his d. 345

doctrine blast of vain d. 109; by their d. 122; d. and holy life 112; d. of thy blessed Apostle 13; enlightened by the d. 13; heavenly d. 109; holy d. 104, 105; life and d. 147, 156; wholesome medicines of his d. 119; the d. delivered by him 120

dominion d. of sin and death 496

doubt the hope of those who d. 499; without all d. 103, 203

doubtful d. in thy Son's resurrection 103

doubts d. and dangers that assail us 636; d., dangers and perplexities 628

drink eat and d. with him 500; the cup thou gavest him to d. 171

duties d. of our calling 223

dwell d. in his love 341; so he may continually d. in us 340; with him continually d. 65, 521, 522

dying not in speaking but in d. 14

eager e. faith and love 403

ear give e., Lord 322; give e. to our prayer 3; merciful ears 82

failed   f. to do it 214

faith   a f. like his 593; beholding by f. 384; by f. 331;
by f. attain 304; by f. behold thy glory 11; by f.
in him who suffered 431, 432; by f. in his death
411, 414; by f. in his sacrifice 265; by f. receive
thy precious Body 212; by f. we are born again
514; by f. with thanksgiving 167; by steadfast f.
433; confess the f. of Christ crucified 185; confessing thy f. 176; confession of a true f. 71; confirmation of the f. 103; constancy of our f. 15; deny
the f. of Christ crucified 469; express thy f. 14;
eye of f. 263; eyes of our f. 58, 490, 492; f. and
hope and love 304; f. and love 240, 403, 500; f.,
hope and charity 87, 572; f. to know . . . that he
abides with us on earth 529; f. to know that he
lives in his Church 519; f. to perceive his glory
412, 413; f. to perceive that . . . he abides in his
Church 520; finish our course in f. 146; firm f.
233; firm in this f. 541; flame of f. and love 343;
full assurance of f. 207; gift of f. 584; giving us
such f. in thee 211; help us in f. 511; hold firmly
and joyfully to this f. 209; in f. beholding the light
of his countenance 128, 129; inward f. 166; keep
the f. which he taught 148; know thee/you now
by f. 21, 178, 362, 363, 364; light of f. 337; lively
f. 124, 170; may we, who have not seen, have f.
499; mercifully give us f. 529; one f. in their hearts
173; our f. may never be reproved 203; our f. may
not be found wanting 636; profess by their f. 493;
profess by our f. 494; proof of our f. 301; seed of
f. 623; shield of f. 620; so firm a f. 234; steadfast
f. 39, 264, 408, 433, 548, 571; steadfast in f. 175;
stedfast/steadfast in this f. 71, 540, 607; stedfastness of this f. 71; that our f. in thy sight may never
be reproved 103; true f. 71, 540; turn in f. to him
436; walk by f. and not by sight 301, 610; witness
to our f. 610

faithful   be found f. 223; f. Abraham 233; f. and true pastors 107, 149; f. departed 140, 142; f. disciples
194; f. in the fellowship of his sufferings 262; f.

gladly

g. suffer for his sake 448; g. suffer shame and loss 139, 446; suffer g. 152

glistering

raiment white and g. 127

glorify

g. his name 357; g. thee by their deaths 15; g. thee in thy works 196; g. thy holy Name 15, 218; g. your name 598

glorified

g. in thy Saints 154

glorious

g. fellowship of thy saints 131; g. fulfilment of your kingdom 281; g. Godhead 21, 363, 364; g. kingdom 28, 230, 394, 395; g. liberty of the children of God 578; g. liberty of the sons of God 577; g. liberty of your children 600; g. majesty 1, 237, 309; g. passion 41, 182; g. resurrection 57, 440, 474, 489

glory

by faith behold thy g. 11; come again in g. 310; comes again in g. 316, 317, 326, 327; confident of the g. 449, 450; crown of everlasting g. 113; declare your g. 246; entered his g. 422; entered not into g. 45, 444, 445; eternal g. 359, 489, 540, 541, 641; excellent g. 129, 199; faith to perceive his g. 412, 413; fill the whole world with your g. 368; fill us with the vision of your g. 542; filled with thy/your g. 245, 246; from g. to g. 128, 199, 384, 413, 416; g. in the cross of Christ 139, 446, 448; g. in thy name 200; g. of his endless life 186; g. of his marvellous works 377; g. of his resurrection 108, 266, 642; g. of his victory 434; g. of Israel 350; g. of the eternal Trinity 71, 540; g. of the Lord's resurrection 483; g. of the Trinity 607; g. of the Word made flesh 246; g. of thy great Name 5; g. of thy holy Name 159; g. of thy/your Name 29, 70, 97, 180, 215, 307, 468; g. of your Father 518; g. of your kingdom 518; g. that shall/will be revealed 46, 449, 450, 451, 616; g. that should be revealed 471; honour and g. 33, 111, 407; King of g. 201; life and g. 416; live and reign with him in g. 271; love and g. 281, 525; make known your heavenly g. 389; may be filled with thy/your g. 246, 367; may behold your g. 365; may know your g. 366; may reflect his g. 350;

may see his g. 415; our g. and our hope 526; power and g. 397; power and great g. 28, 394, 395; promised land of your g. 236; radiance of Christ's g. 374; radiance of his g. 375, 376; radiance of your heavenly g. 334; reign with him in g. 475, 476; reveal his g. 128; reveal your g. 390; revealed his g. 384; revealed in g. 263, 414; revealed the g. of your Son 268; revealed your g. 571; saints in g. 596; see his g. 519; see thy g. 214; see your g. face to face 362; saw your Son in g. 411; seek only thy g. 164; set forth thy g. 156; share his g. 263; shew/show forth thy/your g. 155, 425; splendour of your heavenly g. 335; tell of your g. 539; the g. of all who believe in you 360; the revelation of your g. 255; thy g. may be revealed 195, 251; to the g. of your Name 563; use them to thy g. 160; vision of thy heavenly g. 178; whose g. it is always to have mercy 408; witness to thy g. 397

glorying   ever g. in his Name 134

God   children of G. 173, 578; Father, Son, and Holy Spirit, one G. 542; Lord and G. 281; Son of G. 193; sons of G. 20, 193, 577; sons of G. and heirs 28, 394; the living G. 197; the only G. 91, 92, 261, 409, 410, 417, 603, 622; three persons in one G. 541

godhead   glorious G. 21, 363, 364

godliness   author of all g. 98; in continual g. 97, 307; serve you in g. 604; way of g. 286

godly   g. discipline 299; g. life 61, 285, 561, 562; g. living 123; g. motions 33; g. quietness 77; g. serve thee 51; g. sorrow 170

good   all that is g. 517; do anything g. 81, 253; do no good thing 72, 393; do nothing g. without you 254, 380, 560, 608; every g. work 501, 502; from whom all g. proceeds 547; fruitful for g. 38; g. confession 152; g. desires 56, 479, 480; g. effect 56, 479; g. example 141, 215; g. gifts 5; g. news 625; G. News 377; g. news of your love 581; g. of thy holy Church 164; g. providence 74; g. shepherd 503,

504; g. things 64, 78, 79, 85, 215, 515, 564, 569;
g. works 90, 97, 100, 131, 155, 308, 564, 570, 597;
pleasing and g. 501; things that be g. 64

goodness bountiful g. 94, 95, 99; by thy g. 29; crowned the
year with thy g. 161; ever thankful for your g. 638;
govern it always by your g. 558; great g. 37; in
your g. 544; help and g. 89; nourish us with all
g. 79, 564; of your g. 298; perfect in all g. 275;
source of all g. 420

gospel boldness to preach the G. 536, 538; everlasting
G. 396; freedom of thy g. 311; g. of salvation 452;
g. of your love 601; light of the G. 105, 130; preach
thy G. 151; preaching of the g. 190, 532; revealed
in the G. 53; set forth in the G. 121; truth of thy
holy G. 109; whose praise is in the G. 119, 120

govern direct, sanctify and g. 398; g. all things both in
heaven and on earth 378; g. all things in heaven
23; g. it always by your goodness 558; g. the hearts
and minds 575, 604; g. them whom thou dost
bring up 73, 74; g. those whom you have set upon
the sure foundation 549; guide and g. the minds
of thy servants 156

governance ordered by thy g. 77

governed g. and preserved 37; g. and sanctified 51, 468;
peaceably g. 545

grace adoption and g. 8, 176, 179, 181, 338; bountiful
g. and mercy 6, 7, 319; by your g. 480; comfort
of thy g. 36; didst give such g. 102; fill us with
your g. 323; full of g. 323; fullness of your g. 568;
gifts of his g. 289; give thy g. 5; give to all men
g. 603; give unto us abundantly thy g. 83; give
us g. 61, 109, 124, 160, 201, 309, 310; give us
g. —always to receive him with thankfulness 285;
—faithfully to bear his name 354; —rightly to use
them 160; —so to meditate on thy power 196; —so
to put away the leaven of malice and wickedness
495; —that we may always thankfully receive the
immeasurable benefit of his sacrifice 562; —that
we may cast away the works of darkness 1; —that

we never presume to sin 124, 170; —to accept joyfully the sufferings 449; —to answer readily the call of our Savior 377; —to bear our sufferings 616; —to cast away the works of darkness 237, 309; —to dedicate our freedom to your service 577, 578; —to discipline ourselves 260, 403, 405; —to do your will 601; —to follow in his steps 503; —to heed their warnings 314; —to love one another 512; —to love what you command 428; —to obey your commands 598; —to receive thankfully the fruits of his redeeming work 561; —to turn away from darkness 310; —to use our freedom in your service 600; —to use such abstinence 33; —to use such discipline 407; —to walk in his way 513; given g. to . . . 115; given such g. 101; g. alone 250, 385, 386, 387; g. and heavenly benediction 156; g. and power, 22, 145, 146, 555; g. of his coming 315; g. of that Sacrament 166; g. of your Holy Spirit 551; g. to accept suffering 450; g. . . . to acknowledge the glory 71, 540; g. to believe 603; g. to endure the sufferings 451; g. to forgive 198; g. to love what you command 426; g. to set our minds on things above 478; g. to use them 111; g. to witness a good confession 152; g. truly to believe 116, 294; grant that by thy g. we may be healed 126; grant thy/your people g. 91, 92, 279, 409, 410; grant unto us such a measure of thy g. 84; grant us g. 46; grant us g. so to follow thy blessed saints 123; grant us g. to receive him with thankfulness 617; grant us like g. 194; grow in g. 231, 267, 458; heavenly g. 27, 147, 388, 589; help of thy/your g. 72, 380; in the g. of thy Son 153; means of your g. 461; multiply thy g. upon us 143; plentiful g. and mercy 320; pour thy g. into our hearts 108; power of thy g. 175; riches of his g. 580; riches of thy/your g. 195, 251, 389, 390; seeds of his g. 614; singular g. 138; special g. 56, 479; strengthen us by/with thy g. 15, 397; the spirit of g. and peace 297, 552; through your g. we may proclaim your truth 548; thy g. may always prevent 90; your g. may always precede 570; witness to his g. 447

graces   gifts and g. 153

gracious   be g. to all who have gone astray 408; g. favour 218; g. promises 84; g. rule 302, 626; g. visitation 3, 322; g. will 219; g. work 212; most g. rule 574

graciously   g. to behold 465

graft   g. in our hearts the love of thy/your Name 79, 564

grateful   give us g. hearts 161

grave   g. and gate of death 55, 270, 472, 473; in triumph from the g. 481

great   g. dangers 25, 26; g. gift 609; g. goodness 37; g. High Priest 207; g. humility 1, 44, 237, 266, 309, 437, 440, 642; g. love 460; g. might 6, 7, 319; g. mercy 79, 498, 564; g. shepherd 275, 501, 502; g. triumph 66, 527, 528, 529; power and g. glory, 28, 394, 395; the wise and the g. 191

greatest   g. gift 381

greatness   g. of your gift 303, 621

grow   g. in grace 231, 267, 458; g. up into him 514; g. up into him in all things 459; g. up into the maturity of the true man 287; g. up into thee in all things 167

guardians   g. of your truth 596, 613

guide   g. and govern the minds of thy servants 156; g. by his light 365; g. by thy/your light 245, 366; g. by your truth 246; g. by your wisdom 300; g. the ministers and stewards 317; g. the Wise Men 191; g. their counsels 164; g. them by his example 148; ruler and g. 76, 557

guided   g. by faithful and true pastors 107, 149; g. by the Holy Spirit 192

guiding   by thy/your merciful g. 64, 547

guilt   that we may admit our g. 258

hallow   h. our bodies in purity 138

hallowing   for our h. 216

hand   in all thy works to perceive thy h. 228; recognise your h. in all 229; right h. of thy Majesty 35;

h. and all our members 16; our h. are restless 582,
583; our h. may always be attentive 172; our h.
may be firmly fixed 279, 427; our h. may ever
there be fixed 430; our h. may surely there be fixed
426, 428, 429; penitent h. 408; pour into our h.
31, 78, 288, 381, 515; pour this great gift into our
h. 609; pour thy grace into our h. 108; pure and
clean h. 106; pure h. 410, 486, 585; pure h. and
minds 92, 409; purify our h. 326; rule our h. 93;
rule their h. 164; sanctify our h. 175; send . . .
thy Holy Spirit into our h. 69; sow in our h. the
seeds of his grace 614; take away all vices from
our h. 174; thankful h. 166; trust you with all our
h. 565; with h. prepared 189; working in our h.
219

<dl>
<dt>hearty</dt>
<dd>h. desire to pray 75; h. desires 35; h. thanks 160,
165</dd>

<dt>heaven</dt>
<dd>ascended into h. 521, 531; came down from h.
423; enjoy him perfectly in h. 333; fellowship also
with them in h. 143; fulness of his joy in h. 242;
govern all things in h. 23; h. and earth 80, 546,
614; home in h. 361; in h. and on earth 378; look
up to h. 11; on earth as in h. 244; reigns in h.
340; reigns supreme in h. 281; throne of h. 523,
524; thy/your Kingdom in h. 66, 527, 529; true
bread that comes/cometh down from h. 163, 272;
wind from h. 537, 538</dd>

<dt>heavenly</dt>
<dd>h. benediction 156; h. blessing 158; h. comfort
141, 142; h. desires 486; h. doctrine 109; h. glory
178, 334, 335, 389; h. grace 27, 147, 388, 589;
h. home 632; h. inheritance 208; h. kingdom 201;
h. promises 86, 573; h. treasure 83, 84, 568; love
things h. 567</dd>

<dt>heavens</dt>
<dd>ascended far above all h. 282, 520; ascended into
the h. 65, 522; created the h. and the earth 196,
228, 592; far above the h. 519</dd>

<dt>heirs</dt>
<dd>h. of eternal life 28, 230, 231, 394, 395; h. of ever-
lasting salvation 165</dd>

<dt>help</dt>
<dd>by thy h. 25; come quickly to h. us 404; continual
h. 56, 218, 478, 480; continued h. 479; grant us</dd>
</dl>

your h. 254; h. and defend 257; h. and goodness
89; h. and govern 73, 74, 549; h. and salvation
39, 433; h. of thy/your grace 72, 380; h. us by faith
331; h. us so to proclaim the good news 581; h.
us to hear 238, 312; keep us ever by thy h. 88;
saving h. 586; speedily h. and deliver us 7, 319,
320; thy right hand to h. 24; to h. ourselves 418,
421; without your h. 558

herald   to h. the coming 239

heralds   h. and evangelists 151

hide   did not h. his face from shame 451; h. us from
                the light 382, 383

high   great H. Priest 207; h. honour 101

hinder   remove those things which h. 321

hindered   h. and bound by our sins 320; sore let and h. 6,
                7; sorely h. by our sins 319

hindrances   free from all h. 307

hold   h. fast 2, 208, 280, 312, 408, 516, 567; h. firm
                313; h. firmly 209

holiness   h. becometh thine house 158; in h. and righteous-
                ness 435; in h. and truth 273, 468; in righteous-
                ness and h. 407; law of h. 173; true h. 33

holy   h. and acceptable to the Father 212; h. and ac-
                ceptable unto thee 158; h. Angels 118; h. Apostle
                103, 111, 114; h. Apostles 110, 508; h. Baptism
                165; h. Child 337; h. Church 5, 51, 109, 164, 180,
                283, 629; h. city 201; h. comfort 67, 533, 534; h.
                commandments 102, 114; h. Cross 275; h. doc-
                trine 104, 105; h. family 361; h. function 156; h.
                Gospel 109; h. in life 175; h. in thought and deed
                517; h. inspiration 64; h. life 112, 247, 248, 285,
                561, 562, 617; h. lives 260; h. Martyr 145, 146;
                h. mount 128, 199, 415; h. mountain 384; h. mys-
                teries 48, 183, 267, 454, 458; h. name 15, 73, 74,
                155, 159, 161, 218, 549; h. name of Jesus 352;
                h. night 242, 243, 333, 334, 335, 336, 483, 487;
                h. place 207; h. Sabbath 470; h. Sacrament 167;
                h. Scriptures 2, 238, 312; h. temple 122, 550; h.
                Virgin 152; h. will 323, 560; h. wisdom 239; h.

women 153; h. word 2, 102, 113, 172, 238, 312; most h. life 61; nothing is h. 76, 306, 557

Holy Spirit/Ghost anointed him with the H. 369; anointed Jesus at his baptism with the H. 371; anointed your Son Jesus Christ with the H. 452, 453; anointing him with the H. 372; by the/thy/your H. 70, 213, 563; coming of the H. 187; daily increase in thy H. 187; Father, Son, and H. 209, 541; fellowship of the H. 576; filled with the H. 11; gift of the H. 532; gifts of the H. 149; given thy H. 208; grace of your H. 551; guided by the H. 192; indwelling of thy H. 68; inspiration of thy H. 157; light of thy/your H. 67, 533, 534; partakers of thy H. 179; renewed by the H. 8, 181; renewing us through the H. 396; send the/thy/your H. 31, 69, 164, 381, 527, 528, 609; send us your H. 527; sent the/your H. 289, 518, 530, 538, 614; strengthen us by your H. 385; the H. came upon him 373; the H. hath made thy children 176; through your H. 542; through your Word and H. 542; thy H. 93, 111; when he H. came down 249; with the H. 219; your H. 566

home a h. prepared 326; an earthly h. 221, 299, 361; at h. with thee 190; bring them h. to thy fold 185; fetch them h. 52, 53, 469; heavenly h. 632; h. in heaven 361

homes h. of your people 299

honour high h. 101; h. and glory 111, 407

hope faith and h. and love 304; faith, h. and charity 87, 572; having this h. 28, 230, 394, 395; h. and zeal 214; h. of eternal glory 489; h. of eternal life 313; h. of everlasting life 2, 312; h. of Israel 188; h. of those who doubt 499; h. of thy heavenly grace 27; our glory and our h. 526; our pattern and our h. 421; uplifted by this h. 231

house holiness becometh thine h. 158

household h. the Church 97, 307, 548; thy Church and h. 27

human h. family 587; h. nature 439; h. race 437, 642

humanity share in our h. 345, 346; share our h. 348; shared our h. 347; shares our h. 241, 349; you created h. anew 436

indwelling	i. of thy Holy Spirit 68
inestimable	i. benefit 61
infant	an I. who is the Light of the world 368; i. Son 246
infants	madest i. to glorify thee 15
infections	i. of the devil 91
infinite	i. merits 38
infirmities	healed of all our i. 126; look upon our i. 24
inflamed	i. with the same spirit 150
inherit	i. thine everlasting kingdom 202
inheritance	heavenly i. 208
innocency	i. of life 5; i. of our lives 15
innocent	miseries of the i. 38
innocents	the young i. 14
inordinate	i. love of riches 117
inspiration	by the i. of thy Holy Spirit 157; holy i. 64; your i. 517, 547
inspire	i. all who minister 318; i. our hearts 537; i. the guardians of your truth 596, 613; i. thy servant Luke 121; i. us to work for the coming of his kingdom 351; i. us with such love 305; i. us your children 371
inspired	you have i. us 607
institute	i. the Sacrament 48
instituted	i. the Sacrament 454
instrument	i. of shameful death 139, 446, 447, 448
intercede	i. on our behalf 207
inward	i. faith 166
islands	shine in these i. 130
Israel	all I. shall be saved 168; hope of I. 188; New I. 355
Jerusalem	accomplish at J. 129, 199; all who love J. 54; citizens of the J. which is above 172; in J. 187
John Baptist	thy servant J. 136
John the Baptist	who sent J. 239; you sent J. 317; your servant J. 316
Jordan	in J. 181, 370; in the J. 249, 373; River J. 179, 369
joy	bring us to eternal j. 336; bring us to eternal light and j. 591; celebrate with j. 477; come with j. 169; crown of everlasting j. 584; enter with j. 47; eternal j. 167, 223, 304, 336, 422, 459, 496; filled with

kingdom	at his table in his k. 500; authority of his k. 525; blessing of your k. 452, 453; coming of his k. 351; coming of your k. 528; enter into his k. 310; entered into his k. 269; eternal and glorious k. 230; eternal joy in his k. 336; eternal k. 142, 187; everlasting k. 202; fulfilment of your k. 248; glorious fulfilment of your k. 281; glorious k. 28; glory of your k. 518; heavenly k. 131, 201; heralds and evangelists of thy k. 151; k. of light 237; k. of your Son 496, 497, 631; knowing that your k. shall come 641; presence of your k. 295; share in his k. 633; thy blessed k. 157; thy/your k. in heaven 66, 527, 529; word of his k. 589; your k. extends beyond space and time 516
knee	every k. may bow 191
knit	k. together thine elect 123
knock	come and k. 227
know	do not k. the redeeming work 629; faith to k. 529; k. and do your perfect will 612; k. and keep thy laws 224; k. and understand what things they ought to do 555; k. him and love him 630; k. him and understand his teachings 255; k. him who calls us each by name 504; k. that they are at home with thee 190; k. the fulness of his joy 341; k. the glorious liberty of the children of God 578; k. the power of his resurrection 40; k. thee/you now by faith 21, 178, 362, 363, 364; k. thy/your Son Jesus Christ 110, 508; k. within ourselves 183, 455; k. you in all your ways 541; learn to k. thee better 43; may we k. thee 259; minds that k. thee 204; perceive and k. 22; so perfectly to k. 278, 507; so to k. thee that we may truly love thee 204; truly to k. is eternal life 508; truly to k. is everlasting life 110, 278, 507
knowest	as thou k. our weaknesses 259
knowing	k. his presence and power 518; k. that your kingdom shall come 641
knowledge	k. of his presence 498; k. of our salvation 267, 458
known	k., adored and obeyed 222; k. the revelation 242, 243, 334, 335; k. thy mystery 333; k. thy will 214;

life   a share in your l. and love 542; after this l. 21, 363, 364; all the days of our l. 17, 23, 177, 220, 232; amendment of l. 42; bread of his l. 589; bread of l. 500; brought l. and immortality to light 489; dimness of this l. 172; divine l. 346, 348, 349; doctrine and holy l. 112; earthly l. 178, 219, 237, 238; endless l. 126; ensample of godly life 61; eternal l. 28, 110, 230, 231, 238, 255, 278, 284, 301, 303, 313, 394, 395, 419, 420, 481, 482, 507, 508, 511, 532, 576, 587, 618, 624, 630; everlasting l. 2, 101, 145, 146, 218, 312, 478, 479, 480, 507; example of godly l. 285, 561, 562; faithfully serve thee in this l. 86; fulness of life 256; gate of everlasting l. 56; gave up his l. 462, 463, 464, 627; give his l. 503; give l. to the world 200; gives l. to the world 272, 423; giving his l. for us 441; glory of his endless l. 186; godly l. 285; holy in l. 175; in losing l. we save it 611; innocency of l. 5; laid down his l. 636; liberty of abundant l. 379; l. and doctrine 147, 156; l. and immortality 47, 489; l. and labours 130; l. and light 487; l. and light of your Church 580; l. and power of your Church 289, 614; l. immortal 1, 309; l. of an earthly home 221, 361; l. of his divinity 345; l. of righteousness 276, 277, 505, 606; l. of the souls that love thee 204; l. of the world to come 306; l. with thee 216; light and l. of all believers 176; light of everlasting l. 13; means of l. 139, 446, 447, 448; mortal l. 1, 309, 382, 383; most holy l. 285; new l. in Christ 435; new l. in your love 576; newness of l. 202, 470; our l. here 201; our l. may express thy faith 14; pattern of his holy l. 617; pattern of his l. 351; pledge of l. eternal 48; power and l. 360; raise us to new l. 587; recalled us to l. 496, 497, 631; resurrection and the l. 276, 277, 505, 506, 606; risen l. 498, 509, 513; so ordered our l. 610; the l. you alone can give 611; the way, the truth, and the l. 110, 205, 278, 507, 508, 509, 510, 511, 512, 513; thee, who art the L. 205; true l. in him 506; way of l. 444; way of l. and peace 45, 445; way of l. eternal 539; who holdest all souls in l. 141, 142; whole l. 478; wholeness of l. 399

life-giving   l. Spirit 477

light   a burning and a shining l. 150; armour of l. 1, 237, 309; bright beams of l. 12, 13; bright beams of thy l. 141, 142; brightness of your one true l. 334; brilliance of your one true l. 335; bring l. to the darkness of our hearts 325; bring us to eternal l. and joy 591; brought life and immortality to l. 489; children of l. 150, 425; l. enkindled in our hearts, 18, 342, 344; feast of everlasting l. 486; from darkness to l. 197; giver of life and l. 487; giver of l. 367; guide by his l. 365; guide by thy/your l. 245, 366; help us to walk in his l. 341; his l. may shine forth in our loves 343; kingdom of l. 237; let his l. shine on every nation 368; life and l. 487; life and l. of your Church 580; l. and joy 591, 605; 639; l. and life of all believers 176; l. of a star 246; l. of Christ 310; l. of everlasting life 13; l. of faith 337; l. of his countenance 128, 129, 384; l. of life 333; l. of that love 382, 383; l. of the faithful 148; l. of the Gospel 105; l. of the minds that know thee 204; l. of the nations 350; l. of the world 368, 374, 375, 376, 424, 591; l. of thy/your Holy Spirit 67, 533, 534; l. of thy/your truth 13, 62, 286, 360, 367, 579; l. of your Spirit 535; l. to all the nations 364; l. to mankind 222; marvellous l. 154; may this l. so shine within the Church 485; mystery of that l. 333; new l. of thine/your incarnate Word 18, 341, 342, 343, 344; one true l. 242, 243, 334, 335, 486; power of your l. 586; revelation of his/that l. 242, 243, 333, 334, 335; revelation of that l. on earth 334, 335; shine as a l. in the world 154, 487; the true light 333; walk in this l. 425; world's true l. 336

lighten   l. the darkness 3, 322

lightened   l. by the doctrine 12

likeness   changed into his l. 128, 199, 219, 384, 413, 416; conformed to his l. 20; l. of men 19

live   love and l. together 632

lusts	worldly and carnal l. 16
made	m. us for yourself 582, 583
magnify	worthily m. thy holy Name 161
maintain	m. among us 153; m. peace 300
majesty	beholding his m. 416; divine m. 71, 124, 170, 209, 263, 540; glorious m. 1, 237, 309; revealed his m. 415; revealed in m. 412, 413; right hand of thy M. 35; we humbly beseech thy M. 106
malice	grant that m. may not affect us 273; leaven of m. and wickedness 60, 495
man	became m. 20; bring to m. the blessings 452; create m. in thine own image 19; frailty of m. 88; give to each m. his appointed work 223; in your love for m. 266; lay hands suddenly on no m. 156; made m. in thine/your own image 196, 228, 592; making m. in your own image 229; m. doth not live by bread alone 163; obedient to the law for m. 16; taste death for every m. 171; the New M. 287; the true m. 287; to suffer and to die for m. 296
man's	for m. sake 354; m. frailness 25; m. understanding 78, 305
manhood	the m. which thou hast assumed 226
manifest	m. Christ 401; m. himself to his disciples 58; m. in thy Church 121; m. thy love 168; m. thy only-begotten Son 21, 178; m. thy power 70
manifested	blessed Son was m. 28, 230; m. as thy children 140; m. thy Son Jesus Christ 222; m. to us in your Son 382; m. your only Son 362
manifold	m. gifts 111; m. temptations 259
mankind	all m. 44; all m. acknowledge his authority 281; all m. may be brought to the glorious liberty of the sons of God 577; assured m. of eternal life 284, 576; delivered and saved m. 265, 431; draw all m. to the fire of your love 538; is for all m. the way 509; light to m. 222; maintain peace for all m. 300; m. may be drawn to thy blessed Kingdom 157; opening for all m. the way 481; salvation of m. 400; save and deliver m. 39, 264;

Saviour of m. 354; suffer for all m. 43; tender love towards m. 44, 438, 439; turn m. from darkness to light 197; you saved m. 434; your love reaches out to all m. 601

mansion	a m. prepared for himself 324, 325
mark	read, m., learn 2, 312
marriage	m. feast 152
martyr	holy M. 145, 146; thy first M. 11; thy m. 10
martyrs	noble army of m. 145
marvellous	into thy m. light 154; m. works 377
master	Lord and M., Jesus Christ 600; our M. and our God 125
maturity	grow up into the m. of the true man 287
meal	this m. of bread and wine 460
means	m. by which the work of his incarnation shall go forward 461; m. of life 139, 446, 447, 448; m. of your grace 461
measure	m. of thy grace 84
mediation	merits and m. 85, 569
medicines	m. of his doctrine 119; m. of the doctrine delivered by him 120
meditate	to m. on thy power 196
meditation	the m. of those mighty acts 47
meekness	in m. 201
member	every m. 51
members	all m. of your holy Church 283; all our m. being mortified 16
memorial	m. of his passion 456, 457; m. of the passion 455, 459; m. of thy passion 49, 183, 184; perpetual m. of thy Son's resurrection 220
men	all estates of m. 51; angels and m. 118; bring all m. to the light 367; draw all m. to the fire of your love 536, 538; give to all m. grace 603; hands of m. 157; known to m. in your Son 255; least of m. 293; likeness of m. 19; loving you and our fellow m. 552; made all m. 52, 53, 469; m. and nations 256, 399; reconciling m. to yourself 581; set forth to all m. 147; set forward the salvation of all m. 156; sinful m. 63, 193, 269, 279, 428, 429, 430; thy witnesses to all m. 208; united m. of every na-

tion 166; wicked m. 50, 467; Wise M. 191, 245, 246, 365, 366, 367, 368

mercy
abundance of thy/your m. 85, 569; always to have m. 408; bountiful grace and m. 6, 7, 319; by thy m. 218; by whose m. we are redeemed 637; continual m. 558; God of all m. 32, 402; great m. 79, 498, 564; have m. upon all Jews 52; have m. upon all who know thee not 53; have m. upon your ancient people the Jews 469; in your m. 358, 363; increase and multiply upon us thy/your m. 76, 557; look with m. 256, 257, 466, 467; loving m. 623; made their boast of your m. 565; m. and pity 83, 84, 568; plentiful grace and m. 320; whose m. is shown 258; works of your m. 571

merits
infinite m. 38; m. and mediation of Jesus Christ 85, 569; m. of Christ Jesus 67; m. of his death 40; m. of his sacrifice 433; m. of your Son Jesus Christ 637; through the m. of your Son 640

message
m. of an angel 108; m. of repentance 189

messenger
didst send thy m. 4, 189

messengers
we your m. 295; your m. the prophets 314

Messiah
welcome the M. 316

might
come in m. 311; great m. 6, 7, 319; power and m. 79, 604

mighty
m. acts 47; m. aid 75; m. power 27, 257, 320, 388; m. protection 398; m. resurrection 475, 476; m. to save 259, 404, 620

mind
all our m. 554; body and m. 483, 590; give us the m. to follow you 443; give us the same m. 442; heart and m. 65, 91, 521, 522; keep us in m. 303; m. and body 484, 485, 544; one m. in belief 213; quiet m. 96, 252, 391, 392; set our m. on things above 478; singleness of m. 307; whose m. is revealed in Christ 291

minds
darkness of our m. 322; enlighten our m. 175; govern the hearts and m. 575, 604; m. of people 396; m. of thy servants 156; m. purified 315; m. that know thee 204; pure hearts and m. 92, 409; purify our hearts and m. 326; put into our m. good desires 56, 479, 480

minister	all who m. in your Church 318; m. your justice with compassion 548; willing to m. to the needs of others 292
ministers	m. and stewards 4, 239, 316, 317; we to whom he m. the cup 171
ministrations	diversity of m. 215
ministry	called to thy m. 215; m. of reconciliation 157; offer themselves for this m. 157; sacred m. of thy Church 156; vocation and m. 51, 283, 468
miracles	signs and m. 257, 388
miseries	m. of the innocent 38
mission	share your Church's m. 601
mortal	m. life 1, 309, 382, 383; m. nature 72
mortified	being m. 16
mortify	m. and kill all vices 14, 15
mortifying	m. our corrupt affections 55
Moses	M. and Elijah 129, 199; your/thy servant M. 224, 235, 236, 594, 595
mother	m. of our Lord 138, 144, 323; m. of our Saviour 240; M. of the Lord 132, 137
mother's	the shelter of a m. love and the protection of a m. prayer 153
mount	holy m. 128, 129, 199; on the m. 127
mountain	holy m. 384
mourn	all who love Jerusalem and m. for her 54
mouths	out of the m. of babes and sucklings 15
multiply	m. thy grace upon us 143; dost continually m. thy Church 166; increase and m. 76, 557
multitudes	m. created in your image 629
murderers	prayed for his m. 11
mutual	m. love 221; m. trust 299
mysteries	holy m. 48, 183, 267, 454, 458; m. of our Lord's Passion 169; sacred m. 49, 184, 455, 456, 457, 459; stewards of thy m. 4
mystery	m. of that light 333; Paschal m. 493
mystical	m. body 123
name	baptised in his n. 249; baptized into his N. 369; bear his n. 354; calls us each by n. 504; come together in his n. 615; comfort and peace in his N.

placed	p. among things that are passing away 567
plant	p. in every heart 352, 353
planted	p. within us the seed of faith 623
please	not able to p. thee/you 93, 566; p. you both in will and deed 254, 380; such things as shall p. thee 72; we may p. thee 72
pleased	p. to redeem us 169
pleasing	p. and good 501
pledge	p. of eternal life 454; p. of life eternal 48; p. of thy love 167
plenteously	p. bringing forth the fruit of good works, may of thee be p. rewarded 100
plenteousness	fill all things living with p. 638
plentiful	p. grace 320
poor	didst become p. 225; the p., the humble, and the forgotten 190
possess	for ever p. thee 510
pour	p. into our hearts 31, 78, 288, 381, 515; p. this great gift into our hearts 609; p. thy grace into our hearts 108; p. thy Spirit upon thy Church 168; p. upon us the abundance of thy/your mercy 85, 569
poured	p. on us the new light 341; p. upon us the new light 342
poverty	by thy p. we might become rich 225; p. of our nature 195, 251, 389, 390
power	almighty p. 83, 84, 568; by thy p. we may be defended 30; defended by thy mighty p. 27; divine p. 607; endue us . . . with the same p. 146; gift of p. 174; grace and p. 22, 145, 146, 555; healing p. 121, 256, 399; Holy Spirit and with p. 452, 453; joy and p. 537; judge of all who wield p. 300; life and p. of your Church 289, 614; living in his p. 208; love and p. 535; manifest thy p. 70; mighty p. 257, 388; no p. in ourselves 418, 421; no p. of ourselves 34, 418; p. and glory 397; p. and great glory 28, 394, 395; p. and life 360; p. and love 121; p. and mercy 321; p. and might 79, 290, 564, 604; p. of darkness 497; p. of death 482; p. of evil 605, 639; p. of him who lives and reigns 605; p.

of his endless life 126; p. of his resurrection 40; p. of his sacrifice 434; p. of his victorious cross 436; p. of his victory 39, 264, 265, 268, 411, 414, 431, 432, 433; p. of our enemy 57, 474; p. of Satan 197; p. of sin 631; p. of the devil 417; p. of the Divine Majesty 71, 540; p. of the same Spirit 536, 538; p. of the Spirit 290; p. of thy grace 175; p. of your Divine Majesty 540; p. of your light 586; p. of your Spirit 435; p. to live 393; p. to save 405, 406; p. to speak the truth 628; p. to transform our lives 625; p., wisdom and love 196; presence and p. 518; raise up thy p. 6, 7; raise up your mighty p. 320; show forth your p. 563; source of all p. 261, 622; stir up your p. 319

praise	always serve and p. you 542; always to p. thee 229; ever to p. thee 228; living in p. of thy divine majesty 209; p. and glory of thy Name 180; p. and thanksgiving 268; p. of thy holy Name 155; we may always p. you 607; we p. you 271; whose p. is in the Gospel 119, 120; whose p. this day 14; year by year we p. you 159
praises	rejoicing in his p. 227; show forth thy p. 154
pray	hearty desire to p. 75; more ready to hear than we to p. 85, 569
prayed	p. for his disciples 261, 417; p. for his enemies 198; p. for his murderers 11; p. to thee for his persecutors 10; your Son p. that you would keep his disciples 622
prayer	hear our p. 269, 283, 466, 468; love and p. 313; protection of a mother's p. 153; thoughts that pass into p. 216
prayers	devout p. of thy Church 98; give ear to our p. 3, 322; mercifully accept our p. 72, 380; p. and labours of your holy Church 629; p. of thy humble servants 82; p. of thy people 22, 29, 159; p. of thy servants 137, 144; p. that pass into love 216; receive the p. of your people 555; supplications and p. 51
preach	boldness to p. the Gospel 536, 538; p. and receive the same 116, 294; p. his name in all the world

r. in signs and miracles 257, 388; r. in splendour 416; r. in the Gospel 53; r. Jesus as your beloved Son 373; r. the source 400, 401; r. thyself/yourself as Father, Son and Holy Spirit 209, 541; r. to the three Apostles 129; r. your will to all people 586; the glory that shall be r. 11, 46, 451, 616; thy glory may be r. 195; who r. your love 295; whose mind is r. in Christ 291

rule
direct and r. our hearts 93, 566; direct and r. us according to thy will 69; gentle and loving r. 574; just and gentle r. 575; most gracious r. 302, 574; r. in love 281, 525; r. over all things as Lord 523, 524; r. their hearts 164; under his gracious r. 626

ruler
r. and guide 76, 557

run
r. the way of your commandments 584; r. without stumbling 573

running
r. the race 7, 624; r. the way of thy commandments 84; r. to obtain your promises 568; r. to thy promises 83

Sabbath
this holy S. 470

sacrament
grace of that S. which they have received 166; s. of his Body and Blood 48, 267, 454; s. of holy Baptism 165; this holy S. 167; wonderful s. 49, 183, 184, 267, 455, 456, 457, 458, 459; word and sacraments 222, 374, 375, 376

sacred
s. ministry 156; s. mysteries 49, 184, 455, 456, 457, 459

sacrifice
commemoration of that s. 169; faith in his s. 264; immeasurable benefit of his s. 562; living s. 212, 612; made fit by Christ's s. 633; merits of his s. 433; merits of that holy s. 39; power of his s. 434; s. for sin 61, 275, 285, 561, 562; s. on the Cross 265

safety
continue in s. 89, 558; preserved us in s. 159

saints
blessed S. 123; fellowship of thy S. 131; glorified in thy S. 154; made one with your s. 613; s. in glory 596; s. of our nation 143

sake
for his s. 303; for the s. of the joy that lay ahead 616

salvation
for our s. 443; gift of s. 640; good news of his s. 377; gospel of s. 452; heirs of everlasting s. 165; help and s. 39, 433; in the Name of Jesus Christ alone is s. 134; knowledge of our s. 267, 458; Lord God of our s. 47; make thy/your s. known to all 134, 357; name is our s. 353; overcome death for our s. 41; point the way to s. 313; prepare the way of s. 314; profitable to our s. 88; rejoice in thy/your

234, 593; s. of all 462, 463, 464; s. of others 462, 463, 464; thy blessed s. 130; thy s. 131, 147, 149; thy s. John the Baptist 112, 136; thy s. Saint Luke 121; thy/your s. Moses 224, 235, 236, 594, 595

servants brought thy s. to the beginning of another year 17, 177; give your s. grace 450; hear the prayers of thy s. 137, 144; humble s. 35, 64, 82, 517; mercifully behold thy s. 215; minds of thy s. 156; present with thy s. now assembled 164; s. of all 193, 249, 373; thy s. who bear the cross 200; us thy/your s. 71, 128, 129, 540; we thy s. 415

serve always s. and praise you 542; evermore s. thee 207; faithfully s. before thee 5; faithfully s. thee in this life 86; joyfully s. thee/you 77, 215, 545; s. in the sacred ministry 156; s. thee faithfully 220, 315; s. thee in good works 97; s. thee in the power of his endless life 126; s. thee with a more perfect will 43; s. thee/you in pureness of living 60, 495; s. thee/you with a quiet mind 96, 252, 391, 392; s. you continually in holiness and truth 273; s. you continually in righteousness and truth 498; s. you in godliness 604; s. you in holiness and righteousness 435; s. you in holiness and truth 468, 599; s. you in sincerity and truth 283; s. you with all our being 485; s. you with our whole heart 552; s. you with reverence and thanksgiving 592; s. your loving purpose 232; the will to serve you in them 619; truly and godly s. thee 51; wills that s. thee 204

served s. thee here and are now at rest 141

service accept us in your s. 387; called to your s. 250, 385; called us to thy/your s. 210, 386, 543; dedicate our freedom to your s. 577, 578; find peace in your s. 583; loving s. 318; offer ourselves to your s. 582; surrender our lives to your s. 371; strengthened for thy s. 68; thankful s. 303, 621; thy holy Angels always do thee s. 118; true and laudable s. 86, 573; use our freedom in your s. 600; whole-hearted s. 484; whose s. is perfect freedom 204; yield ourselves to your s. 291; you call us to your s. 602

services	s. of Angels and men 118
serving	s. thee here in newness of life 202
shame	accepted the s. 616; agony and s. of the cross 634; did not hide his face from s. 451; hid not his face from s. 46; open s. 42; suffer s. and loss 139, 446
shameful	s. death 139, 446, 447, 448
share	s. his body and his blood 460; s. his divine life 349; s. his glory 263; s. his risen life 509, 513; s. in his divine life 241; s. in his eternal joy 422; s. in his glorious resurrection 440; s. in his kingdom 633; s. in his resurrection 437; s. in his suffering 452; s. in his sufferings 453; s. in our humanity 345, 346; s. in the glory of his resurrection 642; s. in your Church's mission 601; s. in your life and love 542; s. our humanity 346, 348; s. the divine life 346, 348; s. the fulness of eternal life 255, 630; s. the life of his divinity 345; s. with him in the glory of his resurrection 266
shared	s. at Nazareth the life of an earthly home 361; s. our humanity 347
shares	s. our humanity 241, 349
sharing	s. in his humility 442; s. one another's joys and burdens 298
sharp	s. and painful death 101
sheep	feed thy s. 148; great shepherd of the s. 501, 502; great shepherd of your s. 275
shelter	s. of a mother's love 153
shepherd	didst call shepherds to the cradle 190; good s. 503, 504; great s. of the sheep 501, 502; great s. of your sheep 275; one flock under one s. 53, 185, 469; one fold under one s. 52; s. of souls 148; S. of thy people 274
shield	s. of faith 620
shine	made this holy night to s. 483; s. as a light in the world 154, 487; s. forth in our lives 18, 342, 343, 344; s., . . . in our hearts 154; s. in our words and deeds 337; s. in these islands 130; s. in this our land 130; s. with brightness 334; s. with the brightness of thy/your one true light 242, 243; s. with the radiance of Christ's glory 374; s. with the

s. 424; deliver us from the s. which threaten 311; die for our s. 60, 203, 273, 495; forgive the s. 32, 402; forsake our s. 314; free us from our s. 617; hindered and bound by our s. 320; hindered by our s. 319; lamenting our s. 32, 402; remission of all our s. 124; remission of our s. 170; save us from our s. 358; s. and wickedness 6, 7; suffer for our s. 25; truly sorry for our s. 402

slain   s. for truth 136

slave   status of a s. 291

slavery   out of s. 594; out of s. and affliction 235, 236, 595

sleeping   s. in our sin 227

sloth   unbelief and s. 214

smiters   gave his back to the s. 46, 451

snares   s. of the enemy 40

son   dearly-beloved S. 478; declared to be your S. 275; thy/your beloved S. 302, 369, 370, 371, 373; your dear S. 470, 471; your only S. 295; your S. 372; your S. is the resurrection and the life 606 [*see also* only-begotten]

sons   s. and daughters 588; s. of God 20, 193, 371, 577; s. of God and heirs 28, 231, 394; thy s. and heirs 230; your s. and the servants of all 249

sonship   s. of sonship 484

sorely   s. hindered by our sins 319

sorrow   godly s. 170

sorrows   s. of the bereaved 38

sorry   truly s. 402

soul   all our s. 554; body and s. 25, 37, 94, 95, 182, 398; hurt the s. 34, 418; physician of the s. 119, 120; s. and body 220; travail of thy s. 173

souls   bodies and s. 121; diseases of our s. 119, 120; hallow . . . our s. in humility and live 138; holdest all s. in life 141, 142; inwardly in our s. 34, 418; shepherd of s. 148; s. that love thee 204; s. thereby being born again 165

source   revealed the s. 400, 401; s. of all power 261, 622; s. of all power and might 604; s. of all virtues 288; s. of living water 419; spring and s. of goodness 420

thankfulness	receive him with t. 285, 617; shew forth our t. 105, 130
thanks	give t. for/in all things 217, 382; hearty t. 160, 165; humble t. 153
thanksgiving	by faith with t. 167; praise and t. 268; serve you with reverence and t. 592
think	the spirit to t. 81, 253, 393, 559, 560, 608; t. those things that are right 547; t. those things that be good 64
third	t. day 470
thirst	may we always t. for you 420
thought	every t. brought into captivity 191; t. and deed 51
thoughts	evil t. 34, 418; t. that pass into prayer 216
threaten	sins which t. 311
three	t. Apostles 129; t. Persons in one God 541; when two or t. come together 615
throne	earthly t. 131; t. of heaven 523, 524
time	as at this t. 8, 339; at any t. 124; at this t. 533, 534; bide thy t. 214; end of t. 519, 529; hasten the t. 168; in our t. 378; present t. 46, 449, 451, 471; space and t. 280, 516; suffering of the present t. 46; t. and space 229; t. of this earthly life 237; t. of this mortal life 1, 309
today	in our celebration t. 482
tomb	laid in the t. 202, 470, 471
tongue	every kindred and nation and t. 173; every t. may tell of your glory 539; may every t. confess 359; with our tongues we do confess 14
tongues	fiery t. 174; t. of flame 537
torn	divided and t. apart 575
towel	girded himself with a t. 464
train	t. us to be faithful 262
traitor	the t. Judas 107
transfigured	t. on the holy mount 129, 199; wonderfully t. 127
transform	t. our lives 625; t. the poverty of our nature 251, 389, 390; t. those who turn in faith 436; t. us by the renewal of our minds 612
transformation	the t. of our lives 195
transformed	t. by his passion 447; whole life be t. 478
transgressions	t. in the past 17, 177

sincerity and t. 283, 483, 487; slain for t. and righteousness 136; teaching of thy t. 175; testimony of thy t. 11; the Spirit of T. 175; the way, the t. and the life 110, 205, 278, 507, 508, 509, 510, 511, 512, 513; to distrust thee, who art the T. 205; t. and peace 291; t. of thy holy Gospel 109; t. of thy salvation 147; unchangeable t. of your word 408; way of t. 518; witness to your t. 536, 538; worship you in sincerity and t. 483, 487, 590; worship you in spirit and in t. 585

tumults	t. of this world 641
turmoil	t. of this world 127
twelve	t. Apostles 107
two	when t. or three come together 615
tyranny	t. of evil 290, 620; t. of sin 577, 578; t. of sin and death 236, 594, 595

unbelief	delivered from u. 629; preserve us all from u. 588; superstition and u. 180; u. and sloth 214
unchangeable	u. truth 408
understand	hear, read and u. 238; know and u. 555; u. his teaching 255
understanding	pass man's u. 78, 305; spirit of u. and wisdom 221; surpass our u. 515; wisdom and spiritual u. 174
unending	u. joy 141
unfeignedly	u. love thee 123; u. thank thee 161
union	in u. with Christ Jesus 271; in u. with him 291; in u. with thee 212; perfect u. with you 236, 595
unite	u. us in your boundless love 607
united	u. in love and obedience 361; u. men of every nation 166; u. to each other with a pure will 297; u. to one another in brotherly love 552; u. to one another with pure affection 551
unity	called into the u. of thy Church 173; closer u. and fellowship 599; gathered together in u. 70, 563; hold fast the u. which he gives 208; joined together in u. of spirit 122, 550; perfect u. of love 209, 541; renew our u. with him 267, 458; to worship the U. 71, 540, 607; u. of the Spirit 523, 524; u. of your Spirit 539

only Son into the w. 295; came into the w. 395; changes and chances of this w. 428; changes of the w. 426, 427, 429, 430; conflicts of the w. 261, 417; course of this w. 77, 545; darkness of this w. 610; delivered and saved the w. 432; disquietude of this w. 127; end of the w. 282; fill the whole w. with your glory 368; fill the w. with your splendour 360; give life to the w. 200; gives life to the w. 272, 423; in a w. estranged from thee 197; in the w. may reflect his glory 350; judge the w. 4, 189, 226, 317; known to the w. in your Son 630; life of the w. to come 306; light of the w. 368, 374, 375, 376, 424, 591; make thy/your salvation known to all the w. 134, 357; nations of the w. 180; preach his name in all the w. 194; Savio(u)r of the w. 352, 353; sending thine only-begotten Son into the w. 168; sent your Son into the w. 244, 340, 351; shine as a light in the w. 154, 487; shine throughout the w. 105; show forth your glory in the w. 425; sundry and manifold changes of the w. 63; taught all the w. 104; the w. and all else you have made 281; the w. has been filled with the new light 343; the w. may be filled with your glory 367; the w., the flesh and the devil 92, 409, 410; this w. of changing things 516; throughout the w. 532; to all the w. 601; tumults of this w. 641; whole w. may be filled with thy/your glory 245, 246; whole w. may behold your glory 365; whole w. may know your glory 366; whole w. may perceive the glory 377; whole w. will see his glory 519; witness to thy glory in the w. 397; w. of transient things 280; w. to come 582, 583; w.'s true light 336; you reveal your salvation in all the w. 542; your Church throughout the w. 571; your Son came into the w. 247, 248, 435

worldly w. and carnal affections 114; w. and carnal lusts 16; w. anxieties 382, 383

worship brought to w. you 629; faith and w. 540; taught to w. Thee 125; to the w. of thy/your Son 191, 245, 365, 366; to w. therein 159; to w. your Son

COMPARISON OF CALENDARS AND COLLECTS

	AmerBCP	ASB	IrAPB	SAAPB	AusAC	CanBAS
9th Sunday before Christmas		592	592			
8th Sunday before Christmas		394	394			
7th Sunday before Christmas		593	593			
6th Sunday before Christmas		594	595			
5th Sunday before Christmas		596	598			
		597	597			
Advent 1	309	309	309	310	327	309
				309		
Advent 2	314	312	312	313	314	316
				312		
Advent 3	319	316	317	318	332	321
				316		
Advent 4	324	323	323	323	323	323
				326		
Christmas Eve	—	329	329	331	—	—
				330		
Christmas Day	328	334	334	336	334	335
	333	340	340	333	340	337
	338		341	338	343	348

	AmerBCP	ASB	IrAPB	SAAPB	AusAC	CanBAS
Christmas 1	342	345 350	345 350	351 338	627	344
The Holy Name	352	354	358	357	354	353
Christmas 2	346	361 365	361 365	349 347	375	360
Epiphany	362	365	367	368 363	365	366
Epiphany 1 / 1st Sunday in Ordinary Time or of the Year	369	371	371	373	371	372
Epiphany 2 / 2nd Sunday	374	385	385	386	385	376
Epiphany 3 / 3rd Sunday	377	388	388	390	379	387
Epiphany 4 / 4th Sunday	378	389	389	391 392	628	389
Epiphany 5 / 5th Sunday	379	393	393	608 253	629	392
Epiphany 6 / 6th Sunday	380	394	395	630	383	399
Epiphany 7 / 7th Sunday	381			553	553	388

	AmerBCP	ASB	IrAPB	SAAPB	AusAC	CanBAS
Epiphany 8	382			609	494	560
8th Sunday						
Epiphany 9				610	584	586
9th Sunday						
Last Sunday after Epiphany	384					
9th Sunday before Easter		509	509			
8th Sunday before Easter		399	399			
7th Sunday before Easter		392	392			
Ash Wednesday	402	402	402	401 402	543	402
Lent 1	404	405	405	406 407	405	405
Lent 2	408	409	417	411 412	413	413
Lent 3	418	445	422	419	594	420 421
Lent 4	423	413	413	424	389	425 423
Lent 5	426	431	434	432 433	497	435 436
Palm Sunday	437	438	439	441 438	445	444 642

	AmerBCP	ASB	IrAPB	SAAPB	AusAC	CanBAS
Monday in Holy Week	445		445		442	444
Tuesday in Holy Week	446		446		431	447
Wednesday in Holy Week	449		451		448	450
Maundy Thursday	454	452	455	453	461	460
		455	463	458	462	
		462		457		
Good Friday	465	467	467	466	451	465
		468				
		469				
Holy Saturday	470	472	473		471	
Easter Eve						
Easter Vigil	483	475	481	485	486	487
Easter Day	474	479	477	476	475	476
	477		491	480		
Monday in Easter Week	488					
Tuesday in Easter Week	489					
Wednesday in Easter Week	490					
Thursday in Easter Week	493					
Friday in Easter Week	495					
Saturday in Easter Week	496					
2nd Sunday of Easter	493	498	500	631	505	499
Easter 1						

	AmerBCP	ASB	IrAPB	SAAPB	AusAC	CanBAS
3rd Sunday of Easter	490	502	491	606	498	492
Easter 2			503			
4th Sunday of Easter	504	505	506	502	502	502
Easter 3						
5th Sunday of Easter	507	428	511	514	581	512
Easter 4						
6th Sunday of Easter	515	569	517	516	580	515
Easter 5				519		
Ascension Eve	520			525	521	
Ascension Day	521	522	522	521	524	523
7th Sunday of Easter	527	527	527	530	513	542
Easter 6				527		
The Sunday after Ascension Day				531		
Pentecost Eve	532	533	534	537		
Pentecost	533	538	536	533	538	539
		540		607		
Trinity Sunday	540	541	541	540	541	542
Proper 1 [US]	543				383	
Proper 6 [Can]						399
Proper 2 [US]	544				553	388

	AmerBCP	ASB	IrAPB	SAAPB	AusAC	CanBAS
Proper 7 [Can]	545			609	494	560
Proper 3 [US]						
8th Sunday of the Year						
8th Ordinary Sunday						
Proper 4	546			610	584	586
9th Sunday						
Proper 5	547			611	474	587
10th Sunday						
Proper 6	548			581	633	566
11th Sunday						
Proper 7	549			612	567	588
12th Sunday						
Proper 8	550			446	634	554
13th Sunday						
Proper 9	551			388	388	462
14th Sunday						
Proper 10	555			577	577	583
15th Sunday						
Proper 11	556			613	596	585
16th Sunday						
Proper 12	557			614	582	557
17th Sunday						

	AmerBCP	ASB	IrAPB	SAAPB	AusAC	CanBAS
Proper 13	558			509	635	589
18th Sunday	559			592	636	580
Proper 14	561			615	401	578
19th Sunday	563			616	451	381
Proper 15	564			617	461	564
20th Sunday	565			399	399	589
Proper 16	566			618	637	581
21st Sunday	567			619	462	592
Proper 17	568			620	301	563
22nd Sunday	569			621	639	550
Proper 18	570			622	585	590
23rd Sunday						
Proper 19						
24th Sunday						
Proper 20						
25th Sunday						
Proper 21						
26th Sunday						
Proper 22						
27th Sunday						
Proper 23						
28th Sunday						

	AmerBCP	ASB	IrAPB	SAAPB	AusAC	CanBAS
Proper 24	571			623	592	584
29th Sunday						
Proper 25	572			442	442	595
30th Sunday						
Proper 26	573			585	639	593
31st Sunday						
Proper 27	395			624	640	312
32nd Sunday						
Proper 28	312			625	641	591
33rd Sunday						
Proper 29	574			627	575	574
34th Sunday						
Christ the King						
Pentecost 2		468	599			
Trinity 1						
Pentecost 3		576	576			
Trinity 2						
Pentecost 4		577	600			
Trinity 3						
Pentecost 5		579	601			
Trinity 4						

	AmerBCP	ASB	IrAPB	SAAPB	AusAC	CanBAS
Pentecost 6		566	566			
Trinity 5						
Pentecost 7		381	381			
Trinity 6						
Pentecost 8		580	580			
Trinity 7						
Pentecost 9		418	602			
Trinity 8						
Pentecost 10		442	443			
Trinity 9						
Pentecost 11		462	462			
Trinity 10						
Pentecost 12		581	603			
Trinity 11						
Pentecost 13		451	451			
Trinity 12						
Pentecost 14		557	632			
Trinity 13						
Pentecost 15		575	604			
Trinity 14						
Pentecost 16		553	552			
Trinity 15						

	AmerBCP	ASB	IrAPB	SAAPB	AusAC	CanBAS
Pentecost 17		564	564			
Trinity 16						
Pentecost 18		582	582			
Trinity 17		584	430			
Pentecost 19		585	585			
Trinity 18						
Pentecost 20						
Trinity 19						
Pentecost 21		524	524			
Trinity 20						
Pentecost 22		597	605			
Trinity 21						
Last Sunday after Pentecost		515	515